AF574583

Constable

and his country

Titlepage: Drawing of cornfield from 1813 sketchbook. Constable made a painting of the same scene after the corn had been harvested (16).

Constable

and his country

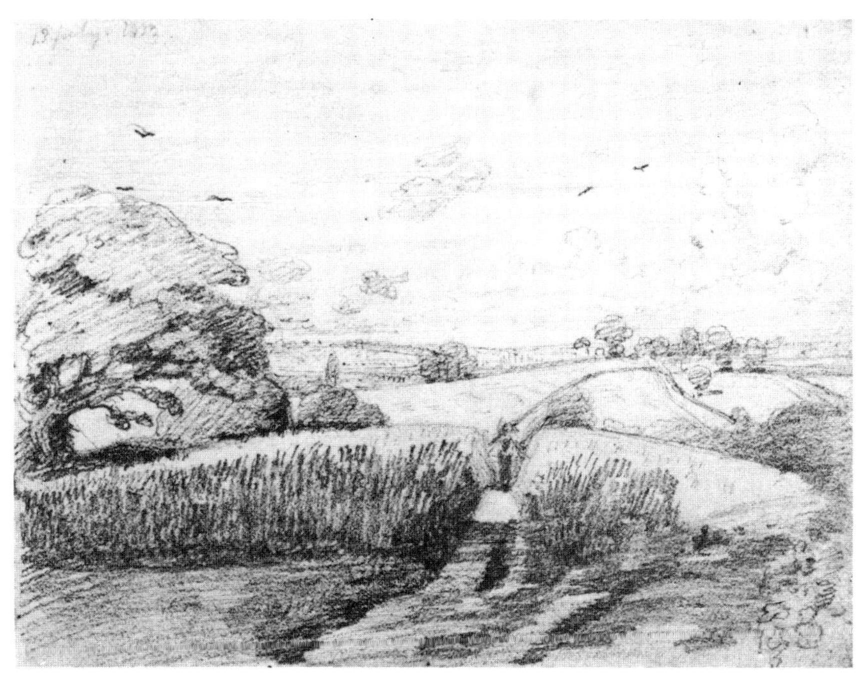

Alastair Smart and
Attfield Brooks

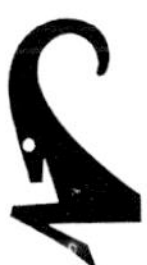

Elek London

For Marita and Rhoda
and for all those who love and cherish
Constable and his country

First published in Great Britain
by Elek Books Ltd
54-58 Caledonian Road
London N1 9RN

Made and printed in Great Britain by
The Garden City Press Limited
Letchworth, Hertfordshire SG6 1JS

Contents

List of plates
6

Preface
10

The topography of Constable's country
by Attfield Brooks
13

Constable and the creative process
by Alastair Smart
31

Notes
133

Appendix: further topographical notes
by Attfield Brooks
135

Selected bibliography
141

Index
143

List of plates

Black and white

1 Drawing of cornfield from 1813 sketchbook. $3\frac{1}{2} \times 4\frac{3}{4}$in. Pencil. Victoria and Albert Museum

2 *Men loading a barge on the Stour*. 1827. 8×13in. Pencil, pen and grey wash. Victoria and Albert Museum.

3 *Portrait of Golding Constable, the painter's father*. 1816. 24×36in. Oil on canvas. Tate Gallery (on loan).

4 *View over the garden of Golding Constable's house*. *c*. 1812–16. $11 \times 17\frac{3}{4}$in. Pencil. Victoria and Albert Museum.

5 *River scene at Mistley, Essex*. 1817. $4\frac{5}{8} \times 7\frac{3}{8}$in. Pencil. Victoria and Albert Museum.

6 *River scene at Mistley, Essex*. 1817. $4\frac{5}{8} \times 7\frac{3}{8}$in. Pencil. Paris, Musée du Louvre.

7 Detail of *A Village Fair at East Bergholt*. 1811. $6\frac{3}{4} \times 14$in. Oil on canvas. Victoria and Albert Museum.

8 Details (re-drawn) from East Bergholt Enclosure Award. Survey by Robert Corby, 1817. Suffolk County Archives.

9 *Self-portrait, aged about 20*. 10×8in. Pencil and watercolour. London, National Portrait Gallery.

10 *East Bergholt Street*. *c*. 1796–9. $7\frac{5}{8} \times 12\frac{5}{8}$in. Pen and watercolour. Victoria and Albert Museum.

11 Photograph of East Bergholt Street. Copyright C. Attfield Brooks.

12 *East Bergholt Church: south archway of ruined tower*. *c*. 1812–16. $10\frac{5}{8} \times 8\frac{1}{2}$in. Pencil. Victoria and Albert Museum.

13 Photograph of East Bergholt Church: south archway of ruined tower. Copyright C. Attfield Brooks.

14 *Dedham Church and Vale*. 1800. $13\frac{5}{8} \times 20\frac{3}{4}$in. Pen, ink and watercolour. Manchester, Whitworth Art Gallery.

15 Photograph of Dedham Church and Vale. Copyright C. Attfield Brooks.

16 *Autumnal Sunset*. *c*. 1812. $6\frac{3}{4} \times 13\frac{1}{4}$in. Oil on paper and canvas. Victoria and Albert Museum.

17 Photograph of site of *Autumnal Sunset*. Copyright C. Attfield Brooks.

18 *Dedham Vale, Morning*. 1811. $30\frac{1}{2} \times 50\frac{3}{4}$in. Oil on canvas. England, private collection.

19 Photograph of site of *Dedham Vale, Morning*. Copyright C. Attfield Brooks.

20 *View of Dedham from the lane leading from East Bergholt Church to Flatford. c.* 1810–15. $9\frac{3}{8} \times 11\frac{7}{8}$in. Oil on paper laid on canvas. Victoria and Albert Museum.

21 Photograph of the lane leading from East Bergholt Church to Flatford. Copyright C. Attfield Brooks.

22 Detail of *Dedham Lock and Mill*. 1820. $21\frac{1}{8} \times 30$in. Oil on canvas. Victoria and Albert Museum.

23 *Scene in Helmingham Park, Suffolk. c.* 1804. $36\frac{1}{4} \times 28\frac{3}{8}$in. Oil on canvas. Toronto, Art Gallery of Ontario.

24 Thomas Gainsborough. Detail of *Cornard Wood. c.* 1748. 48×61in. Oil on canvas. London, National Gallery.

25 Detail of *Salisbury Cathedral from the Bishop's Grounds*. 1823. $34\frac{1}{2} \times 44$in. Oil on canvas. Victoria and Albert Museum.

26 Engraving of Titian's *St Peter Martyr* by Martino Rota.

27 *Dedham Vale*. 1802. $17\frac{1}{8} \times 13\frac{1}{2}$in. Oil on canvas. Victoria and Albert Museum.

28 Claude (1600–82). *Hagar and the Angel*. $20\frac{3}{4} \times 17\frac{1}{4}$in. Oil on canvas. London, National Gallery.

29 *Portrait of Maria Bicknell, the wife of John Constable*. 1816. $11\frac{7}{8} \times 9\frac{7}{8}$in. Oil on canvas. London, National Gallery.

30 Detail of *The Hay Wain*. 1821. $51\frac{1}{4} \times 73$in. Oil on canvas. London, National Gallery.

31 *The Mill Stream*. 1814. 28×36in. Oil on canvas. Ipswich Borough Council.

32 Study for *The Mill Stream*. 1813–14. $8 \times 11\frac{1}{4}$in. Oil on board. Tate Gallery.

33 *Boat-building near Flatford Mill*. 1815. $20 \times 24\frac{3}{4}$in. Oil on canvas. Victoria and Albert Museum.

34 Study for *Boat-building near Flatford Mill*. 1814 sketchbook. $3\frac{1}{8} \times 4\frac{3}{4}$in. Pencil. Victoria and Albert Museum.

35 *Flatford Mill on the River Stour*. 1817. 40×50in. Oil on canvas. Tate Gallery.

36 Photograph of towpath near Flatford Mill. Photograph by Brian Bracegirdle. Copyright Alastair Smart.

37 *Towpath near Flatford Mill*. 1814 sketchbook. $3\frac{1}{8} \times 4\frac{1}{4}$in. Pencil. Victoria and Albert Museum.

38 *Trees at East Bergholt*. 1817. $21\frac{3}{4} \times 15$in. Pencil. Victoria and Albert Museum.

39 *The White Horse*. 1819. $51\frac{1}{4} \times 74\frac{1}{8}$in. Oil on canvas. New York, The Frick Collection.

40 Photograph of a horse on a barge. 1902.

41 *Stratford Mill on the Stour*. 1820. 50×72in. Oil on canvas. England, private collection.

42 Photograph of site of *Stratford Mill on the Stour*. Copyright C. Attfield Brooks.

43 *Study of clouds*. 1822. $11\frac{3}{4} \times 19$in. Oil on paper. Victoria and Albert Museum.

44 *A Heath.* 1831. Mezzotint by David Lucas after *Branch Hill Pond,* 1824.

45 *Willy Lott's House near Flatford Mill.* 1810–15. $9\frac{1}{2} \times 7\frac{1}{8}$in. Oil on paper. *Recto.* Victoria and Albert Museum.

46 *Willy Lott's House near Flatford Mill.* 1810–15. $9\frac{1}{2} \times 7\frac{1}{8}$in. Oil on paper. *Verso.* Victoria and Albert Museum.

47 *Willy Lott's House.* 1830 (?). $10\frac{3}{4} \times 9\frac{1}{2}$in. Oil on canvas. Victoria and Albert Museum.

48 X-ray of detail revealing man on horseback from *The Hay Wain.*

49 *Willy Lott's Cottage.* 1816. $15\frac{1}{2} \times 18\frac{1}{4}$in. Oil on paper on canvas. Ipswich Borough Council.

50 Rubens (1577–1640). *An Autumn Landscape with a View of the Château de Steen.* 1636. $51\frac{3}{4} \times 90\frac{1}{2}$in. Oil on wood. London, National Gallery.

51 Full-scale study for *The Hay Wain.* 1821. 54×74in. Oil on canvas. Victoria and Albert Museum.

52 Full-scale study for *View on the Stour near Dedham.* 1821–2. 51×73in. Oil on canvas. London, Royal Holloway College.

53 *A view on the Stour.* p. 27 of 1814 sketchbook. $3 \times 4\frac{1}{4}$in. Pencil. Victoria and Albert Museum.

54 *A view on the Stour.* p. 52 of 1814 sketchbook. $3 \times 4\frac{1}{4}$in. Pencil. Victoria and Albert Museum.

55 *A view on the Stour.* p. 59 of 1814 sketchbook. $3 \times 4\frac{1}{4}$in. Pencil. Victoria and Albert Museum.

56 *View on the Stour near Dedham.* 1822. 51×74in. Oil on canvas. San Marino, California, Henry E. Huntington Library and Art Gallery.

57 *Flatford.* 1827. 8×13in. Pencil. Dublin, National Gallery of Ireland.

58 *A Boat passing a Lock.* 1826. 40×50in. London, Royal Academy of Arts.

59 *A Lock on the Stour with Dedham Church in the distance.* 1827. 8×13in. Pencil. British Museum.

60 *The Leaping Horse.* 1825. $56 \times 73\frac{3}{4}$in. Oil on canvas. London, Royal Academy of Arts.

61 Photograph of a sluice. Copyright C. Attfield Brooks.

62 Full-scale study for *The Leaping Horse.* 1825. 51×74in. Oil on canvas. Victoria and Albert Musuem.

63 Sketch for *The Leaping Horse.* 8×7in. Chalk and ink wash. British Museum.

64 Detail of *The Cornfield.* 1826. $56\frac{1}{4} \times 48$in. Oil on canvas. London, National Gallery.

65 *A Country Lane.* 1821. $8 \times 11\frac{3}{4}$in. Oil on canvas. Tate Gallery.

66 Photograph of Higham church from Langham. Copyright C. Attfield Brooks.

67 Landscape sketch for *The Cornfield.* 1826(?). $23\frac{1}{2} \times 9$in. Oil on canvas. Private collection, on loan to the City Museum and Art Gallery, Birmingham.

68 Gaspard Poussin (Dughet) (1615–75). *Landscape near Albano: Evening.* 19 × 26in. Oil on canvas. London, National Gallery.

69 *Study of plough.* 1814. $6\frac{3}{4}$ × $10\frac{1}{4}$in. Oil on paper with a brown ground. Victoria and Albert Museum.

70 *Flatford Old Bridge and Bridge Cottage on the Stour.* 1827. $8\frac{7}{8}$ × 13in. Pencil. Victoria and Albert Museum.

71 Photograph of Bridge Cottage. Copyright C. Attfield Brooks.

72 *The Valley of the Stour with Dedham in the distance.* 1800–5. $19\frac{5}{8}$ × $23\frac{3}{4}$in. Oil on paper laid on canvas. Victoria and Albert Museum.

73 Photograph of site of *The Valley of the Stour, with Dedham in the distance.* Photograph by Alan Bower. Copyright C. Attfield Brooks.

74 Detail of *Dedham Vale.* 1828. $55\frac{1}{2}$ × 48in. Oil on canvas. Edinburgh, National Gallery of Scotland.

75 *Dedham Vale.* 1828. $55\frac{1}{2}$ × 48in. Oil on canvas. Edinburgh, National Gallery of Scotland.

76 *The Valley Farm.* 1835. $58\frac{1}{2}$ × $49\frac{1}{2}$in. Oil on canvas. Tate Gallery.

77 Detail of study for *The Valley Farm. c.* 1800–3. $7\frac{7}{8}$ × $11\frac{1}{4}$in. Pencil. University of London, Courtauld Institute of Art.

78 Study of ash trees. 13 × $9\frac{3}{8}$in. Pencil. Victoria and Albert Museum.

79 '*Suffolk Child*': sketch for *The Valley Farm. c.* 1835(?). $7\frac{1}{4}$ × $5\frac{3}{8}$in. Pencil and watercolour. Victoria and Albert Museum.

80 Sketch for *The Valley Farm. c.* 1835. $13\frac{3}{8}$ × 11in. Oil on canvas. Victoria and Albert Museum.

81 *View on the Stour: Dedham Church in the distance. c.* 1832–6. 8 × $6\frac{5}{8}$in. Pencil and sepia wash. Victoria and Albert Museum.

82 Study of water-lilies. 1813 sketchbook. $3\frac{1}{2}$ × $4\frac{3}{4}$in. Pencil. Victoria and Albert Museum.

Map of road access to Constable's country. *Page 25*

Detailed map showing the sites of Constable's viewpoints. *Page 30*

Colour

I *Flatford Mill from a Lock on the Stour. c.* 1811? $9\frac{3}{4}$ × $11\frac{3}{4}$in. Oil on canvas. Victoria and Albert Museum. *Facing page 96*

Flatford Mill. Photograph by Brian Bracegirdle. Copyright Alastair Smart.

II Willy Lott's Cottage. Photograph by Brian Bracegirdle. Copyright Alastair Smart. *Facing page 97*

The Hay Wain. 1821. $51\frac{3}{4}$ × 73in. Oil on canvas. London, National Gallery.

III Lane leading from East Bergholt to Fen Bridge. Photograph by Brian Bracegirdle. Copyright Alastair Smart. *Facing page 112*

IV *The Cornfield.* 1826. $56\frac{1}{4}$ × 48in. Oil on canvas. London, National Gallery. *Facing page 113*

Preface

Many years ago, when I made my first visit to 'Constable's Country' and stood by Flatford Mill at the site of *The Hay Wain,* I was intrigued to discover that Constable had considerably shortened the roof of Willy Lott's Cottage, 11
clearly with the object of accommodating the tall chimney within his composition. C. R. Leslie, his friend and first biographer, visited East Bergholt in 1840, and noticed that whereas the resemblance between the sites of the Suffolk pictures and the paintings themselves was often "startling", in other cases "Constable had rather combined and varied the materials, than given exact views". The whole question of the content of Constable's art is of absorbing interest: to what extent were his pictures topographically accurate, and to what extent did he improvise and invent?

In 1960 Mr Graham Reynolds published the first edition of his catalogue of the Constable Collection in the Victoria and Albert Museum, which, together with the same author's masterly *Constable, The Natural Painter* and the volumes of Constable's correspondence and lectures edited by R. B. Beckett, has a place of special importance in the literature on the artist. The second edition of this work, which appeared in 1973, incorporates many of Lieut.-Colonel Brooks's findings concerning the topography of Constable's paintings and drawings of his native scenes. As Mr Reynolds expressed it, Colonel Brooks had given him "many convincing demonstrations of the artist's accuracy in delineating his homeland". A year later I had the pleasure of meeting Colonel Brooks and the unforgettable experience of being taken by him on a tour of 'Constable's Country'. The bulk of his material—and not least his unique photographs—remained unpublished; and I therefore invited him to collaborate on this book, in order that his quite fundamental work on the topography of the Suffolk pictures might be made more fully available to the public, and so that we might explore together the relationship in Constable's art between truth and imagination.

In writing my own essay on Constable, I have been conscious throughout of my debt, not only to Attfield Brooks, but also to the many scholars who have illuminated Constable's genius, and especially those who have done so much to establish the chronology of his works and to identify the studies for particular compositions. The Bibliography will give some indication of the scope of this indebtedness. I wish, further, to express my thanks to Mr Ian Fleming-Williams and Mr Leslie Parris for kindly answering specific inquiries. The colour photographs of Suffolk sites were taken for me by Mr Brian Bracegirdle: his skills were recommended to me by Mr James Bingley, Warden of the Flatford Mill Field Centre, to whom I am grateful for various kindnesses. I am grateful in addition to Dr Michael Pearson, Senior Lecturer in Botany at the University of Nottingham, for his expert advice upon the trees, plants and flowers represented in some of Constable's Suffolk pictures, and to Mrs Steve Palmer, Photograph Librarian of the Department of Fine Art, for her tireless efficiency. Finally I must express my appreciation of the helpfulness and constructive enthusiasm shown by Miss Janet Haffner and Miss Ann Mitchell of Paul Elek Books Limited.

ALASTAIR SMART, University of Nottingham

Professor Alastair Smart has written above of the tour of 'Constable's Country' which he made with me on a glorious late summer day. For me it was a tremendous experience to show a man who already knew so much of Constable's art the main recognisable sites from where the artist took his views. He gave a new dimension to my understanding of what I had been groping for over the past decade. I accepted his invitation to join forces with him in a book he was planning—although I had never attempted anything of the kind before—because he had made me feel I had a contribution to make to the total sum of knowledge about John Constable in his country. It has been a joy to work with him, and I must express my warmest appreciation to him. Among the people too numerous to name who have helped me I must especially mention the encouragement given to me in the early days by the late Mr R. B. Beckett and Mr Graham Reynolds without which I might never have persevered with my hobby. Recently both Mr Fleming-Williams and Mr Leslie Parris have given me valuable help. My thanks are due to them. Finally I must thank my wife who over the years has been very long-suffering when, because of transient though vital effects of light, I have dashed off at inconvenient moments to secure particular photographs.

ATTFIELD BROOKS, Dedham

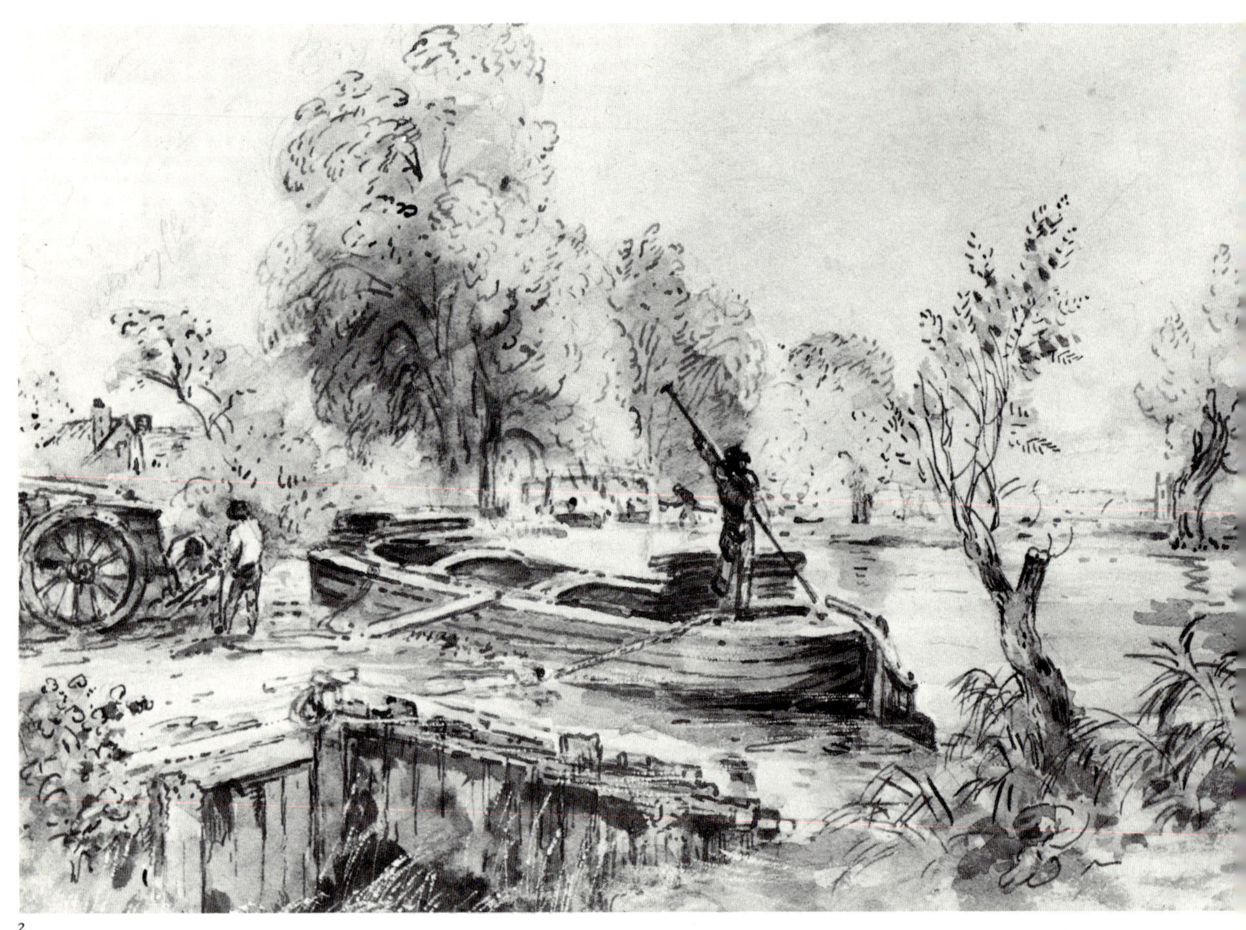

2

Men loading a barge on the Stour
This delightful drawing of normal work in progress at Flatford, made while Constable was on holiday there in October 1827, shows a busy scene near the lock which is visible on the far side of the river. Also shown are the buildings of Flatford Mill and in the foreground the barrier of the little dry dock where the barges were built. Thus it has elements of many of the drawings and paintings considered and illustrated in this volume. These include *Flatford Mill, from a Lock on the Stour* (I), taken from the far side of the lock, *Boat-building near Flatford* (33), taken from a little further back and showing the barge in the dock, *Flatford Mill, on the River Stour,* 1817 (35), taken from a point on the far side of the river out of view in this drawing, and *View on the Stour near Dedham* (56) with the related sketches and drawings, taken from the far side of the dry dock with a line of vision about 90° to the right. In all these works all the main topographical features are in correct relationship one with the other and with their positions today. The one exception is the representation of Dedham Church tower alongside the right-hand willow tree. This is not its geographical position at all and this drawing and the exhibited version of *The Leaping Horse* (60) are the only two works known where Constable has displaced this important landmark. This drawing provides an outstanding example of the way many of Constable's works can be studied topographically with all other even remotely connected works to build up a full commentary on his art.

The topography of Constable's country

Attfield Brooks

John Constable was born in 1776 and grew up in the countryside round East Bergholt in Suffolk. His father Golding Constable was a miller and wanted John to go into his business, so he was trained for milling and worked for a year in the mills. Later he went to London to study as an artist and settled there. Yet his writings as well as his work show that the countryside and the scenes round East Bergholt were the main inspiration for his art. Thus the importance of Constable's Country both as part of the national heritage and for lovers and students of Constable's work can hardly be overstressed.

Over the last ten years or so I have become interested in identifying the exact sites of scenes sketched or painted by John Constable, and this interest stems from several factors. In the eighteenth century my family were farmers at Little Bentley, Essex, five miles south of East Bergholt; in about 1799 my great-grandfather took employment with a firm of maltsters, Edward and Francis Norman, at Mistley on the estuary of the River Stour. He lived in a house in Mistley Street, only a stone's throw from the quay where the Constables' flour and the Normans' malt, both products of locally-grown grain, were loaded into sailing ships for transport to bakeries and breweries in London. Both the Constables and my great-grandfather (on the Normans' behalf) were also engaged in marketing local farmers' grain. Undoubtedly the Brooks family and the Constable family must have been acquainted in those days.

I was born, brought up and have worked all my life in places sketched and painted by Constable. Indeed for forty years I have lived in Dedham in a house which in 1874 replaced one which Constable himself must have visited. I have memories of Dedham and Flatford dating back to 1910 when driving through in horse and carriage. As a boy I developed an interest in maps and recognition of the features they record which was encouraged by my parents. This was further developed by twenty years' service in the Essex

Golding Constable, the painter's father
On 21 May 1815 John Constable wrote to Maria Bicknell in London: 'I find my father uncommonly well which has tempted me to begin a portrait of him—he is pleased and makes quite an amusement of it. It promises to be quite the best I have done which I am very glad of.' The prosperous miller was 76 at the time.

View over the garden of Golding Constable's house
This view shows not only the garden belonging to the Constables' imposing house in East Bergholt (now demolished) but the fields beyond which were farmed by Golding Constable until his death, when the house and land were sold. The house itself was not unlike West Lodge, now known as Stour, depicted in (7).

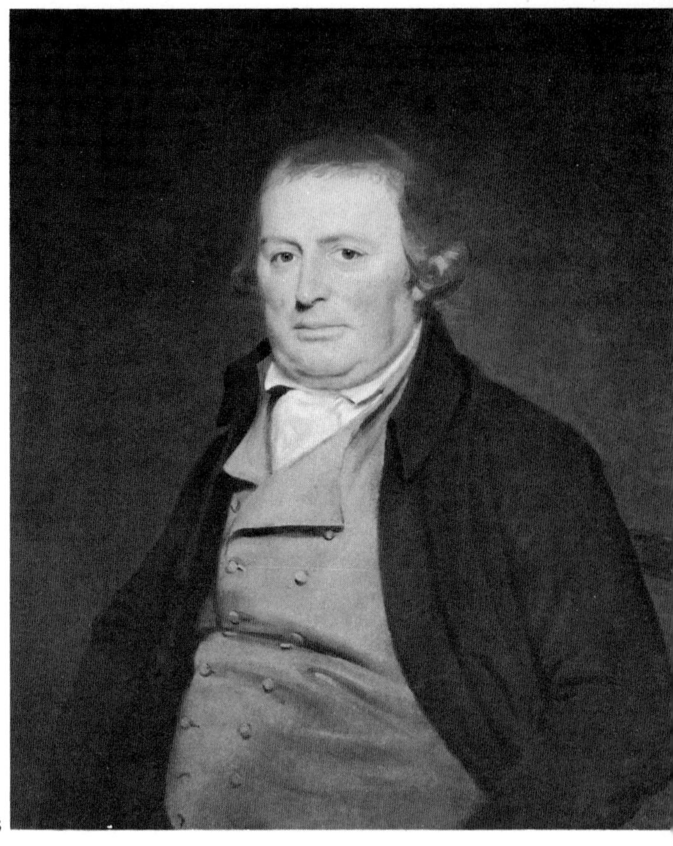
3

5

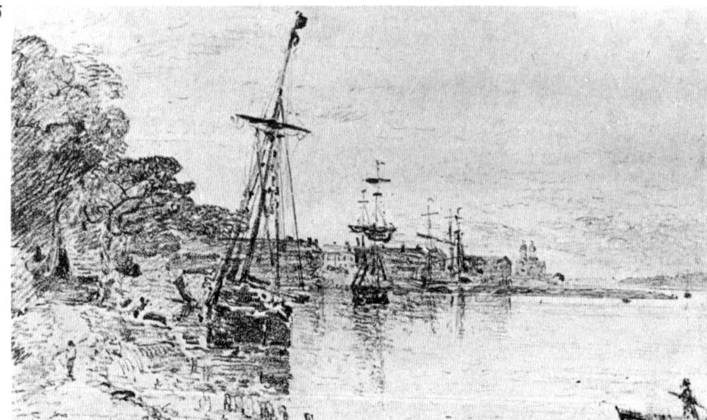

6

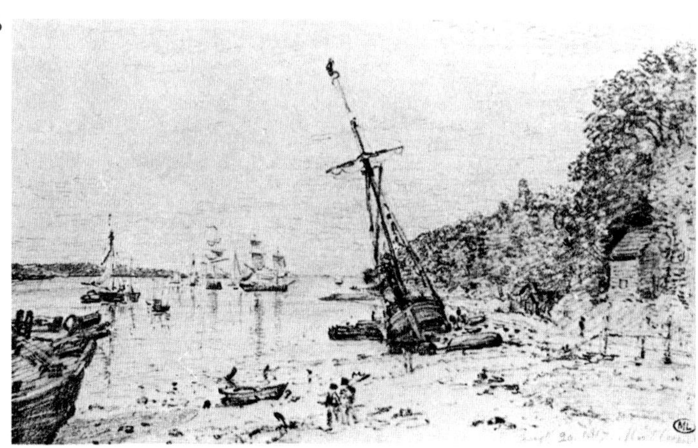

Two river scenes at Mistley, Essex
The vessel aground in the foreshore of each drawing is obviously the same seen from exactly opposite directions, showing that both were made on the same day. The level of the tide is higher in one drawing, while in the other men appear to be examining the planking for possible repairs below the waterline. The tide was probably falling as Constable drew, and we wonder why he made two drawings? Could it possibly be that the ship is *The Balloon* (successor to *The Telegraph*), used by the family milling business for transporting flour to London after transfer from the up-river barges? The scene is much changed by commercial development today, although the towers of Robert Adam's church remain.

Fair at East Bergholt
This view may have been painted from a window in Golding Constable's house. It records the animated side of village life when few could even afford to visit Ipswich.

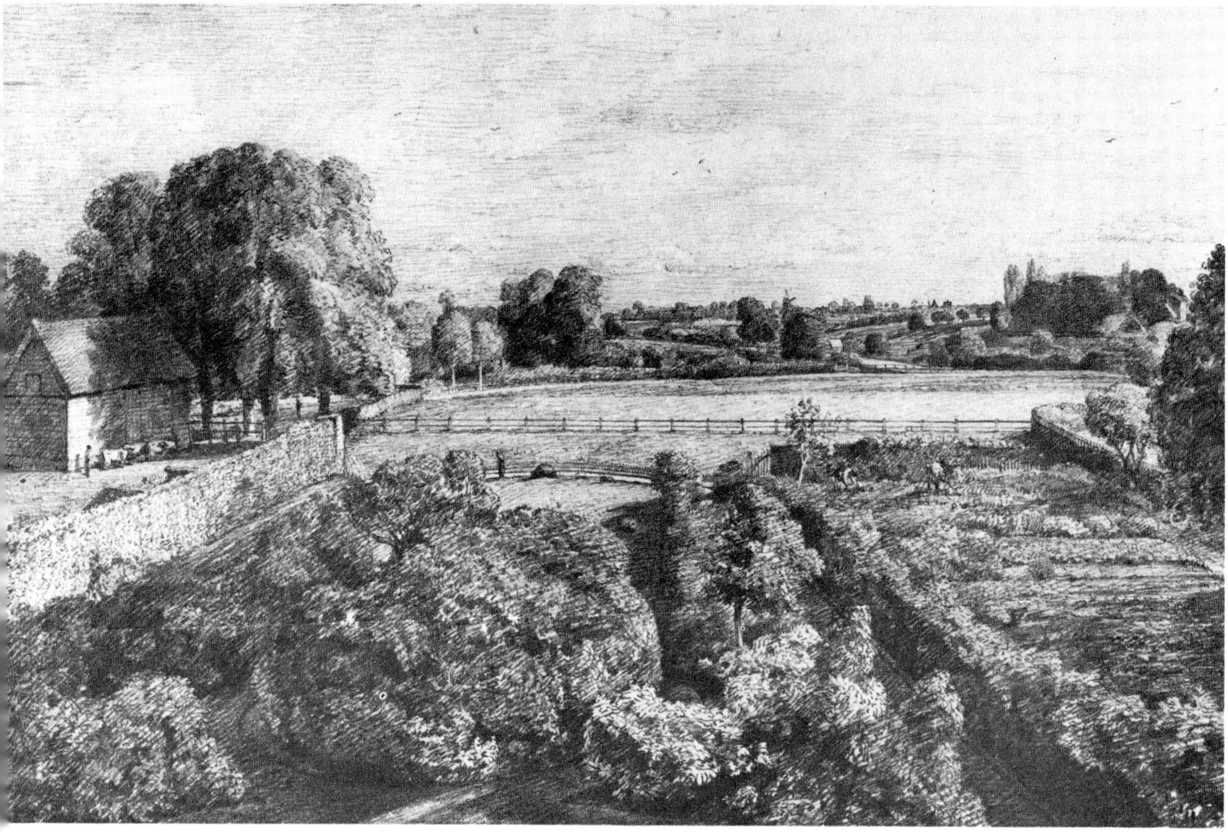

4

7

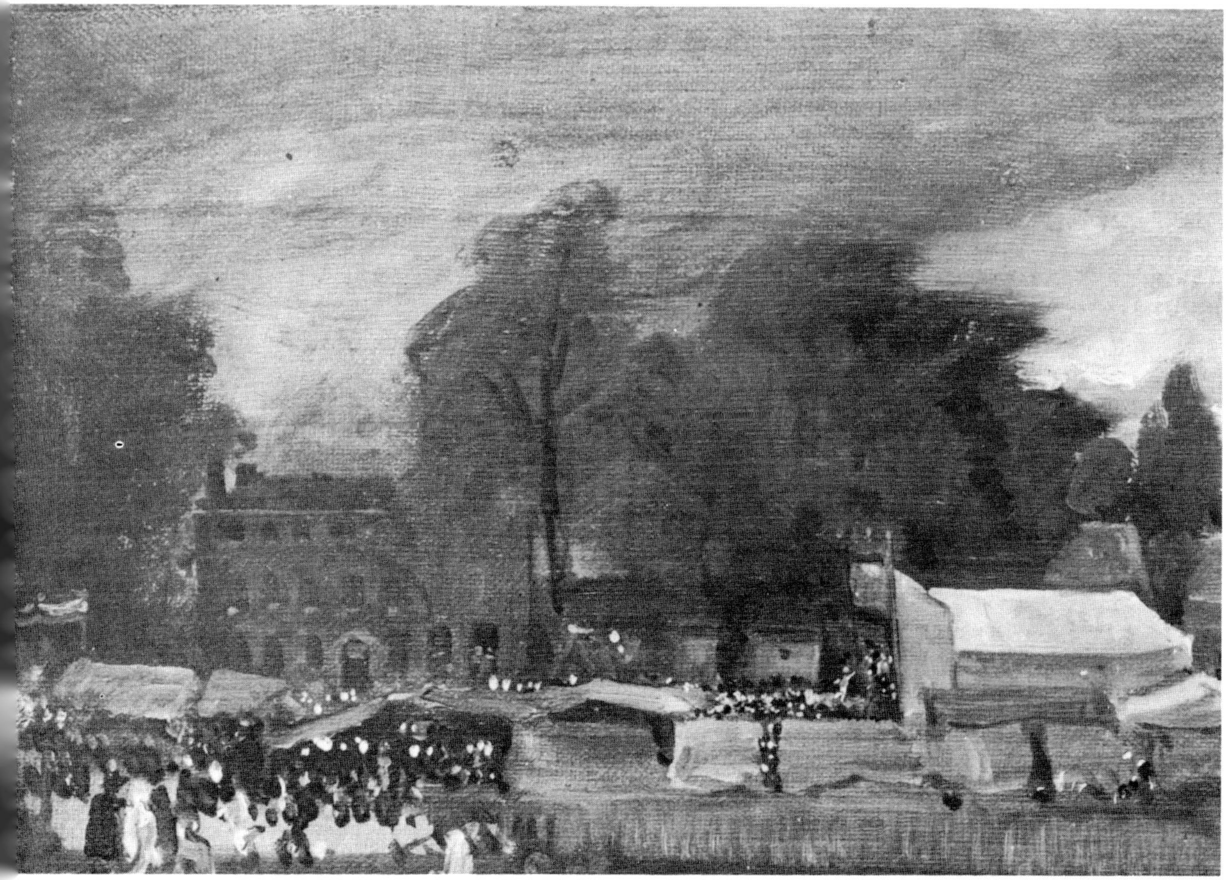

Regiment, Territorial Army, before and during the Second World War.

The incident which triggered off the connection of all these factors into one absorbing hobby took place early in 1963, when I saw for the first time Graham Reynolds's great catalogue of the Constable collection in the Victoria and Albert Museum. Almost at once I recognized that the site of the drawing *Riverside View with Houses* (GR 181) was clearly Mistley on the 5
River Stour about three miles below Flatford, where the Brooks family business was still flourishing. It was here that the barge-loads of flour from Dedham and Flatford were transhipped into Golding Constable's sailing vessel, *The Telegraph*, for transport to London. When this identification was conveyed to Mr Reynolds he said he would welcome any further identifications which might be possible. From this beginning I have extended my knowledge of Constable's work and I have reached a stage where I can often link together his portrayal of scenes from different angles to form an accurate overall picture of the countryside in his time.

Over the years, contact with other interested individuals and with books about the artist has led to some appreciation of his life and artistic qualities. However, it should perhaps be emphasized that my approach to Constable's work has been pragmatic throughout, drawing on my knowledge of the countryside, farming methods, forestry and so on. Sometimes the identification of one view leads to an understanding of another and solves the problem of a hitherto unlocated work. One factor I have discovered is the great importance of viewing the scene at the right time of day and if possible in the type of weather portrayed. For example, the scene of the painting 18
Dedham Vale, Morning, 1811 viewed on a clear sunny day between 9 and 10 a.m., has all the splendour and serenity which Constable gave it, whereas by 1 p.m. it is flat and disappointing and on a dull afternoon worse still with the features barely distinguishable. It is interesting too that, although the pictures almost without exception portray late spring, summer and autumn scenes with the leaves on the trees, the basic features can usually best be studied on a bright March or April day before the buds have burst. The reason for this is that there appear to be many more trees than there were 150 or 160 years ago and they have grown up often in different places. Instances have occurred of my having determined locations and viewpoints with some difficulty; then farming operations suddenly required a hedge to be trimmed: and there is the view in all its glory until in a year or two's time regrowth blots it out again for a long period. This explains why, on occasion, short-stay or day visitors to Constable's Country fail to appreciate how much

that inspired John Constable can still be seen after the gap of two hundred years since his birth.

Constable and farming

John Constable referred to his father not only as a miller but also as a mer- 3
chant. What has been overlooked is that Golding Constable was a farmer as
well. In the advertisement for the sale of his house by auction which appeared
in the *Ipswich Journal* on Saturdays 10, 17, 24 and 31 August 1816 it is described as "Mansion and 15 acres freehold 21 acres copyhold". Leslie in his
biography in 1843 referred to having seen a draft of this advertisement, and
in the East Bergholt Enclosure map of 1817 the various fields are clearly 8
shown. How well these fields were farmed is obvious from the paintings, in
Christchurch Mansion, Ipswich, of Golding Constable's flower garden and
vegetable garden. So from his very earliest days John grew up with his
father's farm over the garden fence and his love of both is shown clearly in the
two meticulous paintings as well as other drawings of the subject. Both as a 4
miller and a merchant Golding Constable needed to keep an eye on the crops
of farmers in the neighbourhood so that he knew what raw materials for the
year ahead would be likely to be available to his mills and also what he might
be asked to market by his neighbours and friends. Young John undoubtedly
accompanied Golding on some of his visits to these neighbouring farms.

An interesting sidelight on the life-style of Golding Constable has recently appeared in the publication by the Essex Record Office of the diary of John Crozier, a miller, of Maldon, Essex. In May 1785, when John Constable was nine years old, Crozier visited East Bergholt for a few days. He did not meet the Constable family but recorded "A Mr Constable, a man of fortune and a miller, has a very elegant house in the street, and lives in the style of a country squire". Another document, in the records of the parish of Ardleigh, recounts the examination before one of His Majesty's Justices of the Peace for the county of Essex on 15 September 1804 of one James Hum, born in the parish of Ardleigh, who stated on oath that "in the year 1800 he hired himself to Golden Constable of East Bergholt, miller, as a servant in livery for one year at the wages of nine guineas, and that he duly served that year complete and received his wages for the same. That he afterwards hired himself to the said Golden Constable for two years more and served the said two years and received his wages for the same".

These new facts not only reinforce the impression that Golding Constable

1

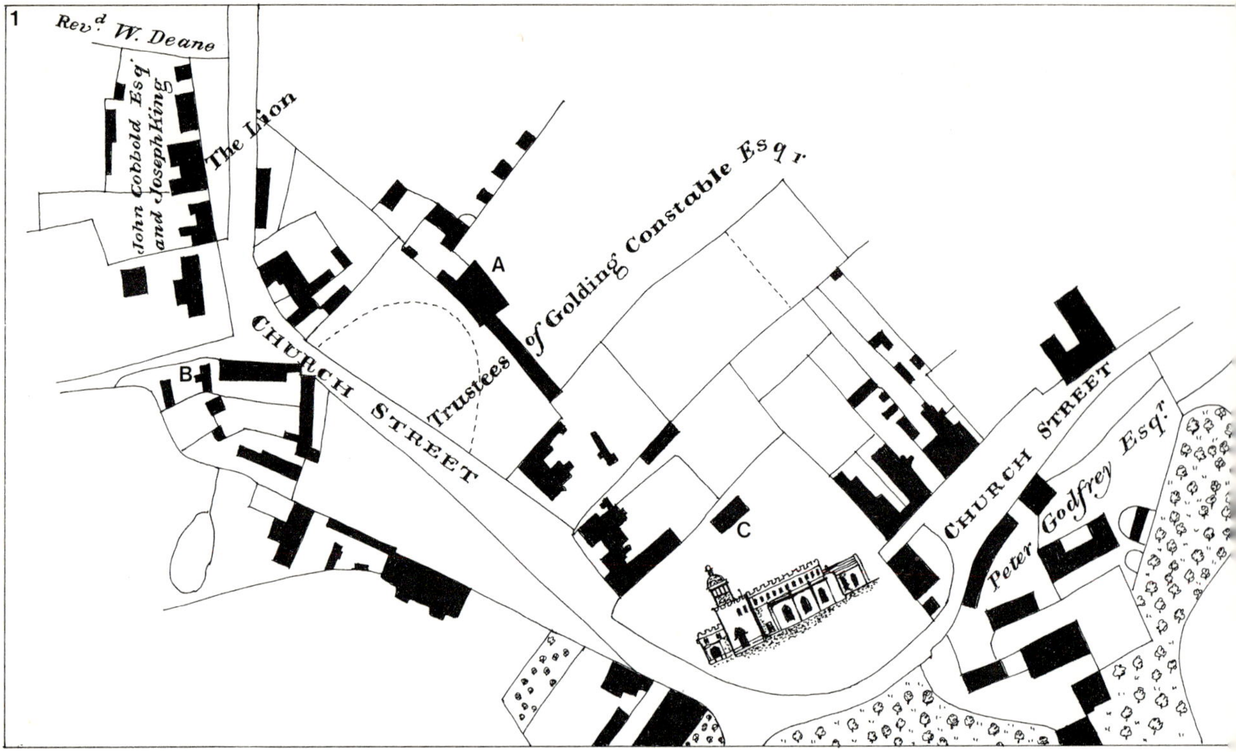

Rev.[d] W. Deane

John Cobbold Esq.[r] and Joseph King

The Lion

Trustees of Golding Constable Esq[r]

A

B

CHURCH STREET

C

CHURCH STREET

Peter Godfrey Esq.[r]

3

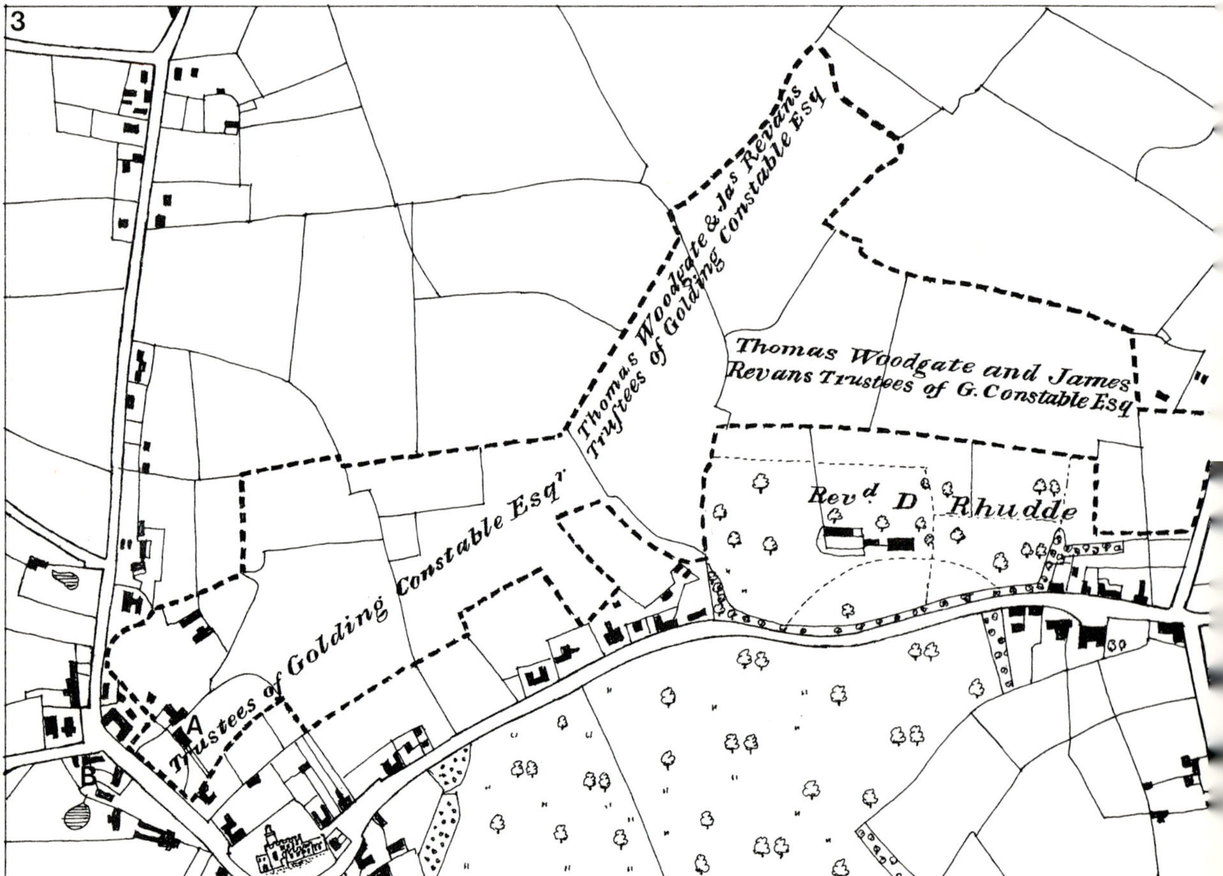

Thomas Woodgate & Ja.[s] Revans Trustees of Golding Constable Esq

Thomas Woodgate and James Revans Trustees of G. Constable Esq

Rev.[d] D. Rhudde

Trustees of Golding Constable Esq[r]

A

B

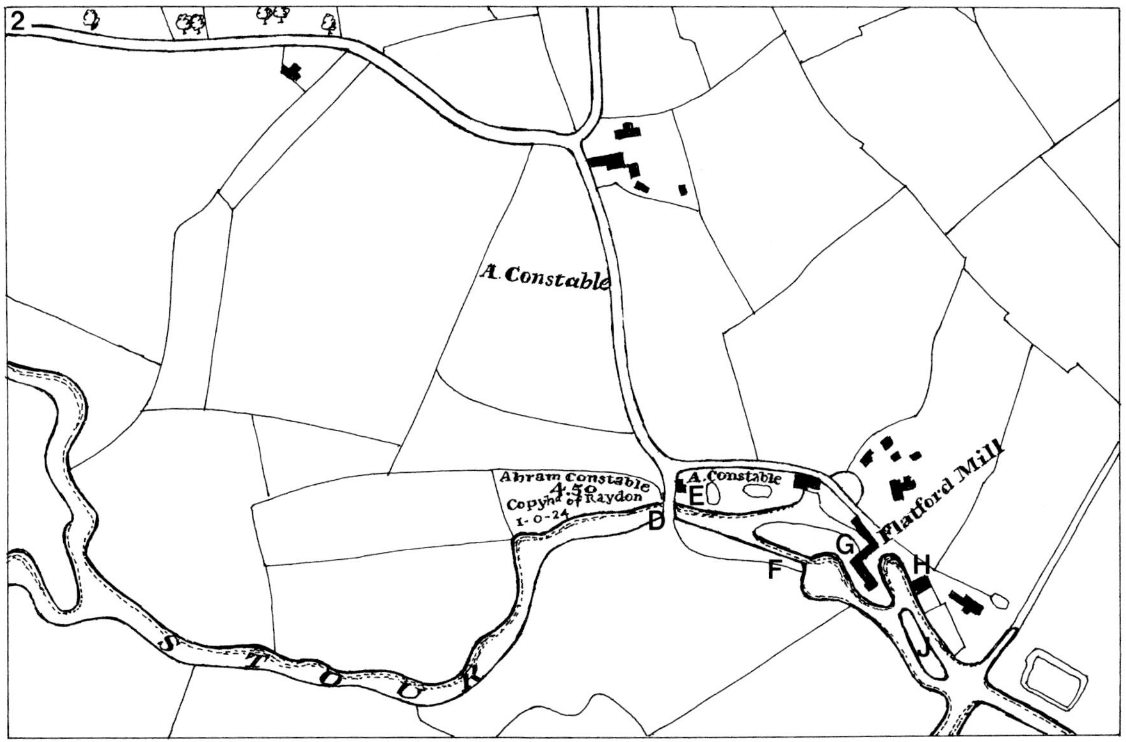

These extracts from a detailed and accurate contemporary survey show very clearly the location of Golding Constable's house, the land he farmed, and John Constable's studio, all in the vicinity of East Bergholt Street. That of Flatford shows the sites of many of the major paintings, such as the bridge and Bridge Cottage, the barge-building dock, the lock, Willy Lott's Cottage, the tailrace of the mill and the water lane or shallow channel leading to the ford across to the fields.

Details taken from *East Bergholt Enclosure Award* 1817

1 CHURCH STREET showing:
A Golding Constable's house
B John Constable's studio
C The Bell Cage in the churchyard

2 FLATFORD showing:
D Flatford Bridge
E Boat-building dock
F Flatford Lock
G Flatford Mill
H Willy Lott's Cottage
J The Spong (island)

3 GOLDING CONSTABLE'S LAND
A Golding Constable's house
B John Constable's studio

was a man of substance but show that as well as being a mill owner he had a wide knowledge of farming and country affairs. Undoubtedly the Constable family went about the countryside to a considerable degree. By the time, therefore, that John went to Dedham Grammar School as a day boy, walking daily through the fields and across the river to Dedham, he already had plenty of knowledge of farming and of the crops to enable his keen observation to take in so much of all his surroundings. These surroundings, as he later recorded, were mainly responsible for his desire to become an artist—"They made me a painter."

Constable's country

The Constable country is an undefined stretch of countryside near East Bergholt in which he grew up and worked. This study will be confined to works occurring in the stretch of the River Stour from just below Flatford Mill to Stratford Mill about three miles higher upstream, together with scenes on the hillsides around. In this stretch of countryside the artist executed hundreds of sketches in both oil, watercolour, pencil, and other media. He returned to these sketches time and time again when composing his great six-foot canvases in London, as Alastair Smart will show later. Some of them are extraordinarily accurate topographically, while others cannot at first sight be related to any known scene. In the following essay associated groups of works will be examined, how much in each is composition and how much relates to the actual site itself will be discussed.

The River Stour rises up in the Suffolk countryside north of the town of Haverhill, flowing down past the towns of Long Melford, Sudbury and Bures to Nayland, forming for the most part the county boundary between Suffolk on the north and Essex to the south. Here it may be said to approach Constable's Country and as it proceeds down through the valley Stoke-by-Nayland Church, a feature of numerous sketchbook drawings, is prominent on the hill to the north. Lower down near Higham Church a tributary, the Brett, enters on its left bank. In rather less than a mile, close by Stratford St Mary Lock, the large pumping station of the South Essex waterworks, erected in 1928, is a very conspicuous object which detracts from the beauty of the scene. Close by the remains of Stratford Mill are visible, and from a reach running southwards can be seen Langham Hills where Constable worked so often, now covered in woods. Flowing close beneath these the river turns past Le Talbooth restaurant, under Stratford Bridge which

replaced the one prominent in many of Constable's pictures. Immediately 73
below this it flows under the new dual carriageway which was so skilfully placed across Constable's Country in 1965, and then on to the very well known Dedham Lock and Mill. The mill-pool is not much changed but is now often used by canoeists who are able to find rapid water escaping from the mill sluices in which to practise for competitions. Dedham Bridge was reconstructed in 1974. About half a mile farther on the county boundary, following the course of the old river, diverges to the right through a modern concrete sluice. The river than takes a bend to the left and comes to the spot where New Fen Bridge used to stand, across which Constable used to walk daily from his home to Dedham Grammar School. Another half mile brings it to the familiar scenes of Flatford Bridge, Lock and Mill, shortly below which it is rejoined by the county boundary and comes to Judas Gap. Here there is a spillway which allows surplus water to escape into the head waters of the southern branch of the estuary. Flowing on, protected from the saltings by a sea-wall, it comes to the Lock and Mill at Brantham. This Lock was the point where the barges coming down from Sudbury and Dedham used to enter the salt water in the northern branch of the estuary. They continued down under Cattawade Bridge, whence they proceeded to Mistley Quay. In 1973, this branch of the estuary has been dammed below Cattawade Bridge, and is now all fresh water. There are an intake and a pumping station near Brantham Mill to take the water (much of which has been pumped over from the Ely Ouse to join the Stour near Haverhill) to Abberton reservoir for purification and pumping on to consumers in south Essex. The southern branch of the estuary has been protected from tidal flooding by a special sluice. A map of approaches to the area is reproduced on page 25, and a detailed map of Constable's Country on page 30.

The importance of the topographical studies

John Constable's compositions under consideration later in this volume are those painted during the period in which he was at the height of his powers and in which he aimed to achieve the highest expression of his artistic vision—*The Hay Wain,* the *View on the Stour near Dedham, The Leaping Horse, The Cornfield, Dedham Vale* and others. Whilst, as will be shown, he always had an actual scene in mind and desired the end result to be a credit to his aim to be a "natural painter", topographical accuracy was not necessarily such an important matter to him as it seems to have been in his earlier work. Therefore,

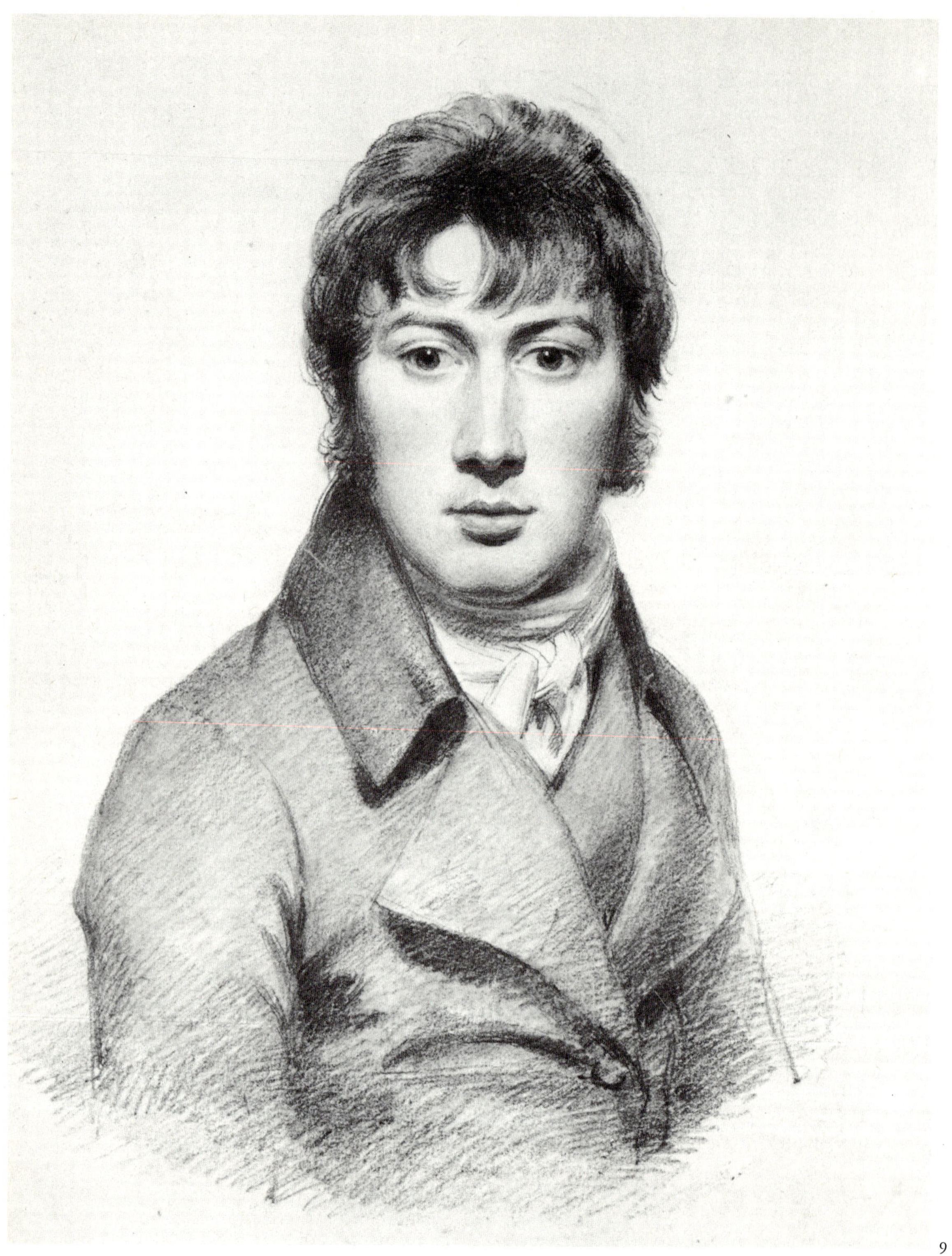

9

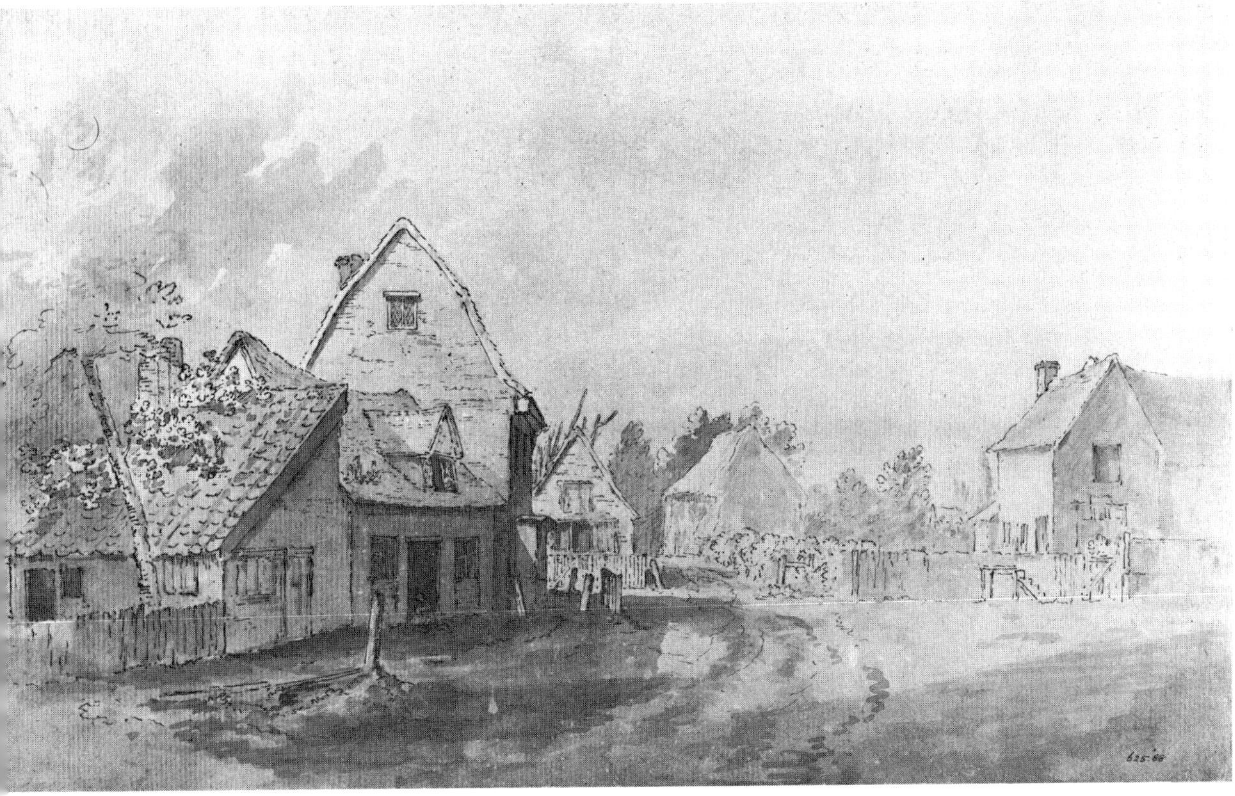

10

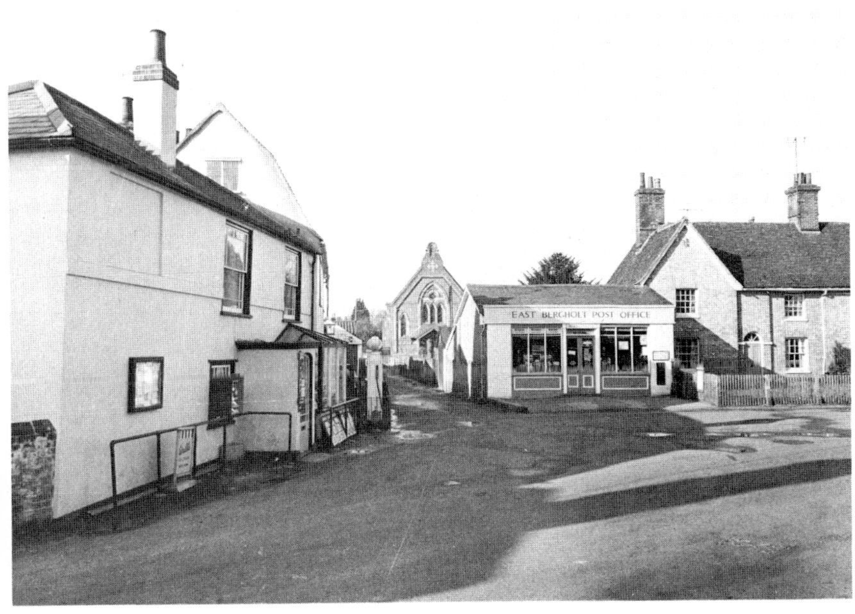

11

Self-portrait of John Constable, aged about 20

East Bergholt Street
In 1802 Constable bought a cottage to use as a studio—presumably with his father's help—behind this group of buildings, which are still present as a group today. The windowed gable on the left is unmistakable, as is the house on the right side on to which the Post Office has now been added. The site of the old barn is now occupied by the United Reformed Church.

12

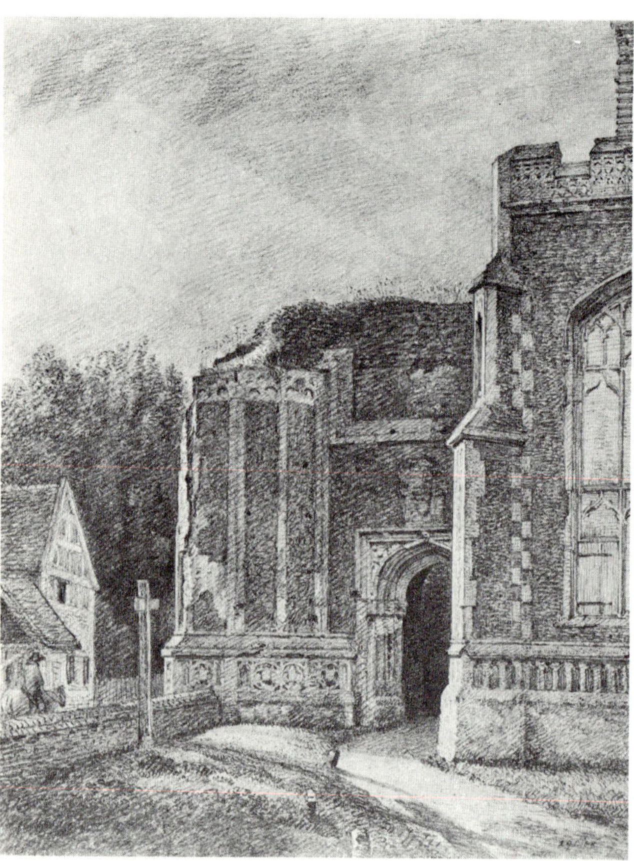

13

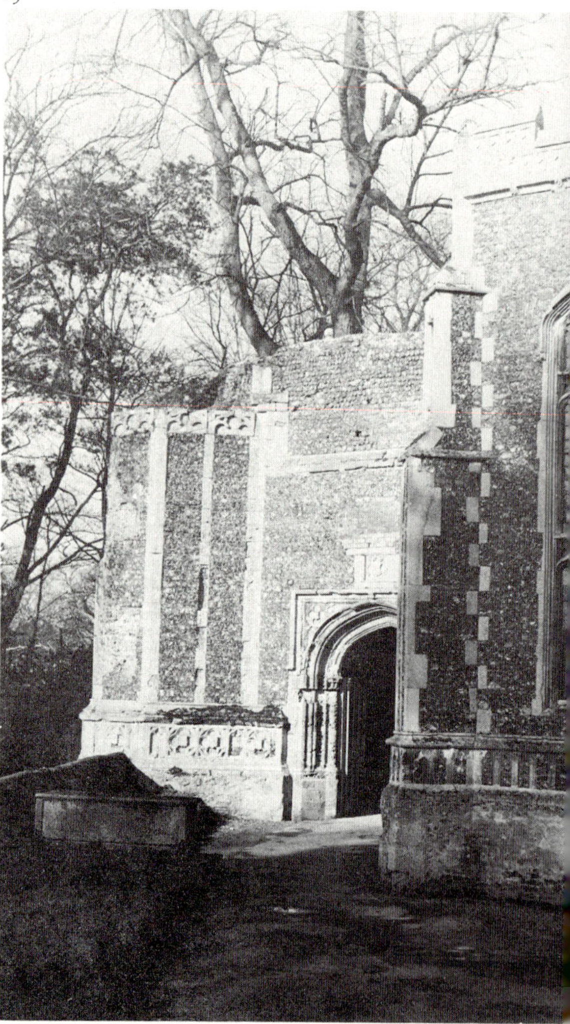

East Bergholt Church: south archway of the ruined tower
This is a masterpiece of detailed drawing, typical of many which Constable executed of the church. Careful examination and comparison with details in the photograph, especially the corner dressings of the buttress, the brick toothing of the top of the west end of the church ready to be joined to the tower, and the scars on the tower where flints have fallen away, reveal the artist's meticulous accuracy.

before proceeding to the detailed examination of the topography of the great works and comparison of the drawings and sketches used in their final composition, it is desirable to show how he began as an artist and to discuss a few representative examples of earlier and simpler items. The plates that follow show a selection of sketches, drawings and oil paintings outside the mainstream of the works examined in this volume (14-21). Each is accompanied by a photograph of the scene taken within the last few years from very close to Constable's viewpoint. The correspondence between these and the original works will need no emphasis. In some of the later works it has also been possible to obtain similar photographs. These, with notes about them and about contemporary practices in agriculture and the countryside given in the Appendix, provide valuable additional material for the proper understanding of Constable's methods. Indeed this evidence can often offer possible solutions or even positive answers to puzzling problems.

Map of road access to Constable's Country

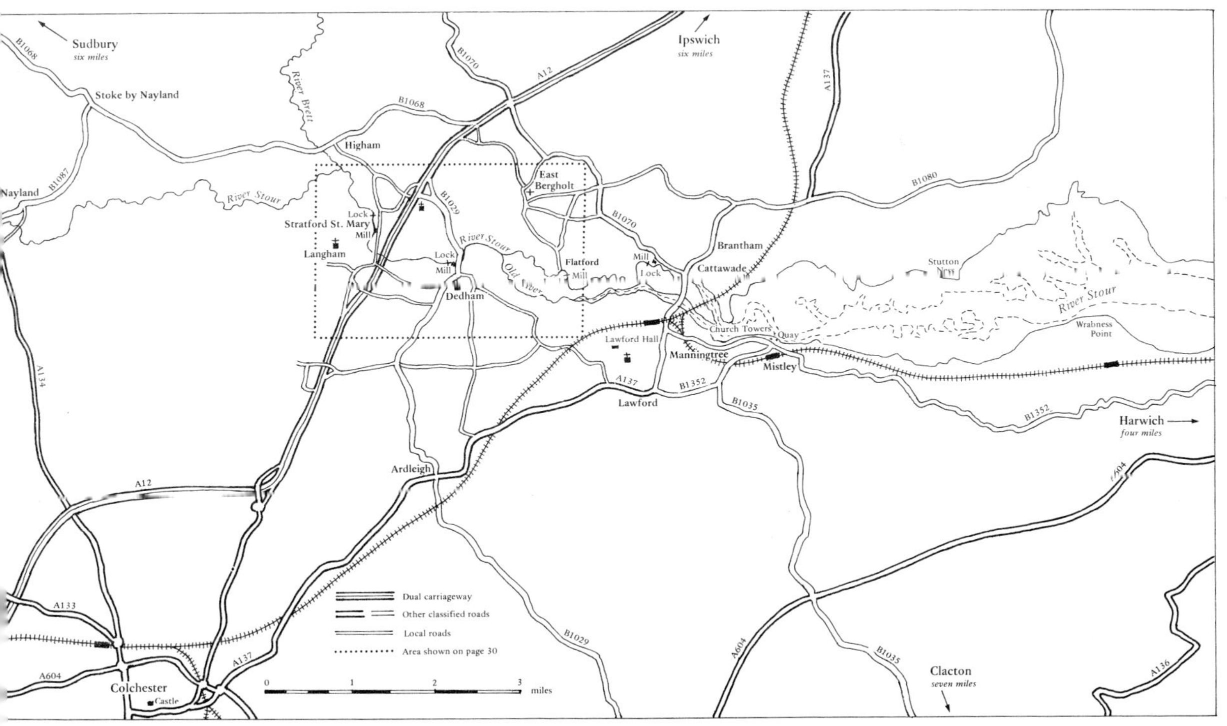

14

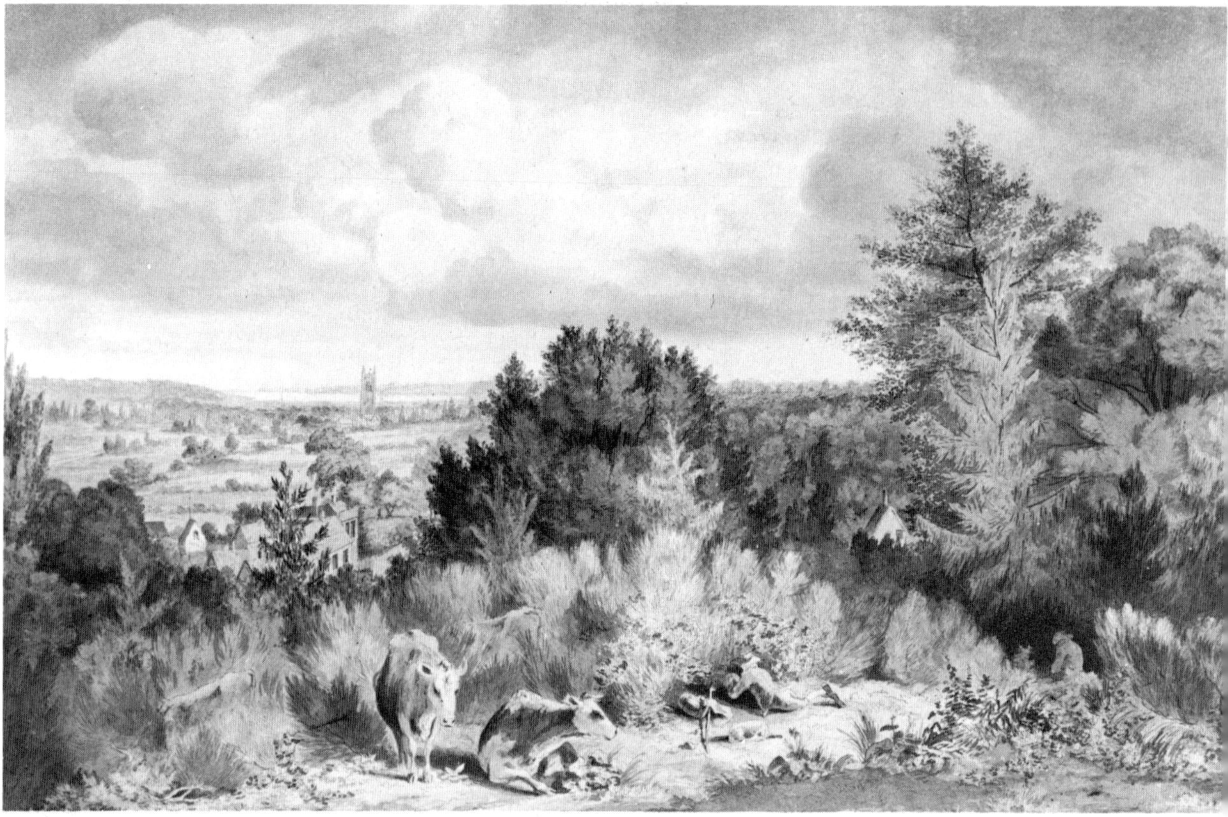

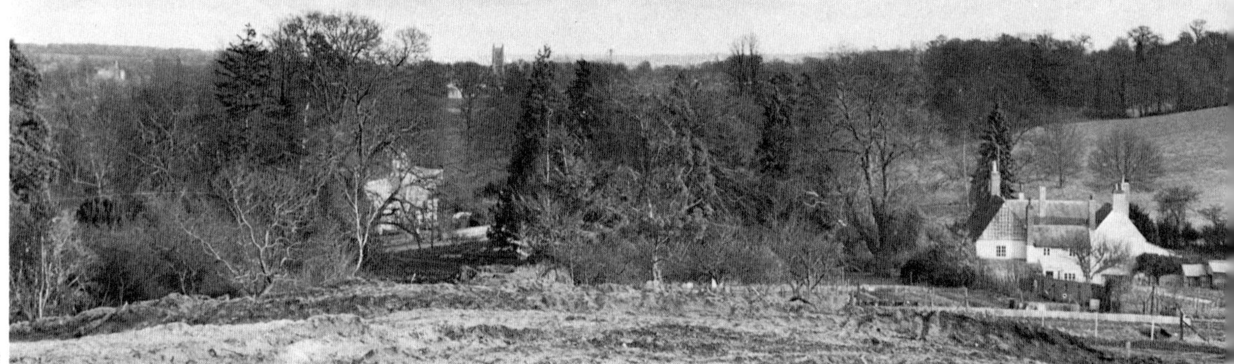

15

Dedham Church and Vale
In 1800 Constable executed a series of four watercolours giving a panoramic view of the scene from the hill above Gun Hill, Dedham, as a wedding present for Lucy Hurlock, daughter of the curate of Langham Church nearby. They are all extremely detailed and meticulously accurate, though much of the view, taken from the edge of the wood at the top of the bank above Stratford Road, adjacent to the bridge, is now obscured by trees. However, in both the painting and the photograph Dedham Church tower, the house called Dalethorpe below it, the hills in the far distance down the estuary of the Stour, and the chimney and gable of the house to the right called The Rookery may be clearly identified.

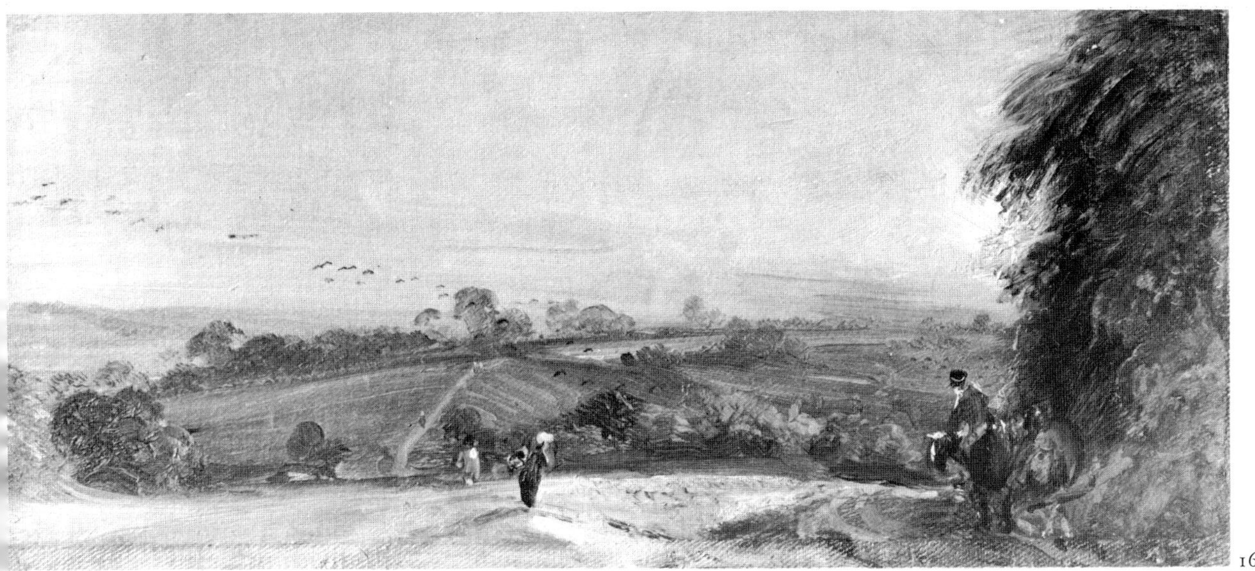

16

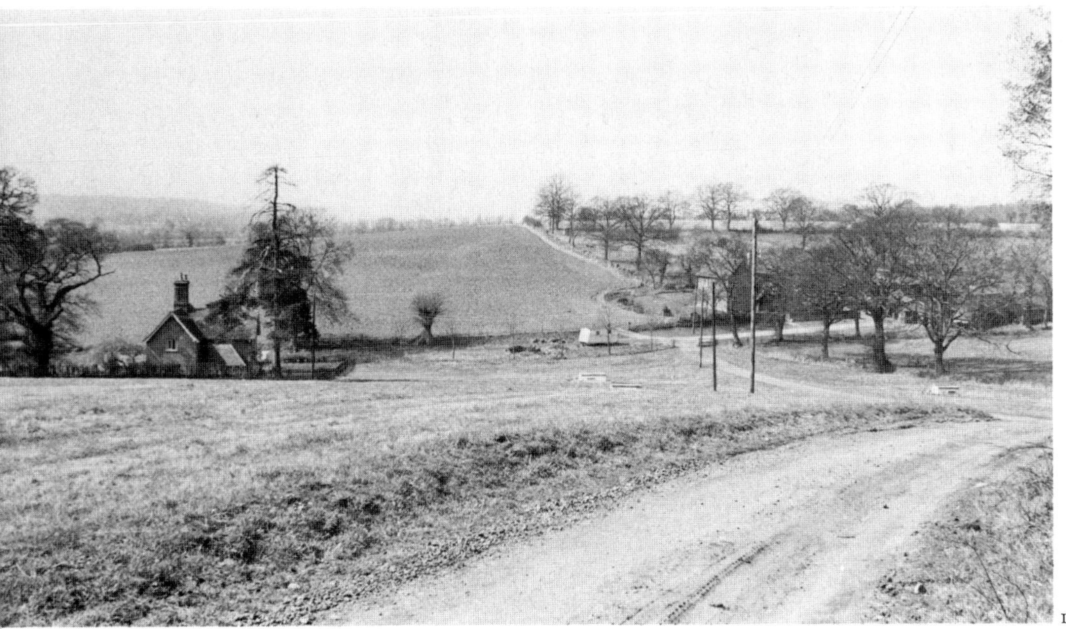

17

Autumnal Sunset
A sketchbook drawing of the same scene (reproduced on the titlepage) shows a crop of wheat in ear, whilst this oil sketch seems to show stubble after harvest, in which case they are both likely to have been done in the same year, 1813, and not as dated elsewhere. The scene is from the lane leading down from East Bergholt Post Office to Vale Farm. Just inside the farm gate the lane becomes private but the footpath continues to Stratford St Mary Church. The path has been diverted in recent years so that instead of proceeding across the middle of the fields as shown in the painting it continues along the lane towards the farm and up the side of the further field. In the photograph, taken in 1963, the remains of the stile in the valley and the track of the old path across the ploughed field on the far side are just visible.

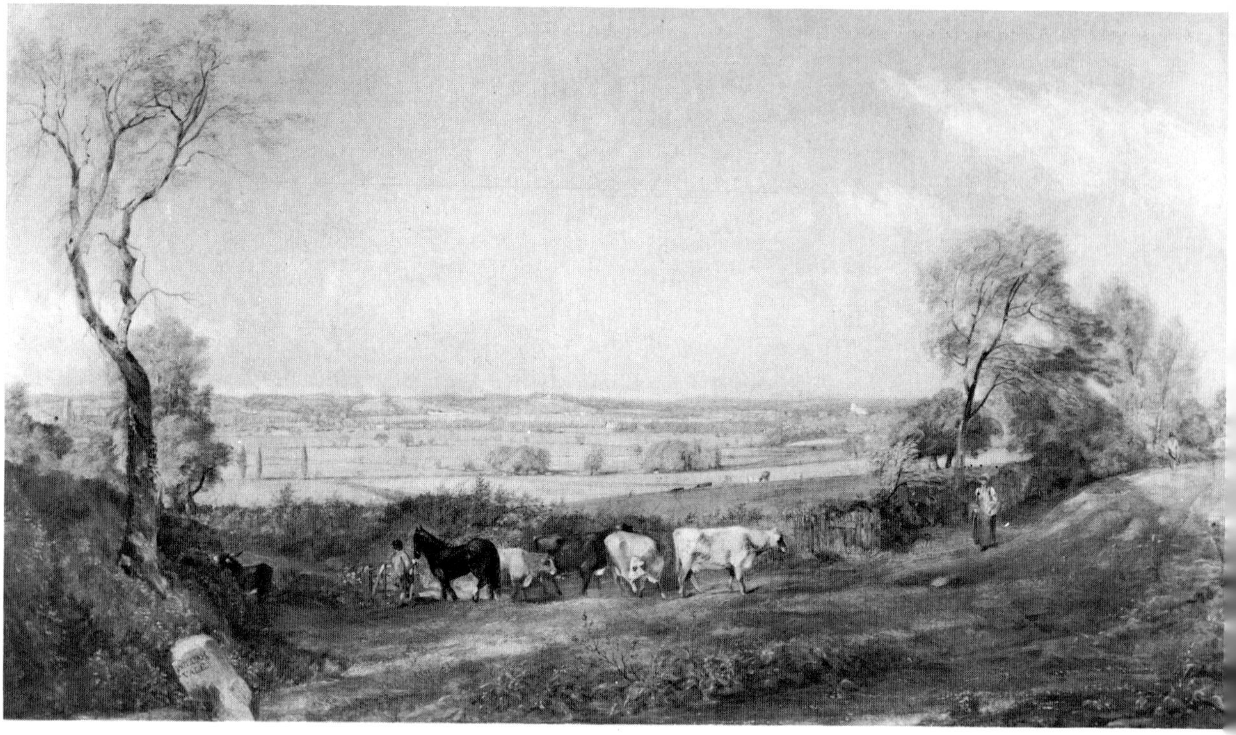

18

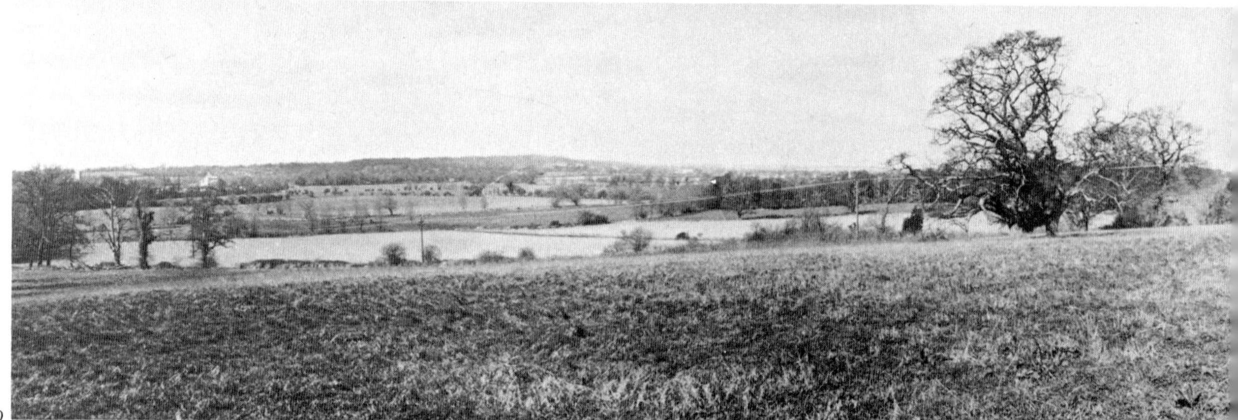

19

Dedham Vale, Morning
This painting is one of the rare instances where it is possible today to identify trees shown by the artist. Near the right-hand middle distance of the painting, under some larger trees in the hedge of the lane, may be seen two young oak trees. Their trunks are at a very recognisable angle which serves to identify them with the two large oak trees in the photograph taken more than 160 years afterwards from a nearer viewpoint. Other identifiable features are the cornfields and many hedges as well as the towers of Dedham and Stratford St Mary churches. This view, like a number of other of Constable's landscapes, is very wide and cannot be taken in by an ordinary camera lens or by a single exposure.

20 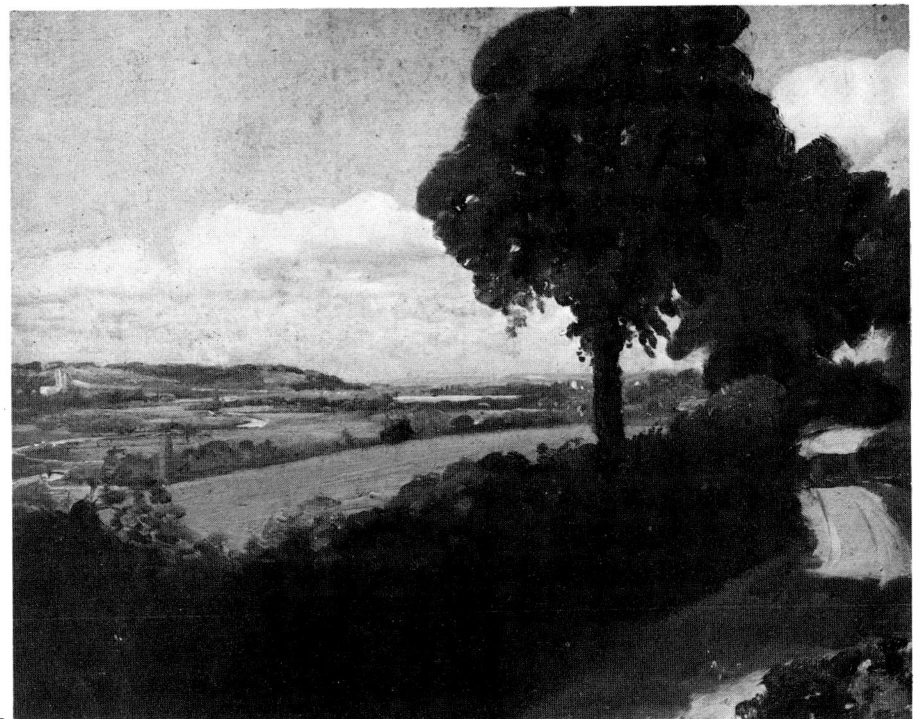

21 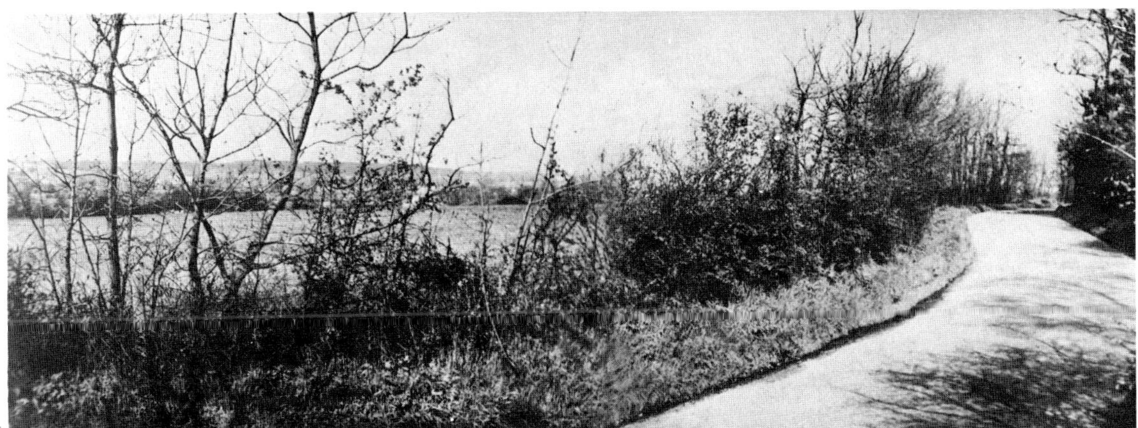

View of Dedham from the lane leading from East Bergholt Church to Flatford
Barely visible in the summer because of the growth of the roadside hedge is this view of Dedham Vale. It occurs along the lane from East Bergholt towards Flatford about 400 yards from the church. Constable has clearly compressed the features on the left in order to keep these details in the picture and to emphasise the slope of the hills: but the bends in the river and distant features, such as Stoke-by-Nayland Church on the skyline and Stratford St Mary Church a little further to the right close to the trunk of the tree, are precisely located.

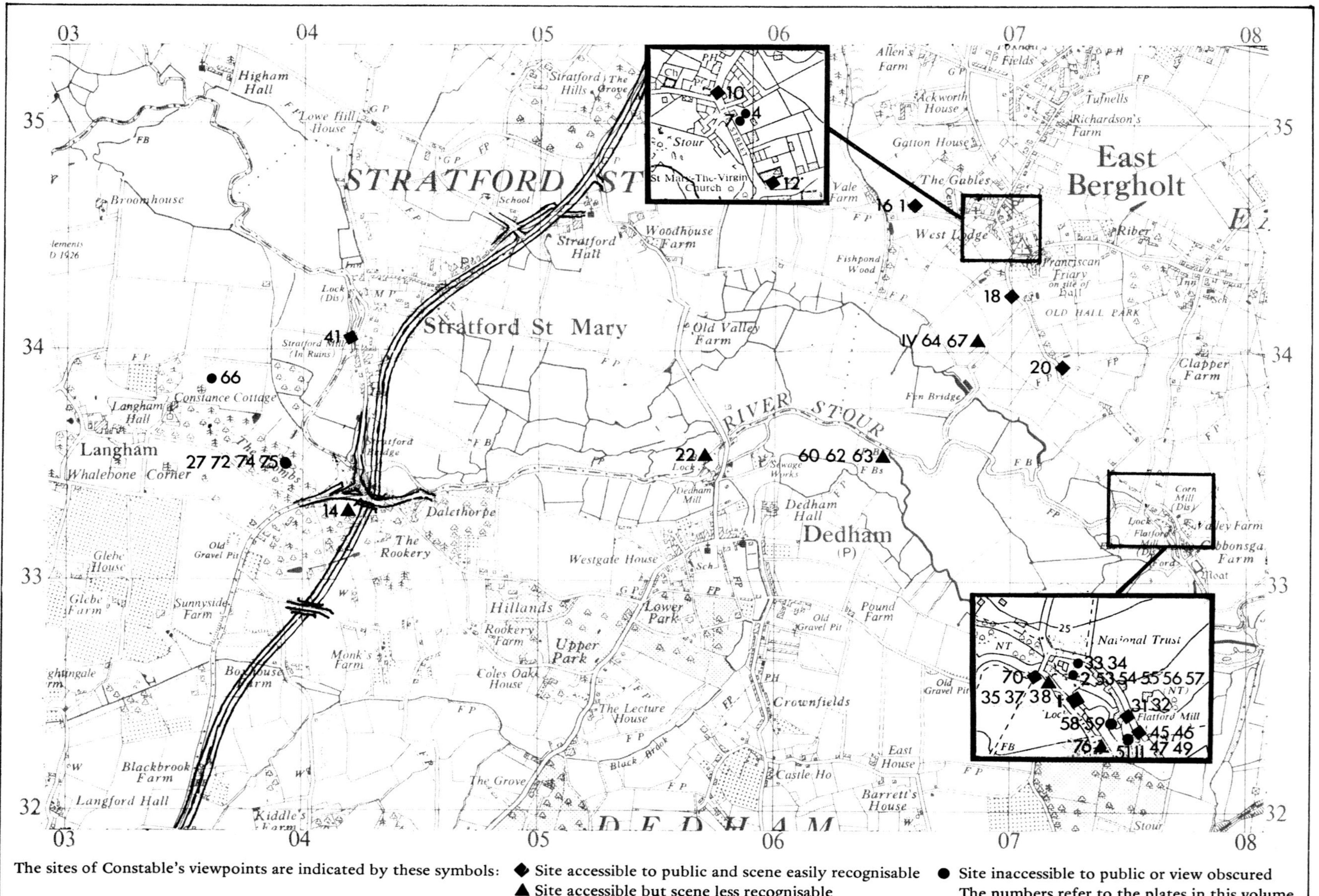

The sites of Constable's viewpoints are indicated by these symbols: ◆ Site accessible to public and scene easily recognisable ▲ Site accessible but scene less recognisable ● Site inaccessible to public or view obscured

The numbers refer to the plates in this volume

Constable and the creative process

Alastair Smart

A great painting, however complex it may be, is capable of making an overwhelming impression in an instant: only on reflection do we begin to guess at the creative processes which shaped its final form. We may then embark upon an adventure of absorbing interest—the attempt to probe the secret workings of imaginative genius. Such an inquiry will always tell us much, not only about the mind of an individual artist, but about the nature of art itself.

There is no more familiar English painting than Constable's *Hay Wain.* It is so familiar that we tend to take it for granted, like Nelson's Column or any other national monument. At first sight it seems to be merely an uncomplicated view of a pleasant corner of the English countryside, and we might think that there was little to say about it. But in this we should be deceived; for *The Hay Wain* is far from being a mere glimpse of a particular scene: it is an imaginative composition that gradually took shape as Constable brooded over the subject, and its genesis and evolution can be traced over a period of many years. Although it is based on an actual view, it is much more than that: it is a crystallization of memories and experiences going back to the days of the artist's boyhood in Suffolk.

You can still stand on the spot where Constable once stood, and you can II
look out on the scene that inspired the picture. Although sycamores, firs and scrub have replaced the elms that once grew there, surprisingly little has changed: there, on the left of the pond—across which once lay the ford—is the cottage known as Willy Lott's House; on the right, the red-brick wall (only just visible in the picture) by Flatford Mill, one of the properties owned by the painter's father, Golding Constable of East Bergholt; and broad meadowlands still stretch back to a distant fringe of poplars, although from this precise viewpoint the prospect is largely obscured by a cluster of hedges and trees. Yet *The Hay Wain* was not painted here at all, but in London; and as Constable worked upon his picture he played variations,

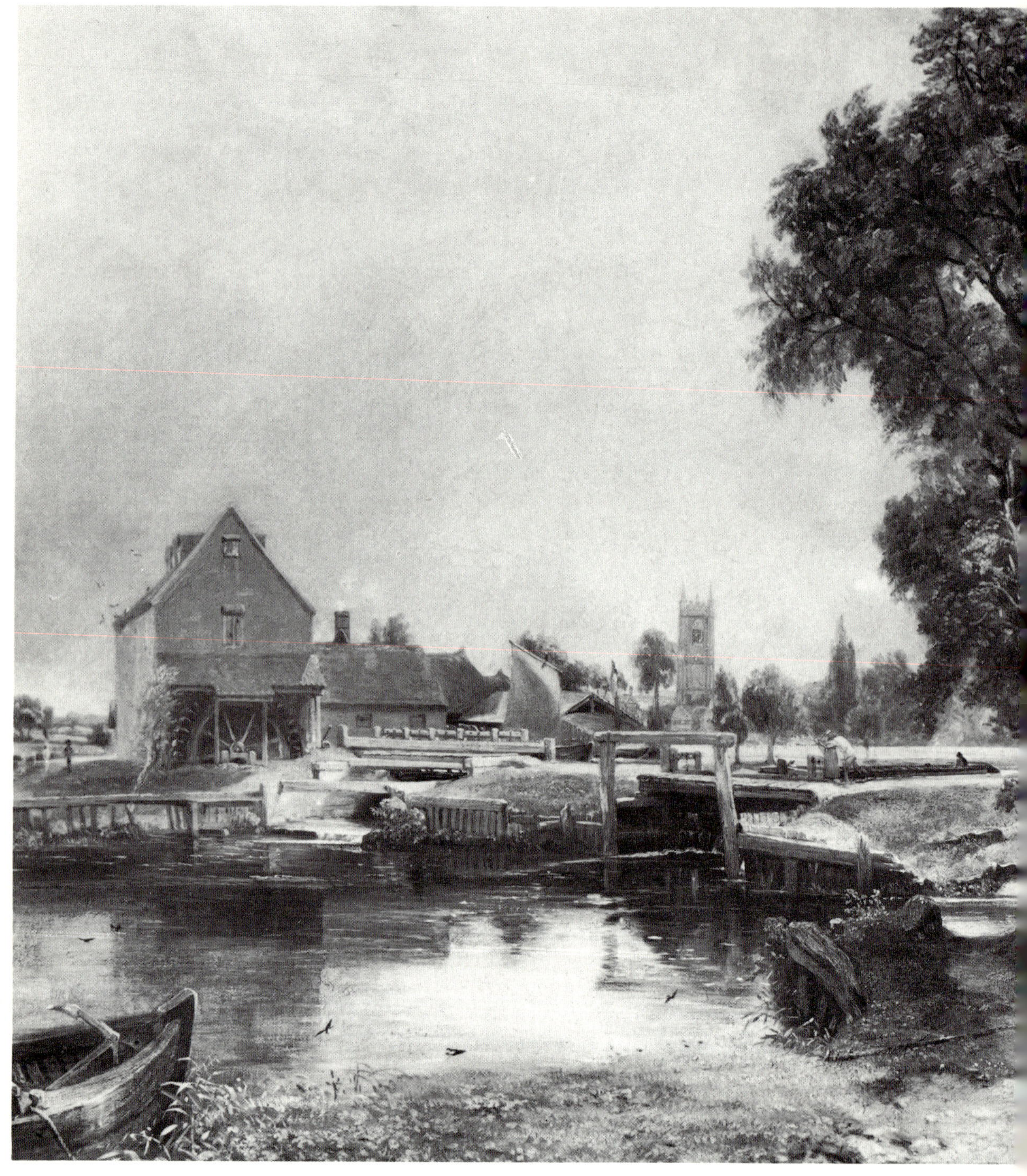

Detail of *Dedham Lock and Mill*
Constable painted four other known versions of this work. The mill belonged to his father and undoubtedly he worked there and at Flatford before he went to London to study painting. The charming building shown here was demolished in about 1848 and the present large brick structure was erected after 1908. The lock was reconstructed in 1931 and at the same time slightly realigned but not significantly. By taking the footpath along the north side of the mill pool it is possible to come to a spot where one sees the lock at the same angle as painted by Constable, and at th same time to see Dedham Church in exactly the same relationship as he shows it.

as it were, upon his theme, transforming an intimate and in some ways ordinary scene into a majestic landscape. It is curious to reflect that this summery picture was painted in Constable's studio during the course of a London winter. In a truly Wordsworthian sense, it is an expression of "emotion recollected in tranquillity".

What is still more interesting is that the stages by which the composition was developed can be deduced from a study of earlier sketches, considered in relation to the finished picture on the one hand and to the actual *motif* on the other. A number of other paintings by Constable can be analysed in this way; and in the masterpieces of his maturity, among which *The Hay Wain* of 1821 has a central place, we discover two processes at work: first, there was that concern for the truth which is epitomized by Constable's famous declaration to his boyhood friend John Dunthorne, "There is room enough for a natural painter" (the spelling 'painture' apparently used by Constable in the original letter has been variously interpreted: see Note 2); and secondly, there was the more purely aesthetic impulse which required that profound visual and emotional experiences should be given their perfect artistic expression. We are concerned with the pull, on the one hand, of Nature, and, on the other, of Art.

In Constable's early works, there is generally a much greater fidelity to the 10–21
topography of a given scene, as can be demonstrated by Attfield Brooks's photographs taken on the sites of many of the Suffolk paintings. But in the late works imaginative composition plays an increasingly important role in Constable's method as an artist. By selecting a few of the major pictures in this second category—such as *The Hay Wain*, *View on the Stour near Dedham*, *The Cornfield* and the Edinburgh *Dedham Vale*—and by examining them in relation to the scenes that originally inspired them, I shall attempt to explore the nature of this process of imaginative reformulation.

This is not to suggest that purely 'compositional' elements never occur in early paintings, as though Constable was not an *artist* from the beginning, deeply affected by the art of the past; not is it to ignore the problems posed by the psychology of pictorial representation. In his illuminating *Art and Illusion*, Sir Ernst Gombrich frequently turns to Constable's work and thought in order to illustrate the complexities of the processes involved in artistic creation, choosing as a prime example a painting which, despite its modernity of treatment, belongs to the venerable tradition of English topographical painting—the beautiful *Wivenhoe Park, Essex*, of 1816 (in the National Gallery of Art, Washington). No one familiar with Gombrich's

book is likely to imagine that Constable's naturalism was simply a matter of
matching an image that appeared on his retina, or that *Wivenhoe Park*—or
(for instance) the *Flatford Mill, on the River Stour*, of the following year—is "a 35
mere transcript of nature": even in his most naturalistic paintings, the process
of 'making', as distinct from 'matching', was in any case intimately bound up,
as Gombrich emphasises, with his response to his wider experience, to
traditional modes of representation, and not least to the conventions
developed in the art of his great predecessors.

All this must be allowed for when, within the strict limits of the present
inquiry, we contrast the 'truthfulness' of Constable's renderings of particular
scenes or *motifs* with the role of 'imaginative composition' in his art; for we
shall be concerned primarily with those moments of conscious choice, when
he either retained or discarded—or transfigured—particular features of a
known landscape. It may, however, be apposite at this point to draw attention to one of the many interesting fruits of Attfield Brooks's photographic
alignments, which in itself underlines the difference between the eye of the
camera and the eye of the artist: this is Constable's tendency towards what
may be called 'vertical exaggeration'. For instance, not only do we find that
Dedham Church, which is so frequently represented by Constable as an
emphatic background feature of a landscape, often appears more prominent
in his pictures and drawings than it does in a photograph (which gives us the
key to the actual scale), but landscape features themselves can sometimes be
shown to have been expressed in a similar manner; a good example is the
early *View of Dedham*, where the panoramic prospect beyond the lane in the 20
foreground assumes an added impressiveness due to the vertical 'distortion' 21
of the image.

When all this has been said, it is nevertheless important to recognise that,
even in works of the late period in which imaginative composition has a
dominant role, a concern for topographical accuracy can remain an essential
feature of Constable's approach to his subject (and usually does). For
instance, as Attfield Brooks has proved, the central area of the Edinburgh
Dedham Vale is a remarkably faithful rendering of the Stour Valley: yet this 74
becomes the core of a richly inventive composition. We might regard it as the
symbol of that fundamental commitment to the truth which lies at the heart
of Constable's work, even in his most imaginative flights, and which can be
related to his conviction that painting could properly be regarded as a branch
of natural philosophy. To these questions we shall constantly be returning.
First, however, it will be necessary to place Constable within his own times

and to say something about his life, his personality and his artistic development.

Constable and Turner

In trying to define Constable's position in our great tradition of landscape painting it is almost inevitable that we should compare him with Turner, his almost exact contemporary but in many ways his opposite. Both were revolutionary figures; and both exerted, sooner or later, a profound influence upon European painting. Yet in Turner's case there is nothing quite comparable with the almost immediate impact made by the works of Constable's maturity upon the French Romantics, such as Géricault and Delacroix, and on the painters of the Barbizon School (the precursors of the Impressionists), who admired and copied his pictures when they were exhibited in Paris. This is something of a paradox, since there could be no more English a painter than Constable. And there could scarcely be a more English picture the *The Hay Wain*. Yet it was the technical innovations of *The Hay Wain*,
and its revolutionary treatment of atmospheric light and colour, that made 30
Delacroix and his contemporaries stand in front of it in admiration when it was shown at the Paris Salon of 1824. Partly because of its influence upon European art, but also on account of its intrinsic virtues, *The Hay Wain* has claims to be regarded as the most important single landscape of the English School, and may be compared with the best of Rubens, the best of Claude, and the best of Ruisdael.

Yet beside the vaulting imagination of Turner the humbler naturalism of Constable may seem a smaller thing. Constable, we may be sure, never dreamt of such subjects as Turner created, with visionary eye, out of a unique mixture of realism and poetic fancy: to fashion the most glorious of all sunrises from the magic of ancient myth, as in Turner's *Ulysses deriding Polyphemus,* where the Horses of the Sun mount the skies with the spreading blaze of the dawn; or to dare a demonstration of the frightening littleness of man in the face of the elemental, indifferent forces of Nature, as in his two great evocations of snowstorms on land and sea, the *Snowstorm*: *Hannibal crossing the Alps,* and the *Snowstorm with a Steam-Ship*—such expressions of the mythopoeic imagination and of the sublime are not to be found in the art of Constable, which is closer to common experience, but which transcends it by a profound contemplativeness akin, in many ways, to the brooding quality of the landscapes of Rembrandt and Ruisdael.

To compare any such picture by Turner with *The Hay Wain* or *The Cornfield* is to remind ourselves both of Constable's insularity and of his singlemindedness. Turner crossed the Channel many times; several of his journeys abroad took him to Italy; and he painted the mountains, the rivers and the vistas of many countries: so far from crossing the Alps, Constable never once ventured across the English Channel, even to receive from King Charles X of France the Gold Medal which *The Hay Wain* had won him on its exhibition at the Paris Salon of 1824. His working life was chiefly spent in London, at his country house in Hampstead, and in his native Suffolk; and his single-mindedness was such that he found almost all that he ever needed for his art in the scenes of his boyhood and early manhood at East Bergholt and the surrounding countryside. His youthful sketching expeditions to the Peak District and the English Lakes were unimportant and unsuccessful attempts to comply with a fashionable taste for pictureque subjects such as these regions afforded to the painter and the traveller; the pictures that he painted in Dorset and at Salisbury, although including some of his masterpieces, were—so to speak—the accidental products of his friendship with Bishop and Archdeacon Fisher; and his Brighton paintings were the fruit of personal circumstance and tragedy, the outcome of visits to the sea necessitated by his wife's relentlessly deteriorating health; nor, without his wife's need to escape from the climate of London, might he have spent as much time as he did at Hampstead, where he discovered the skyey vistas and the melancholy beauties of the Heath. It may be said above all that, in dwelling upon the scenes of his boyhood in Suffolk, and by transmuting them in recollection, over the space of many years, into the fabric of an intensely personal art woven from deeply felt memories, Constable achieved a profundity of expression which is no less telling than the vast range of Turner. Moreover, the Suffolk pictures in themselves have been proved by time to possess a quality of universality which may remind us, for example, of the virtues that Johnson discovered in Gray's *Elegy*: "The *Churchyard* abounds with images which find a mirror in every mind, and with sentiments to which every bosom returns an echo."

Unlike Turner, Constable was slow to establish himself. It was not entirely because he rebelled against fashionable taste, and it was not entirely because he was a mere landscape painter in an age which placed portraiture and history-painting in a higher category, that he had to wait until 1829, when he was well over fifty, for his election to full membership of the Royal Academy. He was born in 1776, only a year after Turner; but Turner was already an Academician by 1802, so that there was an interval of twenty-seven years between Turner's election and Constable's—over a quarter of a century during which, in most people's eyes, Constable stood in a quite inferior position to Turner. Yet in these years he had forged a style which can be seen in retrospect (however much it was misunderstood by his contemporaries as a whole) to mark a turning-point in the history of landscape painting—a decisive liberation from the artificialities and conventions of eighteenth-century taste. Later developments in England and on the Continent fully justified Constable's observation to Dunthorne (in the familiar form of the statement given in Leslie's *Life*), "There is room enough for a natural painter." There was room enough for a whole school of natural painters.

The scenes of his Suffolk boyhood, Constable once remarked, "made me a painter". These were not the scenes of romantic solitude or inspiring sublimity that caught the imagination of Turner, although certain aspects of the sublime enter into Constable's art and play an important part in it. The constant source of Constable's inspiration was Nature in her more domesticated aspects, Nature cultivated by man through long centuries. In his pictures the evidences of man's presence and of his cultivation of the land—as Graham Reynolds has beautifully shown elsewhere—are normally present; so much so that in a sense they are not merely landscapes but narratives: a barge-horse is being ferried across the river; a boy is pushing a barge out towards the lock-gate, in preparation for the next stage in its long and slow progress down the canalised river; a well-trained barge-horse leaps a fence on the tow-path; a hay-cart enters a ford, while labourers gather in the harvest in the distant fields; a shepherd-boy leaves the flock he is guiding down a country lane on a hot summer's noonday to quench his thirst at a stream. It is this human element that helps to give Constable's landscapes their congenial intimacy, besides adding to their conviction of truth: it is a far cry from the Arcadian dream-world first imagined by Claude, a world of make-believe peopled by the gods, the heroes and the nymphs of classical mythology, such as still invade the majestic canvases of Turner.

So domestic in character are the Suffolk pictures of Constable—which are the most representative of his art—that their subjects are almost all to be found within a very few miles of his birthplace at East Bergholt, in the green countryside where the River Stour winds eastwards to the sea, past the water-mills at Dedham (just across the Essex border) and Flatford—the mills, both owned by Golding Constable, which his son was to immortalize. Often, when he sketched the scenes of his boyhood, he was standing on land which belonged to his father: there could scarcely be a more domestic art than this! And as Constable looked out, from this vantage-point or that, across the gently sloping Vale of Dedham, he discovered one focal point—Dedham Church itself—which has this function in a large number of his pictures. It takes the place, as it were, of the conventional ruin or classical monument which so often serves a similar purpose in eighteenth-century English landscapes painted in the Claudian tradition.

Early influences

Golding Constable originally hoped that John, his second son and fourth child, would take Holy Orders; he sent him to the grammar school at
Dedham, and the future painter walked there each day from East Bergholt III
down the lane to Dedham Vale which is famous locally as the site of *The* IV
Cornfield, now in the National Gallery; but he showed little academic promise, and it was decided that he should follow his father in the milling trade, his elder brother Golding having shown himself to be incapable. When that hope proved vain, the painter's younger brother, Abram, fell heir to the family business. But it was not until 1799, when John was in his twenty-third year, that he went up to London to study at the Royal Academy Schools. Before this, however, 'the handsome miller', as he was called in the neighbourhood, had already begun to apprentice himself to the calling of a landscape painter, and he seems to have taken some lessons from an amateur artist, Elizabeth Cobbold, the wife of a brewer at Ipswich. But greater importance must be attached to his friendship with John Dunthorne, a master plumber and glazier in East Bergholt who was an enthusiastic landscape painter in his spare time, and who on the evidence of his surviving work might have enjoyed considerable success as an artist if circumstances had been more favourable. In later life Constable always looked back to the happy times he had spent sketching in the fields with his friend, whose son (also John) was eventually to become his studio assistant. Another sketching companion during these early years was the landscape painter George Frost, of Ipswich. Frost, who was a generation older than Constable, founded his landscape style upon that of Gainsborough, whose paintings and drawings he collected. He therefore provides an interesting link between Gainsborough and Constable, both Suffolk men; and Constable's early work (notably in the year 1802) sometimes bears a quite strong resemblance to Frost's exercises in
Gainsborough's manner. As John Hayes has observed, it was from Frost 23

that Constable "learnt the art of massing, and of disposing light and shade". There are also early works by Constable that show Gainsborough's direct influence. 24

By the age of twenty, if not earlier, Constable had determined that he must be a painter. His resolve was strengthened, and his excitable nature stimulated, by a visit in August 1796 to the Edmonton home of an uncle, Thomas Allen, who introduced him to the celebrated 'Antiquity' Smith—John Thomas Smith, the antiquary and engraver who is best known today for his biography of the sculptor Joseph Nollekens. Smith was then living at Edmonton, just before moving to London, and was engaged in preparing a volume entitled *Remarks on Rural Scenery*, which was to be illustrated with etchings, from his own hand, of picturesque cottages. Constable was captivated by his new acquaintance, and overwhelmed by gratitude for the encouragement he received from him. His stay at Edmonton was long enough for him to be frequently in Smith's company, and he must have been deeply impressed by the conversation of a man who had been the pupil of Nollekens and who was acquainted with many of the eminent artists of his time. Further, Smith urged him to read more widely, and Constable wrote to him on his return to East Bergholt that he had brought back with him a number of books, including a recent translation of Leonardo's *Treatise of Painting* and Count Algarotti's *Essay on Painting* (published in London in 1764).

At East Bergholt, Constable began making drawings of cottages in imitation of those by Smith, and also tried his hand at etching. The drawings were sent on to Smith at regular intervals, and much correspondence passed between the two. Smith continued to encourage Constable, supplying him with painting materials and prints: and on occasion he entertained him in London. In the autumn of 1798 Smith went to stay with the Constable family at East Bergholt, and during this visit he may well have persuaded Golding Constable to allow his son to go to London to study to be a painter. Certainly by this time Constable was despairing of ever having the opportunity of following his heart's desire; the affairs of his father's business were pressing, and even Smith had evidently inclined to the view that he should prepare himself to follow in his father's footsteps. In the spring of the previous year Constable had written to Smith disconsolately: "I must now take your advice and attend to my Father's business; as we are likely soon to lose an old servant (our Clerk), who has been with us these eighteen years. And now I certainly see it will be my lot to walk through life in a path contrary to that [in] which my inclination would lead me." Yet, as R. B.

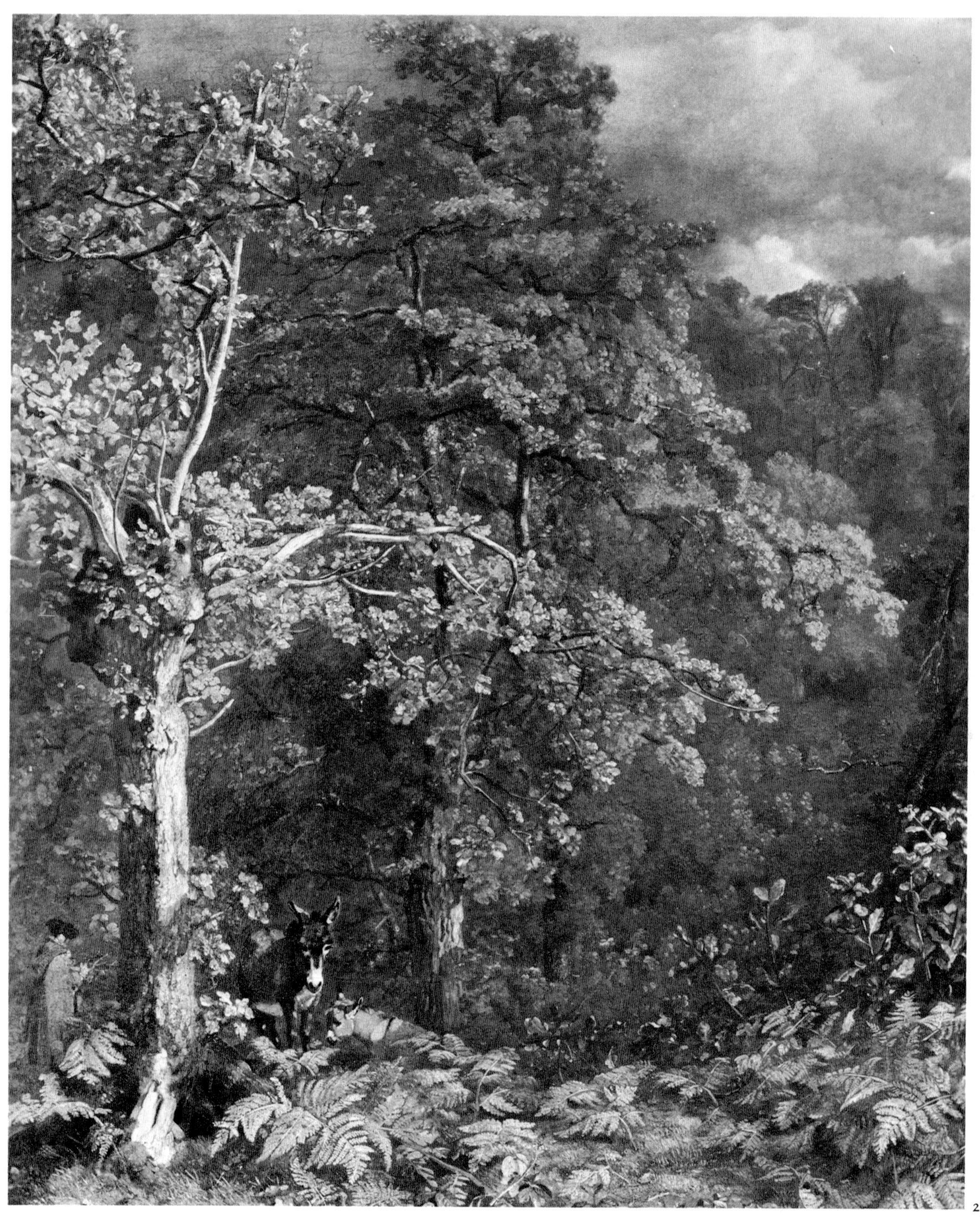

23

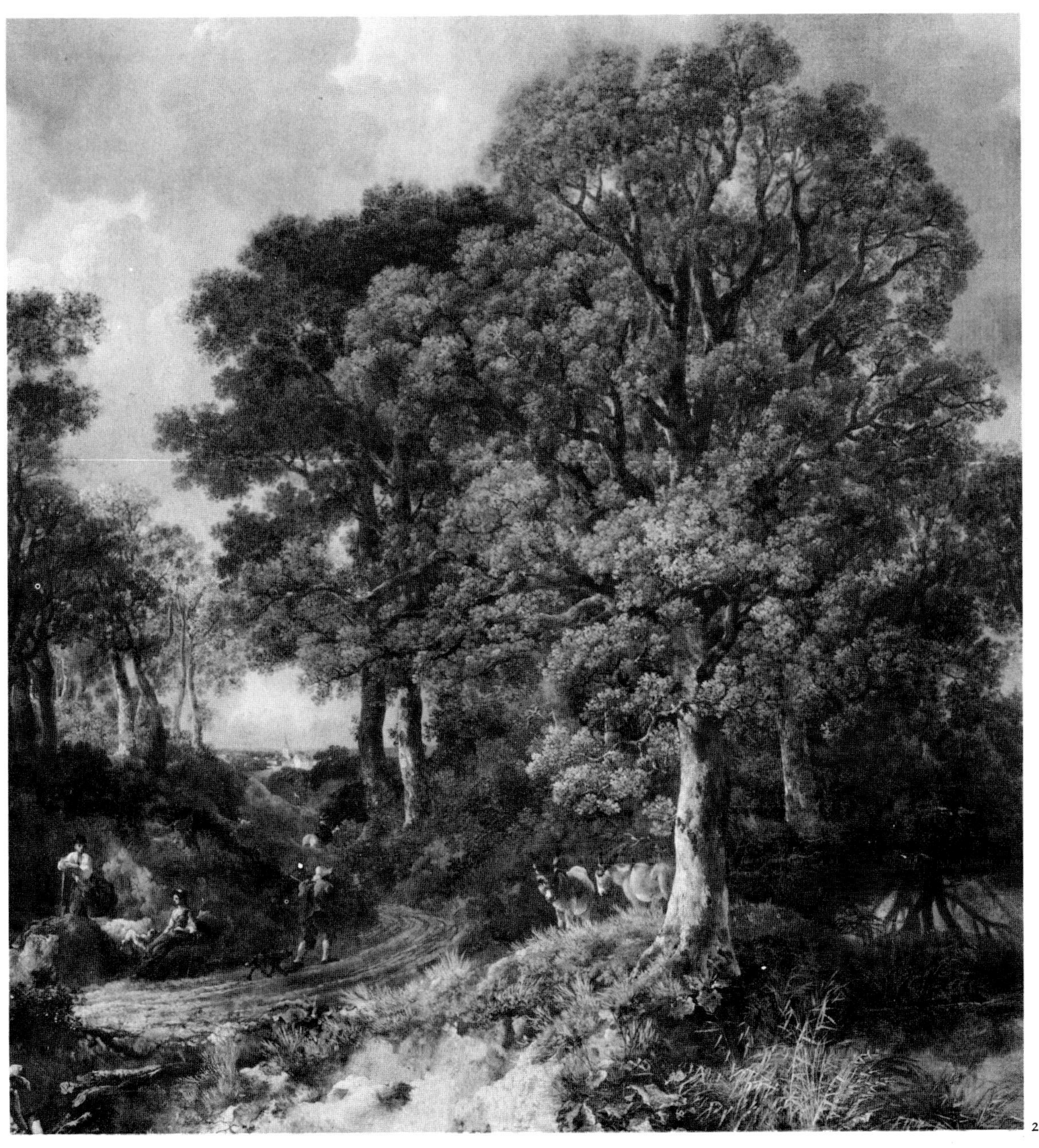

24

Scene in Helmingham Park, Suffolk
Several of Constable's early works show the direct influence of Gainsborough, also a Suffolk man, not only in subject matter but in style. The accompanying detail from Gainsborough's *Cornard Wood* shows how closely Constable followed him on occasion.

Beckett has pointed out, "it may not be without significance that within three months or so of Smith's visit to East Bergholt Constable had obtained his father's permission to go up to London to study art. Possibly the compliments which the visitor was able to pay to his pupil's progress had something to do with bringing this about." At all events, on 4 February 1799 Constable was able to write proudly to John Dunthorne: "I am this morning admitted a student at the Royal Academy. . . ." There is no evidence that by this date he had shown any proof of exceptional gifts, and Golding Constable may have been justifiably sceptical of his son's prospects: but two things he had shown, both of them of ultimately greater value to him than precocious talent—a deep love of Nature and a determination to succeed. There now began the long struggle to achieve facility; and shortly after executing the examination drawing—of the Belvedere Torso—which gained him admittance to the Academy Schools, Constable set about copying a picture by Ruisdael.

In later life Constable intimated to his first biographer, the American-born painter C. R. Leslie, the value he attached to the advice he had so freely received from 'Antiquity' Smith. Leslie cites one instance in particular:

> "Do not," said Smith, "set about inventing figures for a landscape taken from nature; for you cannot remain an hour in any spot, however solitary, without the appearance of some living thing that will in all probability accord better with the scene and time of day than will any invention of your own." Often has Constable, in our walks together, taken occasion to point out, from what we saw, the good sense of Smith's advice.

Furthermore, it is of interest that Smith's *Remarks on Rural Scenery*, which was published in 1797, contains precepts which anticipate Constable's own practice. Smith was aware, for instance, of reflected colour in Nature, which he advised artists to imitate; and one observation upon the colour green in Nature is especially striking when we remember that it antedates *The Hay Wain* by nearly a quarter of a century: "The shades or degrees of this colour as it is distributed in nature are innumerable." Years later Delacroix, upon whom *The Hay Wain* had made so powerful an impression, was to note in his Journal: "Constable says that the superiority of the green of his fields comes from its being composed of a multitude of different greens. What produces lack of intensity and of life in the verdure of most landscapes painters is that they paint it ordinarily in a uniform colour."

The influence of the Old Masters

At the Academy Schools Constable learnt to draw the nude model; he had already begun a systematic study of anatomy. His life drawings, however, are less notable for any remarkable skill in draughtsmanship than for the interest which they reveal in chiaroscuro, that quality which Constable always strove to give his landscapes: indeed, contrasting and blended effects of light and shade became for him one of the primary vehicles for the expression of feeling. Constable's studies at the Academy are not likely to have been of direct benefit to him as a landscape painter; but they would have supplied him with a grounding in drawing which must have been of particular service to him in his portrait commissions, which he accepted chiefly for financial reasons and, as he said, to help him to acquire 'execution'. A landscape painter could not expect the lucrative rewards of the portraitist; and it is not surprising that his parents hoped that he would earn distinction as a fashionable portrait painter.

During his years as an Academy student Constable spent much time in his native Suffolk drawing in the fields with his friend Dunthorne. His consciousness that he was following in the footsteps of Gainsborough is reflected in a well-known comment in one of his letters to Smith, who had fostered his interest in Gainsborough's art and had introduced him to one of Gainsborough's most fervent admirers, a minor artist named John Cranch: " 'tis a most delightful country for a landscape painter; I fancy I see Gainsborough in every hedge and hollow tree." Constable responded warmly to Gainsborough's power of communicating feeling. In later life, in a lecture delivered at the Hampstead Literary and Scientific Society, he remarked:

> The landscape of Gainsborough is soothing, tender, and affecting. The stillness of noon, the depths of twilight, and the dews and pearls of the morning, are all to be found on the canvases of this most benevolent and kind-hearted man. On looking at them, we find tears in our eyes, and know not what brings them.

One could say much the same of many of Constable's early Suffolk pictures,
such as the *Dedham Vale, Morning* of 1811 (Proby collection) and a number of 18
oil-sketches of similar subjects painted in this period or earlier, in which the quality of a particular time of day—morning, noon or evening—is poetically evoked.

Among the connections which Constable formed in his early years, one of the most important was his introduction to Sir George Beaumont, whose

mother lived at Dedham. Beaumont was himself a landscape painter of distinction, in the classical tradition of Claude, and owned a fine collection of pictures. He frequently visited his mother at Dedham, and came to take an interest in the young Constable, having been particularly impressed by some pen and ink copies which he had made from engravings of the Raphael Cartoons. Beaumont remained on close terms with Constable over the years, and at his house at Coleorton, in Leicestershire, Constable was able to study and copy the paintings in his collection. We can even detect in some of
Constable's very early works the influence of Beaumont's own conservative 14
style.

Sir George so admired one picture in his possession, Claude's little *Landscape with Hagar and the Angel* (now in the National Gallery), that he used frequently to take it with him in his carriage when he travelled. Constable first saw this picture on one of Beaumont's visits to Dedham: as his friend and biographer C. R. Leslie informs us, he "looked back on his first sight of this exquisite work as an important epoch in his life". He was later permitted to make a copy of it, and it was a picture he never forgot. One imagines that he often referred to his own copy in later years; certainly Claude's
design influenced many of his own compositions, an important early example 27
being the *Dedham Vale* of 1802, in the Victoria and Albert Museum. And, as 28
we shall see, when in 1826 he chose for the setting of the famous *Cornfield* IV
a familiar lane near East Bergholt, down which he had often walked in his early days on his way to Dedham, he assimilated to his recollections of the scene the noble design of Claude's picture. In the year in which *The Cornfield* was painted, Sir George Beaumont presented the Claude to the National Gallery, which had been founded two years earlier. Constable was not to know that his own *Cornfield*—purchased for the nation by a group of subscribers shortly after his death in 1837—would also hang there.

Beaumont owned a number of modern works, including watercolours by John Robert Cozens and Thomas Girtin, both of whom Constable recognized as two of the major figures in the history of landscape painting. Constable was especially drawn to Cozens because of his lyricism: "Cozens," he once remarked, "is all poetry"; and he went so far as to hail him, in one of his lectures, as "the greatest genius that ever touched landscape". Beaumont was to respond to Constable's admiration for Cozens by presenting him with one of his finest watercolours, the *View on the Galleria di Sopra, above the Lake of Albano* (now in the Williamson Art Gallery at Birkenhead). Something of the delicacy and emotive power of Cozens's landscapes seems to be reflected already in a number of Constable's early watercolours and sepia drawings, such as those which he made on his rather uncharacteristic visits to the Peak District (in 1801) and the Lake District (in 1808). The freshness and sheer spirit of Constable's later watercolours may be said to belong, in a broad sense, to the more modern idiom of Girtin; but they transcend it in the vivacity of the handling, which is due in part to the immediacy of the notation and in part to the desire to suggest movement; for in Constable Nature is never still.

One of the masters who deeply influenced Constable's thoughts on landscape in his early years was Jacob van Ruisdael, the greatest of all the Dutch landscape painters of the seventeenth century. When he began his studies at the Academy, Constable shared rooms with a fellow artist of about the same age, Ramsay Richard Reinagle, who painted the portrait of him as a young man which is now in the National Portrait Gallery; and we find the two friends pooling their resources in order to purchase, for £70, what Constable described as "a very fine picture by Ruysdael". Of this he diligently made a copy. He was still studying the art of Ruisdael when he was at the height of his powers as a painter. In 1818, for example, he made a copy in pen and sepia of Ruisdael's etching of *A Cornfield*, just as, long before him, Gainsborough had copied the famous Ruisdael known as *La Fôret*.

Despite his remark to his friend C. R. Leslie, "When I sit down to make a sketch from nature, the first thing I try to do is to forget that I have ever seen a picture," Constable was the most assiduous of copyists. From his early days onwards he continued to make numerous copies after the Old Masters, and even towards the end of his life, in 1832, we find him making a copy of a Ruisdael in the collection of Sir Robert Peel. He also acquired a very large collection of paintings, drawings and prints; and we must always remember that as he worked on his own pictures in his London studio this vast range of source-material—this constant source of inspiration—was instantly available to him. The full extent of the influence of the Old Masters upon the art of Constable lies outside the scope of the present book; but it may confidently be expected that future studies will reveal it to be even greater than it is already known to be.

When we read his comments on landscape painting in the lectures which he delivered at Hampstead and at the Royal Institution, we are likely to be struck by the breadth of his sympathies. What he could not tolerate was an artificiality, such as he found in Boucher, which denied Nature. Above all, he looked for three characteristics in a good landscape painting—first, the sentiment it conveys; secondly, the reflection in it of the artist's understanding of Nature; and, thirdly, the method of design. At times, in speaking of a particular work, he will mention all these aspects; at other times only one or two of them. Often his observations surprise by the novelty of their perceptions. Thus, in speaking of Claude, he first makes a general statement with which we may easily concur: "In Claude's landscapes all is lovely—all amiable—all is amenity and repose; the calm sunshine of the heart." But then, in describing the *Sea-Port, with the Embarkation of St Ursula*, which by this time had found its home in the National Gallery, Constable goes on to observe: "The *St Ursula* is probably the finest picture of *middle tint* in the world. The sun is rising through a thin mist, which, like the effect of a gauze-blind in a room, diffuses the light equally. There are no large dark masses . . . In no other picture have I seen the evanescent character of light so well expressed." A perception of this nature may entice us to look at Claude again—through the eyes of a painter to whom effects of light and the qualities of skies were all-important.

Constable was less concerned than we are today with stylistic categories: he does not speak of Claude as an exponent of the 'classical' style of landscape, nor of Ruisdael as a 'naturalistic' artist; but he was deeply conscious of the wide differences between the two masters in their interpretation of Nature and in their communication of feeling. "In Claude's pictures," he says, "with scarcely an exception, the sun ever shines. Ruysdael, on the contrary, delighted in, and has made delightful to our eyes, those solemn days, peculiar to his country and ours, when without storm, large rolling clouds scarcely permit a ray of sunlight to break the shades of the forest. By these effects he enveloped the most ordinary scenes in grandeur." Constable clearly recognized in his own intentions as a painter an affinity with those of Ruisdael; and his own skies are usually filled with cloud, and his trees and meadows lit by fitful gleams of sunlight. The concluding words of Constable's appreciation of the art of Ruisdael can be applied with equal truth to such works as *The Hay Wain* and *The Cornfield*; and it is still possible to visit the sites of these paintings, as C. R. Leslie did in 1840, to see how Constable "enveloped the most ordinary scenes in grandeur".

It is interesting that Constable should have been making copies after both Ruisdael and Cuyp at the very time that he was projecting the first of his
large Stour scenes—*The White Horse*, completed in 1819. He admired Cuyp 39
for his treatment of light and shade, that is for his chiaroscuro, which was not (he insisted) to be thought of as a characteristic only of dark pictures, such

as those of Rembrandt. But there can be no doubt that Rembrandt, like Ruisdael, meant far more to him. He said of Rembrandt's *Mill* that it was the first picture in which a sentiment had been expressed "by chiaroscuro only, all details being excluded". Many of the views of Hampstead Heath, painted after Constable first took up residence at Hampstead in the summer of 1819, bring Rembrandt to mind. This affinity with Rembrandt is particularly
striking in the famous *Heath* of which David Lucas made a superlative 44
engraving in 1831, capturing all the freedom and largeness of Constable's sweeping brushwork, in which attention to detail is sacrificed, in a truly Rembrandtesque manner, to general effects of chiaroscuro.

The influence of Rubens's landscapes was no less important: and we see it
especially in *The Hay Wain*; for in a sense *The Hay Wain* is a reinterpretation 50
of Rubens's majestic *Château de Steen* in the National Gallery, with Willy 51
Lott's House replacing the stately castle on the left, the hay wagon replacing the carriage, which is fording a stream, and the meadows of the Stour Valley sweeping into the distance on the right, like the flat pastures of the Flemish landscape which Rubens had painted with such genial affection.[1] The *Château de Steen* was a picture that Constable had known well from his early days, for it had been bought by Lady Beaumont in 1802 as a present to her husband. In his third lecture to the Royal Institution, immediately before his observations on Rembrandt's *Mill*, he said of Rubens: "In no other branch of the art is Rubens greater than in landscape", commending "the freshness and dewy light, the joyous and animated character which he has imparted to it, impressing on the level monotonous scenery of Flanders all the richness which belongs to its noblest features". He then went on to describe the *Château de Steen*, which Beaumont had now presented to the National Gallery along with Claude's *Hagar and the Angel* and other pictures.

Constable only regretted that the *Château de Steen* was still separated from its companion-piece, the *Rainbow Landscape* now in the Wallace Collection (which had come up at Christie's in 1823 at the Watson Taylor sale). These two pictures, he remarked, were two of Rubens's finest works. The very title of the picture in the Wallace Collection now suggested itself to Constable as an apt description of the art of landscape as practised by Rubens: "By 'the rainbow' of Rubens, I do not allude to a particular picture, for Rubens often introduced it; I mean, indeed, more than the rainbow itself; I mean dewy light and freshness, the departing shower, with the exhilaration of the returning sun, effects which Rubens, more than any other painter, has perfected on canvas." 'Dewy light and freshness'—these qualities Rubens

25

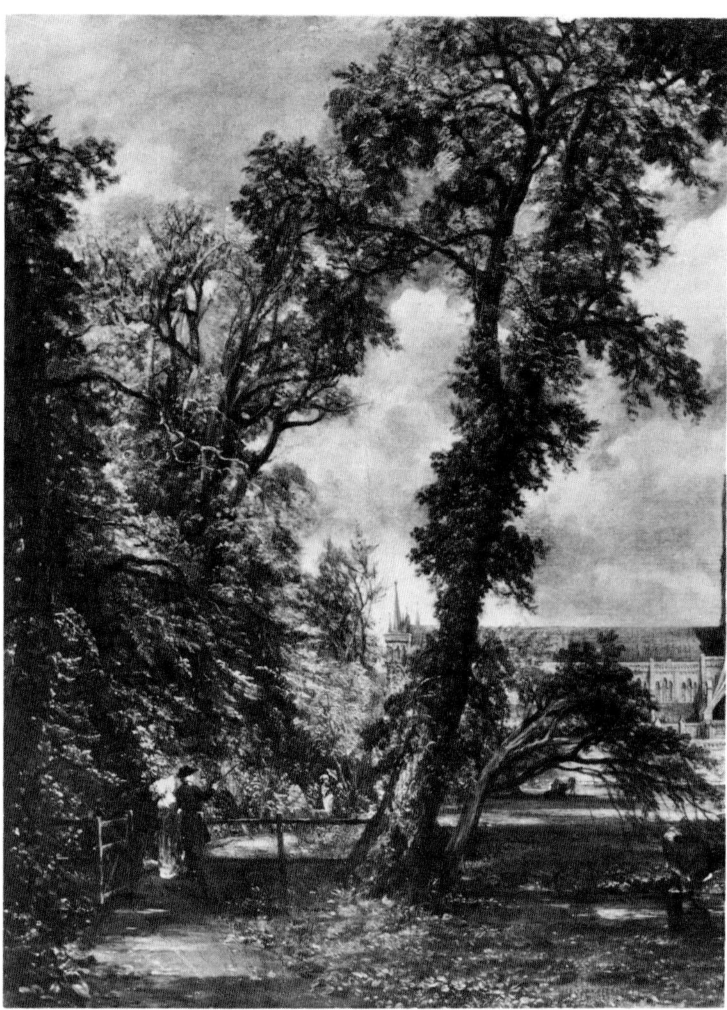

26

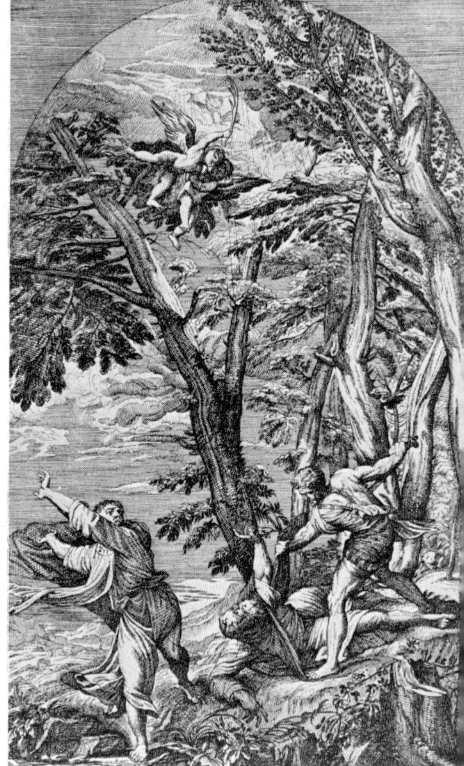

Detail of *Salisbury Cathedral from the Bishop's Grounds*
"Sir Joshua is swayed by his own practice of generalising . . . In Titian there is equal breadth, equal subordination of the parts to the whole, but the spectator finds, on approaching the picture, that every touch is the representation of a reality." So Constable praised Titian's approach to landscape which he knew from examples like this engraving of the lost painting *Death of St Peter Martyr* (*right*): echoes of it may be found in this detail.

27

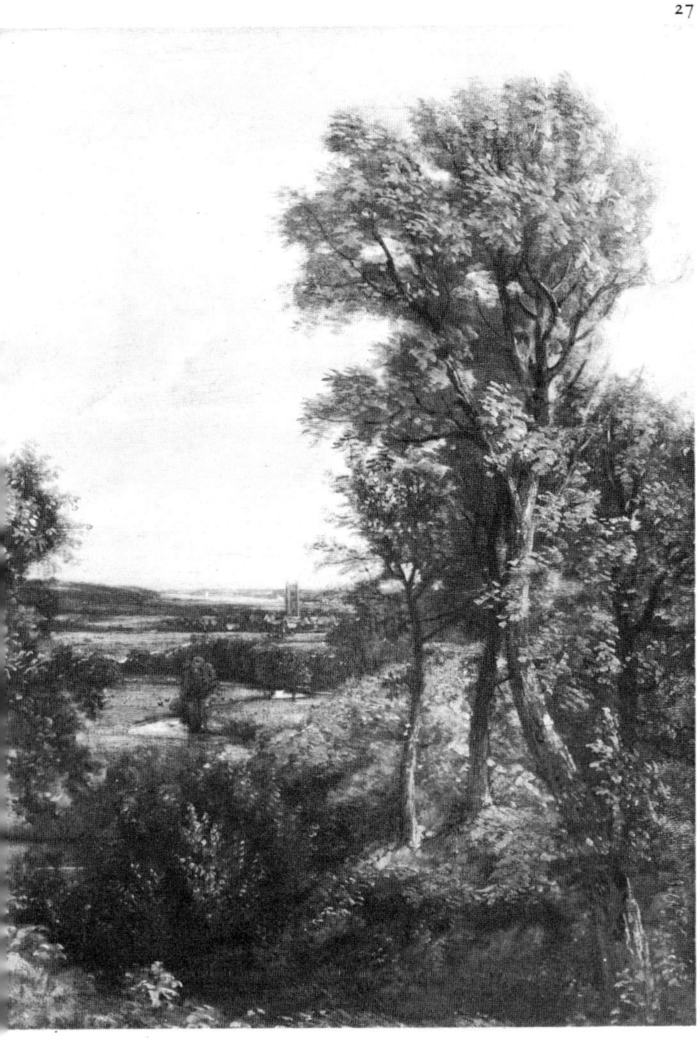

Dedham Vale 1802
This small painting was the first which Constable painted of the view from a spot on the hills between Gun Hill, Dedham, and Langham Church. The same view was to be the inspiration of several more paintings. In its composition he was obviously very much influenced by Claude's *Hagar and the Angel* belonging to Sir George Beaumont whose mother resided at Dedham prior to 1795. He used to bring the painting, one of his favourites, with him when he made an extended visit to her. On one of these visits Mrs Constable obtained an introduction for her son to him, and the picture made a deep and lasting impression on Constable. His painting of Dedham Vale shows rather less of the area immediately at the foot of the hill—possibly because of greater growth of bushes—than later versions, but otherwise the view of the fields, the village of Dedham, the estuary and Mistley beyond are shown with great detail and accuracy. Fuller details will be found in the note on the great *Dedham Vale* of 1828 (75) and in the Appendix.

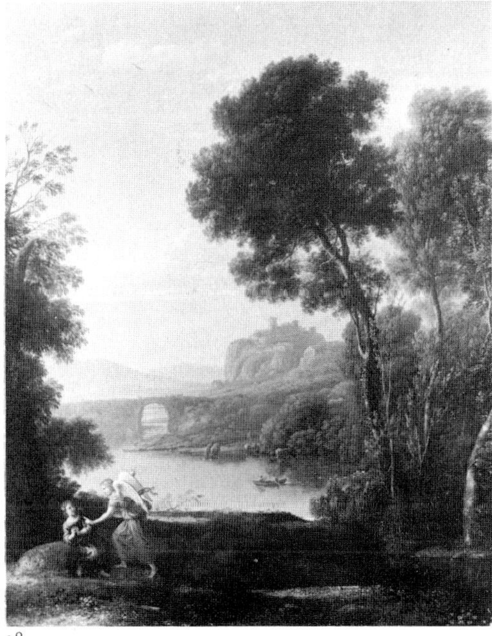

28

sought to convey by sparkling brushstrokes, applying blobs and dashes of crisp paint which anticipate Constable's still more daring technique—the scumblings and impastos and those flecks of pure white which an uncomprehending critic described as 'Constable's snow'. In an earlier lecture at Hampstead Constable had spoken in similar terms about the landscape painters of the Low Countries who meant most to him—Rubens, Rembrandt, Ruisdael and Cuyp—and had added that "on the death of these great men, Landscape rapidly declined"; succeeding painters had looked at art but not at Nature, and had been content to imitate what their predecessors had achieved by original study; but, he concluded significantly, "From this degraded and fallen state it is delightful to say that landscape painting revived in our own country, in all its purity, simplicity, and grandeur, in the works of Wilson, Gainsborough, Cozens and Girtin."

Original study from Nature was not, for Constable, sufficient in itself to make a great landscape painter: we have seen the value he attached to the feeling and poetry expressed in the landscapes of Gainsborough and Cozens. His standard of excellence is succinctly explained in a letter to his friend John Fisher written in April 1821, in which he comments on the art of Gaspard Poussin: "The works of Gaspar Poussin contain the highest feeling of landscape painting yet seen—such an union of patient study with a poetical mind." Gaspard Poussin's sensitive eclecticism, in which were mingled the styles of his master and brother-in-law Nicolas Poussin (whose name he adopted) and of Claude Lorrain, made him one of the painters who were most admired in eighteenth-century England; and although Constable does not appear to have discussed him at any length in his lectures, he was of course very familiar with his work, and in one of his early letters he mentions with special pleasure his recent purchase of "two charming little landscapes by Gaspar Poussin, in his best time". As we shall see, there is some evidence that a landscape by Gaspard Poussin now in the National Gallery influenced 68
the composition of *The Cornfield*.

Before we leave the subject of Constable's lectures, there is one painting which we must consider because he often returned to it when he traced the history of landscape painting in Europe. This was Titian's *Death of St Peter Martyr*, a work of imposing scale which has been destroyed by fire but which is known from copies and from a famous print. In his lectures both to the Literary and Scientific Society of Hampstead and to the Royal Institution in London, Constable devoted much space to this picture, in which, he declared, the landscape background "may be considered as the foundation of

all the styles of landscape in every school of Europe in the following century".
Moreover, Constable made an attempt to demonstrate to his audience how
Titian built up his composition, noting from copies of preliminary sketches
by Titian, or attributed to him, how the master altered features of his original
conception as he gradually perfected his design. We do not know exactly
what Constable said in making this demonstration, since for much of it we
have only C. R. Leslie's brief notes on the general tenor of his remarks, in
supplementation of the record of his own words; but Constable felt certain,
for example, that the tall tree on the right was an afterthought, made neces- 26
sary by earlier changes in the design. It is clear that Constable believed the
painting to have been built up in the course of a prolonged intellectual
process—in much the same way that Constable's later Academy pictures can
themselves be seen today to have been constructed. Constable's close study of
Titian's painting is confirmed by the survival of a drawing by him of one
of the figures. I believe that echoes of this great composition, which Constable
knew by heart (although he never saw the original, which was in a church in
Venice), are to be found in some of Constable's own compositions, such as 25
those views of Salisbury Cathedral in which the cathedral spire is glimpsed
through tall, arching trees.

In addition to its grandeur of design, Constable admired in the *St Peter Martyr* Titian's combination of breadth of effect and truth to Nature in his rendering of the landscape. In his eleventh *Discourse* at the Royal Academy, Reynolds had criticized Count Algarotti for seeing in the picture something that was not there—in Reynolds's words, "the minute discrimination of the leaves and plants, as he says, to excite the admiration of a Botanist". Connoisseurs, Reynolds goes on, "will always find in pictures what they think they ought to find"; but an artist who acquired the name of 'the Divine Titian' never gave his attention to such 'trifling circumstances'. Constable took up this point in one of his own lectures, coming in a sense to the defence of Algarotti, whose *Essay on Painting,* as we have seen, he had read at the time of his early association with 'Antiquity' Smith. More precisely, he sought a middle position between Algarotti's views and those of Reynolds:

> . . . Sir Joshua was swayed by his own practice, of generalizing to such a degree that we often find in the foregrounds rich masses of colour, or light and shade, which, when examined, mean nothing. In Titian there is equal breadth, equal subordination of the parts to the whole, but the spectator finds, on approaching the picture, that every touch is the representation of a reality; and as this carries on the illusion, it cannot surely detract from the merit of the work.

Here Constable must have drawn upon his knowledge of other pictures by
Titian which he knew in the original. His observations upon the balance
achieved by Titian between the particular and the general reflect his own
practice in his central period, as in such compositions as *The Hay Wain* and
The Cornfield, although in his last works the treatment can be as summary as
Reynolds's (but in terms of a different style and intention). He was fond of 76
putting into his foregrounds a few characteristic specimens of plants and
flowers, such as can still be seen growing in profusion by Flatford Mill; and
he was able to suggest their forms by a few decisive strokes of the brush or the
palette knife which sacrificed detail, but not truth, to breadth of effect. While
he was working on *The Cornfield* in his London studio, he seems to have consulted a botanist friend, Henry Phillips, who was a devoted admirer of his
work, about the flowers and plants which it would be appropriate to introduce
into a midsummer landscape; but he painted them broadly, and yet with an 64
eye for their individual character.

The phases of Constable's development

Constable's working life can be divided into four main periods, which are
conveniently connected—and most of them, perhaps, significantly connected
—with his relationship to Maria Bicknell, who became his wife in October 29
1816, when he was forty years old. The first period, which we may call the
period of uncertainty, lasts until about 1809, the year in which Constable
first declared his love. The second comprises the seven years of his courtship,
when he devoted himself principally, as a painter, to studies of Suffolk
scenery, and developed the free sketching style in oils which formed the I
foundation of his later practice. There then follows the third and central
period, from 1816 to the year of his wife's death from tuberculosis in 1828.
This is the period of the large Stour scenes, all completed between 1819 and
1825, and all but one painted on six-foot canvases; and it is ushered in by an
important picture dated 1817 which anticipates the series in subject-matter
and treatment—the famous *Flatford Mill, on the River Stour,* now in the Tate
Gallery. The great series comprises: *The White Horse* (1819); *Stratford Mill*
(1820); *The Hay Wain* (1821); *A View on the Stour near Dedham* (1822); *The
Lock* (1824); and *The Leaping Horse* (1825). To these may be added variants of
The Lock (notably, the famous version of 1826), and two major compositions
inspired by the Stour Valley, *The Cornfield* of 1826 and the Edinburgh *Dedham
Vale* of 1828, which complete a sequence of large-scale Suffolk scenes

terminating in the year of his wife's death. (The first *Lock* and the last two scenes in the entire group differ from the others in having an upright format.)

The final period, from 1828 to the year of his own death in 1837, is characterized, in general, by a sombreness of mood, tending to melancholy. Many of the paintings executed by Constable after his wife's death, which left him desolated by grief, show a quite extraordinary freedom of handling, as the 'Impressionism' of his earlier oil-sketches becomes the vehicle of a new 'Expressionism': the tortured brushwork and the slashing strokes of the palette-knife can now project a state of mind with an immediateness once reserved for the optical effects of sunshine and shade upon glistening leaves and dewy grass. This final manner is, however, anticipated in the large oil-sketches which preceded the completion, in greater detail, of several of the 'Stour Scenes' destined for public exhibition.

The claims of Nature and Art

Constable's art was rooted both in his love of Nature and in his appreciation of such painters as Claude, Rubens, Rembrandt and Ruisdael; but it was only gradually that he learnt to achieve a satisfactory balance between the potentially conflicting claims of Nature and Art. His awareness of the problem is reflected in his famous letter to Dunthorne of 29 May 1802:

For these few weeks past I believe I have thought more seriously on my profession than at any other time of my life—that is, which is the surest way to real excellence. And this morning I am the more inclined to mention the subject having just returned from a visit to Sir G Beaumont's pictures—I am returned with a deep conviction of the truth of Sir Joshua Reynolds's observation that "there is no *easy* way of becoming a good painter". It can only be obtained by long contemplation and incessant labour in the executive part.

And however one's mind may be elevated, and kept up to what is excellent, by the works of the Great Masters—still Nature is the fountain's head, the source from which all originally must spring—and should an artist continue his practice without referring to nature he must soon form a *manner,* and be reduced to the same deplorable situation as the French painter mentioned by Sir J Reynolds, who told him that he had long ceased to look at nature for she only put him out.

For these past two years I have been running after pictures and seeking the truth at second hand. I have not endeavoured to represent nature with the same elevation of mind—but have neither endeavoured to make my performances look as if really *executed* by other men.

I am come to a determination to make no idle visits this summer or to give up my time to common-place people. I shall shortly return to Bergholt where I shall make some laborious studies from nature—and I shall endeavour to get a pure and unaffected representation of the scenes that may employ me with respect to colour particularly and any thing else—drawing I am pretty well master of.

There is little or nothing in the [Academy] exhibition worth looking up to—there is room enough for a natural painture. . . .[2]

The little picture of *Dedham Vale* painted in the summer of that year, and 27
now in the Victoria and Albert Museum, was one of the first-fruits of this new
sense of purpose, although there is no evidence that it was executed in the
open air. The view the picture presents, showing Dedham Church in the
distance, beyond the winding course of the River Stour, was taken from a
wooded hill on the west side of Dedham. Colonel Brooks has established
that it is topographically accurate: yet, as Andrew Shirley pointed out,
the composition has a strong look of Claude, and in particular of the *Hagar*
and the Angel (National Gallery). Indeed, Constable had just seen this picture 28
again at Sir George Beaumont's house; in 1800 he had made a copy of it. The
synthesis between the claims of Nature and the demands of Art is now being
forged; and a quarter of a century later, in the last of his great sequence of
Suffolk views—the superb *Dedham Vale* now at Edinburgh—Constable 75
took up the subject again, using the little picture of 1802 as the basis for a
still more imposing and a more imaginative design.

When Constable painted the early *Dedham Vale* of 1802 he found a theme ideally suited to his genius. Yet it was not for another eight years that he returned consistently to the congenial subject-matter provided by the haunts of his boyhood (although several fine pictures, on a small scale, of Suffolk scenes—including views of Dedham Vale—are certainly datable within the period 1802–10). In 1806, in response to the taste for views of picturesque mountain scenery, he made his ill-advised visit to the English lakes, admitting afterwards that mountains oppressed his spirits; and from 1807 until 1809 he was still working up scenes of the Lake District for exhibition at the Academy. Much of his time in these years was spent on commissions which distracted him from his true vocation. He made copies for the Earl of Dysart of family portraits by Reynolds and Hoppner; he painted an altarpiece in 1805 for Brantham Church—the subject being *Christ blessing Little Children*—and another in 1810, of *Christ blessing the Bread and Wine*, for the church at Nayland; and he accepted commissions for portraits (as in later years also) in order to supplement his small allowance. In this way, apart from a few minor landscapes painted on visits to Bergholt in these years, he allowed himself, largely perhaps owing to financial necessity, to be deflected temporarily from the source and mainspring of his art—the inspiration afforded him by the landscape of the Stour Valley. Two paintings in particular, both probably of about 1809, and both in the Tate Gallery, do, however, anticipate his later development: these are the beautiful prospect of *Malvern Hall, Warwickshire*, painted when Constable was employed in executing a portrait of the owner of the house, Henry Greswolde Lewis, the nephew of Lady Dysart, and the small *View at Epsom*, which although little more than a sketch is remarkable for its freedom of handling, its mastery of simplified tonalities, and the unity in it of sunswept landscape and windblown sky.

The year 1809 may be said to mark the end of this somewhat indecisive
period and the beginning of a new and crucial phase. The direction which his
art would now take was announced, as it were, by his exhibition at the
Academy in 1811 of the lovely *Dedham Vale, Morning* (collection of Sir 18
Richard Proby). Constable's visits to Bergholt in the summer and autumn
months became more and more prolonged, and from July 1815 until October
1816, when he returned to London for his marriage to Maria Bicknell, he was
almost continuously in Suffolk. He was now regularly making sketches in
oil in front of the *motif*, besides filling his sketchbooks with small pencil
drawings; and he must have been recollecting these days when he said in his
last lecture, delivered in 1836 to the Literary and Scientific Society at
Hampstead: "Paley observed that 'the happiest hours of a sufficiently happy
life were passed by the side of a stream'; and I am greatly mistaken if every
landscape painter will not acknowledge that his most serene hours have been
spent in the open air, with his palette on his hand." The oil-sketches include
studies of Willy Lott's House which contain the germ of the great conception 45
realized many years later in *The Hay Wain*. A similar interest attaches to two
sketchbooks of 1813 and 1814, of tiny size ($3\frac{1}{2} \times 4\frac{3}{4}$in and $3\frac{1}{8} \times 4\frac{1}{4}$in respec-
tively), used by Constable during his protracted visits to Bergholt in these
years. The small, and often very free, pencil studies in these two sketchbooks 1
were to be consulted over the years when Constable was working on such 37
compositions as *Flatford Mill, The White Horse, Stratford Mill*, the *View on the* 53
Stour near Dedham and *The Valley Farm*—which are all among the most
important of Constable's evocations of the scenery of Bergholt and Dedham
Vale. It was probably the first of these sketchbooks that Constable half-
seriously described, in a letter to Maria Bicknell, as his 'journal': "You once
talked to me about a journal. I have a little one that I made last summer that

might amuse you could you see it—you will then see how I amused my leisure walks, picking up little scraps of trees, plants, ferns, distances etc etc." These 'little scraps', recorded on a minute scale, were to become the substance of several major compositions executed on six-foot canvases.

It would be difficult, if not impossible, to trace Constable's slow development as a painter without relating his art to his personality; and it is particularly desirable to do so in respect of the period which led up to the painting of the great Stour scenes. Although physically strong, Constable was a man of an extremely delicate nervous constitution, constantly prone—as Basil Taylor has rightly emphasized—to feelings of anxiety and moods of depression. His parents and friends often had cause to express their concern about his states of nervous agitation and self-doubt, which not only left him without peace of mind but at times affected his ability to apply himself to his work. His slowness to establish himself as a painter can be directly connected with his highly strung temperament; and it is not surprising that his kindly father, a man of strong practical commonsense who judged success in life by its monetary rewards, should have sought to prod him, during his early struggles in London, into a greater decisiveness of purpose. "When once you have fixed on a subject," he advised him in a letter of December 1811, "finish it in the best manner you are able, and not through despair put it aside and so fill your room with lumber. I fear your too great anxiety to excel may have carried you too far above yourself; and that you make too serious a matter of the business and thereby render yourself less capable; it has impaired your health and spirits. Think less and finish as you go." (This would be sound enough advice for many an artist.) So also his uncle David Pike Watts, who had paid for his visit to the Lake District, discerned in Constable's work a reflection of the artist's own melancholy. Writing to him about *The Mill Stream* (now at Christchurch Mansion, Ipswich), which Constable exhibited in 1814, and which may be regarded as his first conception of the subject 31
immortalized seven years later in *The Hay Wain*, he observed: "If I may say so, the trees are not green, but black; the water is not lucid, but overshadowed; an air of melancholy is cast over the scene. . . ." But here, without knowing it, Watts put his finger upon an aspect of Constable's art which constitutes one of his most important contributions to English landscape painting—its expressive power.

As Michael Kitson has pointed out, "Although it is true that the love of observed fact is the principal element in Constable's attitude to nature, and although he undoubtedly extended to a significant degree our knowledge of what nature actually looks like, we must never forget that for any great artist imitation is an essentially creative and active, not merely a receptive and passive, process. Nor must we forget that Constable was a Romantic, and that his aim of realism was the outcome of a powerful emotion, not of a spirit of detachment." Kitson has aptly applied to the mood of *The Mill Stream* a remark made by Constable some years later (in a letter to Fisher of 2 November 1823): "A sketch will not serve more than one state of mind and will not serve to drink at again and again—in a sketch there is nothing but the one state of mind—that which you were in at the time." Kitson adds: "The Ipswich *Mill Stream* will serve to drink at again and again." Yet Constable's uncle had detected something else in the picture—a lack of finish which he ascribed not, as we should do today, to a significant development in the painter's style, but to temperamental weakness. There was, he told Constable, much to admire in the picture, but also "this sad Trait to lament, namely hurry and slight of *Finish*. This is the unfortunate sign of an hurried Mind and consequently perplex'd pencil; in short of that fatal habit *Procrastination*." To those who knew him, Constable's proneness to anxiety was one of his most noticeable characteristics: it was a symptom that alarmed his great friend and admirer John Fisher; and he was himself deeply conscious of its fatal power to distract and oppress him.

In his thirties, when he was courting the lovely Maria Bicknell, his anxiety states were exacerbated by the opposition of her family to the proposed marriage. Maria's father, Charles Bicknell, was a man of some standing in society, being solicitor to the Admiralty. Although friendly towards Constable, he was understandably alarmed at the prospect of his daughter's marriage to an indigent landscape painter, and at one point forbade her to answer Constable's letters. By 1813 Constable was even being refused admission to the Bicknells' house in Spring Garden Terrace, and he would spend many hours lingering in the neighbourhood (which was not far from his own lodgings in Charlotte Street) in the hope of seeing her. Charles Bicknell's concern is all the more comprehensible in that Maria, like her brothers and sisters, had inherited from her mother (Bicknell's second wife) an extremely delicate constitution: her younger brother Durand had died in 1811 at the age of twenty, and another brother, Samuel George, was to die at the age of twenty-four; while Mrs Bicknell, at the time of her own death in 1815—two months after the death of Constable's mother—had been an invalid for some ten years.

To the Bicknells' opposition to the marriage there was added that of Mrs

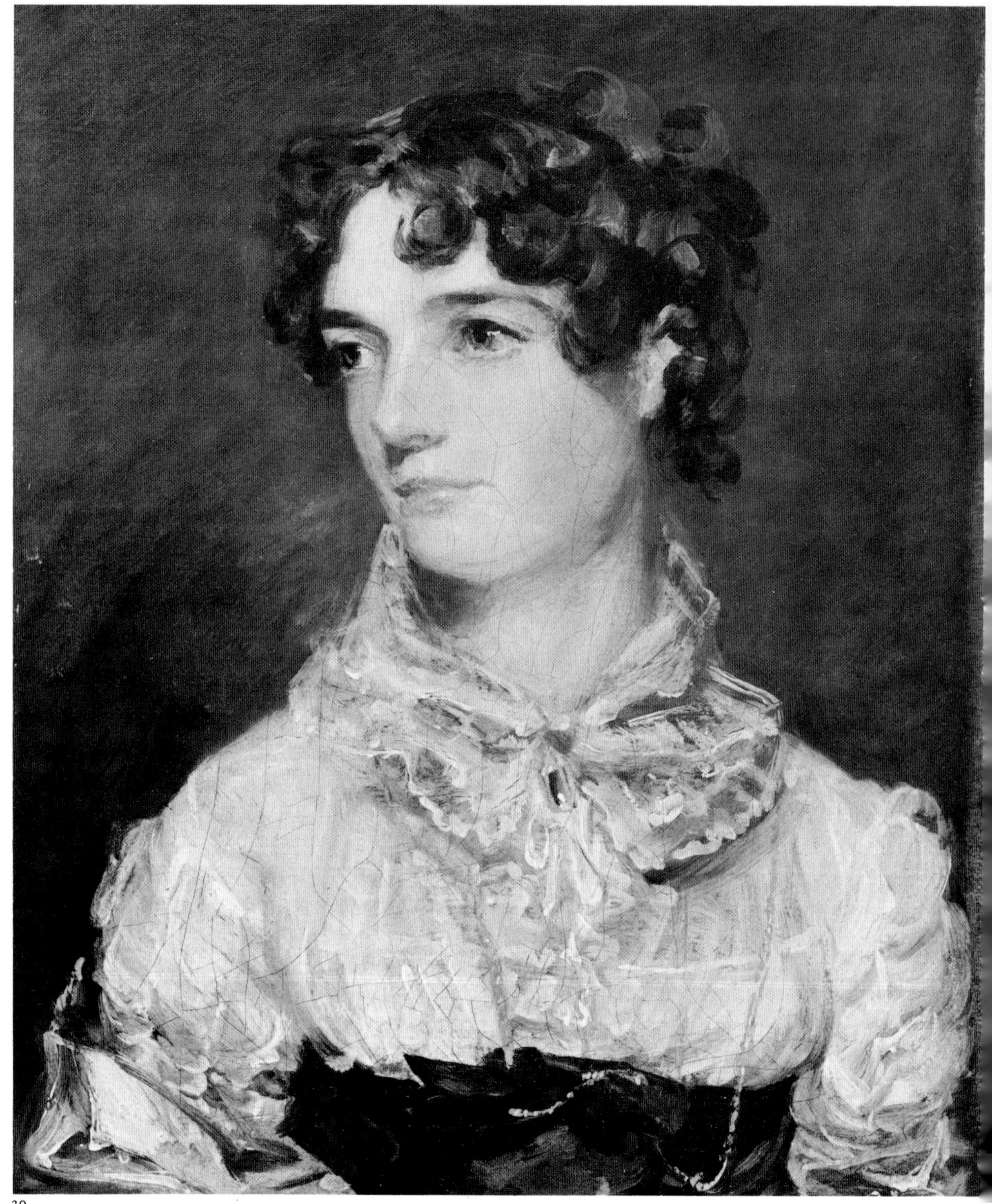

29

Portrait of Maria Bicknell in the year of her marriage to Constable, 1816

Bicknell's father, the Reverend Durand Rhudde, D.D., Rector of East Bergholt cum Brantham and Wenham (whose memorial tablet in the chancel of East Bergholt Church was placed there by John Constable). It appears that Constable, who had known Maria as a child, had fallen in love with her during one of her visits to the Rectory at East Bergholt, probably in 1809. "It is gratifying to me," he was to confide to her, "to think that the scenes of my boyish childhood should have witnessed by far the most affecting event in my life." Dr Rhudde was known to be rich, and the Bicknells confidently expected him to provide handsomely in his will for his surviving grandchildren. But in his eyes there was the greatest possible difference between an ordinary social relationship with the Constables at East Bergholt and the prospect of his granddaughter's marrying the son of a tradesman, although Golding Constable was now a wealthy and eminently successful man. At all events, Dr Rhudde's threat to cut Maria off without a penny, together with the possible implications of his anger for other members of the family, filled the Bicknells with alarm: they had the welfare and dowries both of Maria and of her two sisters to think of; and the fatal inheritance of tuberculosis, from which Maria herself was to die, must have been constantly in their minds. Maria herself—as Constable well understood—knew that it was not only her own prospects that were threatened. But Constable never gave up hope, despite the long periods of enforced absence from Miss Bicknell and all the difficulties of communication even by letter: he never wavered in his attachment to her, nor she in hers to him. Inevitably, however, the seven long years of courtship from 1809 to 1816 were years of strain and uncertainty; and if it had not been for the encouragement and intervention of his friend John Fisher, Constable might well have been in the position of waiting much longer before determining, whatever the difficulties, to press Maria for a final, affirmative answer to his protracted suit.

John Fisher, who was to become Constable's closest friend, had been ordained to the priesthood in 1812; five years later he became Archdeacon of Berkshire, in the diocese of Salisbury, of which see his uncle, Dr John Fisher, was Bishop. Dr Fisher had at one time been Rector of Langham—near Bergholt—and had encouraged Constable in his first efforts in landscape; and in the autumn of 1811 the bishop invited Constable to spend a few weeks at Salisbury. It was then, in all probability, that Constable first met the younger John Fisher, who had lately been ordained deacon. A friendship quickly developed which was to last until Fisher's death in 1832, and which was to be of the utmost benefit to Constable both in his personal life and in his career; for Fisher, although a much younger man by some twelve years, became a sympathetic adviser and a constant support in times of difficulty, and, like his uncle, an enthusiastic and understanding patron. Moreover, it was the young John Fisher, the future archdeacon, who pressed Constable in the autumn of 1816 to take matters into his own hands and to marry Maria Bicknell, offering to perform the marriage ceremony himself: he was in a mood for such assistance, having himself lately married; and so, on 2 October of that year, the wedding took place at St Martin-in-the-Fields. The couple spent their honeymoon with the Fishers at Osmington, in Dorset, where the future archdeacon held the living. It may be added that Charles Bicknell soon became reconciled to the match, forming a close attachment to the painter, and that Maria Constable even received from Dr Rhudde, on his death in 1819 at the age of eighty-five, a legacy of £4000—a considerable sum in those days—which at once eased Constable's financial anxieties. It was in the same year that Constable was elected as Associate of the Royal Academy.

Still more important, 1819 was the year of the exhibition at the Royal Academy of the first of Constable's great Suffolk compositions on six-foot canvases—'A Scene on the River Stour' (as the title appeared in the Academy catalogue), which soon became known, from the white horse in the barge on the left, as 'Constable's White Horse'. *The White Horse*, which was bought by 39
John Fisher, was warmly received by the critics, and it was the quality of this picture that led to Constable's election as an Associate Member of the Royal Academy. Its success was a great encouragement to him as he began work in the following winter upon the second of the large Stour scenes, the 41
Stratford Mill, exhibited in 1820 and bought by Fisher as a present for a friend. And with the third large Stour scene, *The Hay Wain* of 1821, we reach II
the central point of Constable's artistic development. French dealers were already becoming interested in his landscapes, and were showing them in Paris; and in 1821, during his visit to England, the great French Romantic painter Théodore Géricault saw and admired *The Hay Wain* at the Academy, where he was a guest at the annual banquet. Géricault's enthusiastic appreciation did much to establish Constable's growing reputation in France; and in November 1823 the French dealer John Arrowsmith offered to buy *The Hay Wain*. At first Constable refused to sell the picture, which had already been reserved for Fisher; but in the following spring, on Fisher's magnanimous offer to renounce his claim to it, for the sake of the advantage to the artist of its being shown in Paris, Constable agreed to sell it. It thus came about that Constable's

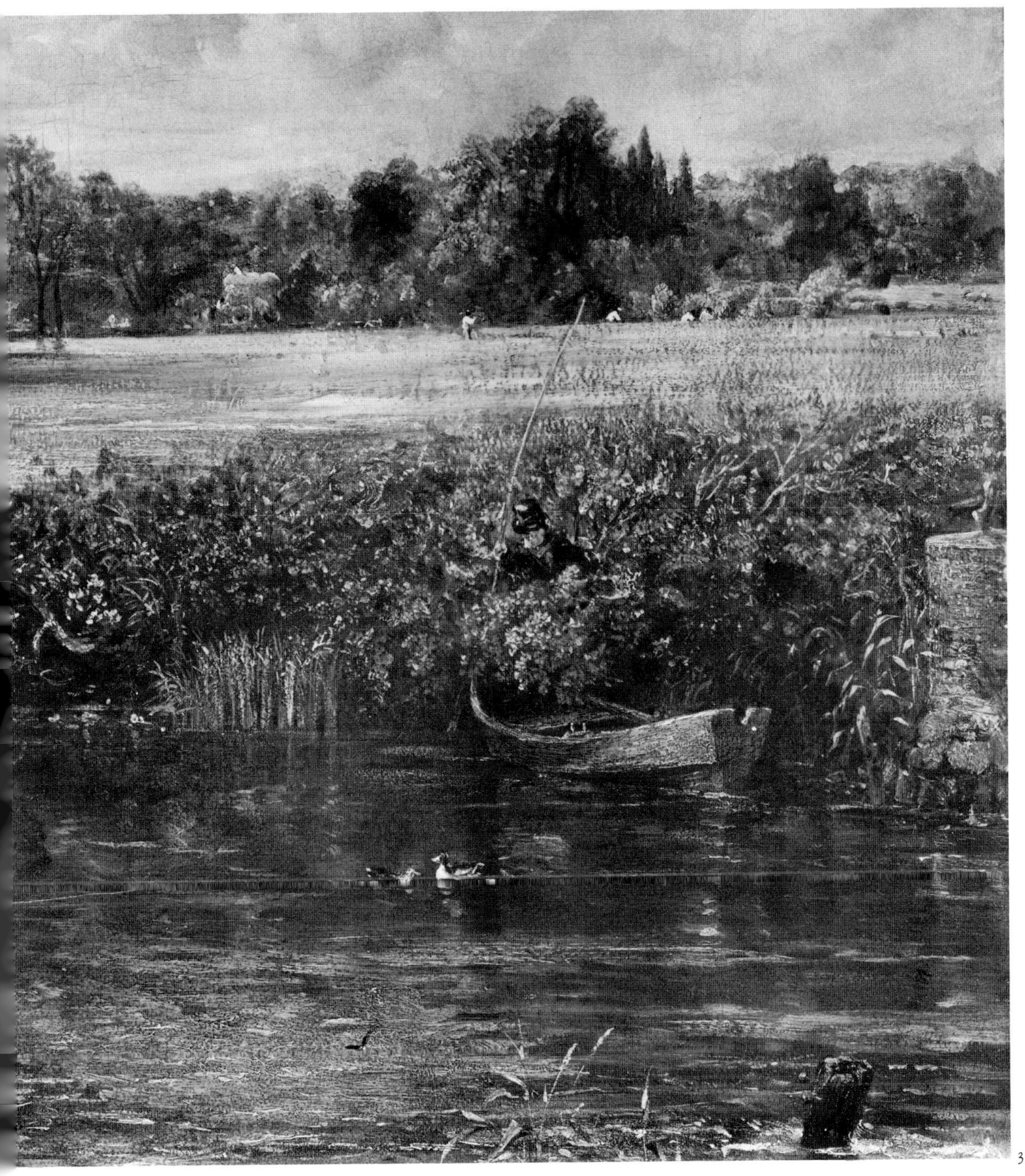

30

Detail of *The Hay Wain*, which caused such a stir at the Paris Salon in 1824, partly on account of the lively brushstrokes which Constable used to represent the play of light on surfaces, and partly because of the directness of his approach to nature. Delacroix and the Barbizon School were greatly influenced by this work.

central masterpiece was exhibited in 1824 at the Paris Salon, where it created a sensation.

Recognition in France

Delacroix, as is well known, was so impressed by *The Hay Wain*, and by other paintings by Constable which he saw in Paris in the winter of 1823–4, that he repainted part of his great composition *The Massacre of Chios*, also exhibited at the Salon of 1824, in order to give his picture something of the freshness and something of the quality of light which he discovered in the work of Constable. The painters of the Barbizon School, such as Théodore Rousseau, Troyon and Daubigny, who adopted the practice of painting their pictures in the open air, in front of the *motif*, were influenced no less directly by Constable's naturalism. And so this insular Englishman, neglected and misunderstood by his own countrymen, had established by 1824 a reputation on the Continent such as he never quite enjoyed in England, except perhaps during his very last years: indeed, when at long last, in 1829, he was elected to full membership of the Royal Academy and called upon the President, Sir Thomas Lawrence (who had himself been elected, as a fashionable portrait painter, at the age of twenty-five), he received the doubtful compliment of being told that, in the President's opinion, he was fortunate—as a mere landscape painter—to have been preferred to one or other of the history painters who were on the list of candidates. As Constable reflected ruefully in a letter to Leslie some two months afterwards, "I am still smarting under my election." Yet to Delacroix and his contemporaries in France, Constable
had shown the way to a new method. The vivacity of Constable's handling 30
of paint—the impact of which, as we look back through our experience of Impressionism and modern art as a whole, we can today appreciate better in his sketches than in his more finished works—together with the immediacy with which he was able to convey his emotions, seemed to open a window, in a quite novel manner, upon the actualities of Nature, upon the freshness of dewy meadows and rain-drenched trees, such as no one had quite painted and interpreted before. Constable was at once elated and surprised by this success. In December 1824 he wrote to Fisher:

A gentleman told me the other day that he visited the Louvre—he heard one say to his friend, "Look at these English pictures—the very dew is upon the ground." They wonder where the *brightness* comes from. Only conceive what wretched students they must have been to be so surprized at these qualities—the fact is they study . . . art only—and think so little of applying it to nature.

At the same time Constable was irritated that some of the French critics, like his uncle, objected to his lack of finish. But he consoled himself with the thought, "Is not some of this *blame* the highest *praise*?" And, anyway, it was not to be denied that his pictures had made "a decided stir", and had "set all the students in landscape thinking—they say on going to begin a landscape, Oh! this shall be—*à la Constable* ! ! !" The reaction of the painters was more significant, as it always is, than that of mere critics; and there can be no doubt that Delacroix, for example, understood the value of a technique which avoided minute finish and definition. For Delacroix, "touch"—the direct brushstroke—was all-important. "Many masters," he was to write in his Journal, "have avoided showing the touch, thinking, no doubt, that by so doing they were coming closer to nature, where there is of course no such thing. Touch is merely one of several means that contribute towards rendering a thought in painting." And it was this for Constable, as much as it was also the means of capturing the fleeting effects and the changing lights of Nature. As he observed to Fisher in 1823: "Painting is but another word for feeling."

The importance of sketching

The origins of Constable's expressive handling in *The Hay Wain* and in the other major works of his maturity lie in the free sketching style which he began to develop about 1809 or 1810 (although he had painted from the *motif* much earlier) and which served the purpose not only of capturing a momentary effect but also of establishing broad relationships of tone and simplified form within a kind of unified 'continuum' of paint. He now regularly adopted the practice of painting rapid oil-sketches from Nature, sometimes on millboard or canvas but frequently on paper. He established a "middle tint" (to borrow the term he used of Claude's *St Ursula*) by painting on a reddish brown or ochre ground, which assisted in the unifying process.
The remarkable *Flatford Mill from a Lock on the Stour*, in the Victoria and Albert I
Museum, and a similar sketch of the same subject in the Diploma Gallery of
the Royal Academy, both of which may possibly be as early as 1810, and two
studies of Willy Lott's House, also in the Victoria and Albert Museum, are 45
well-known examples of oil-sketches of this type. 46

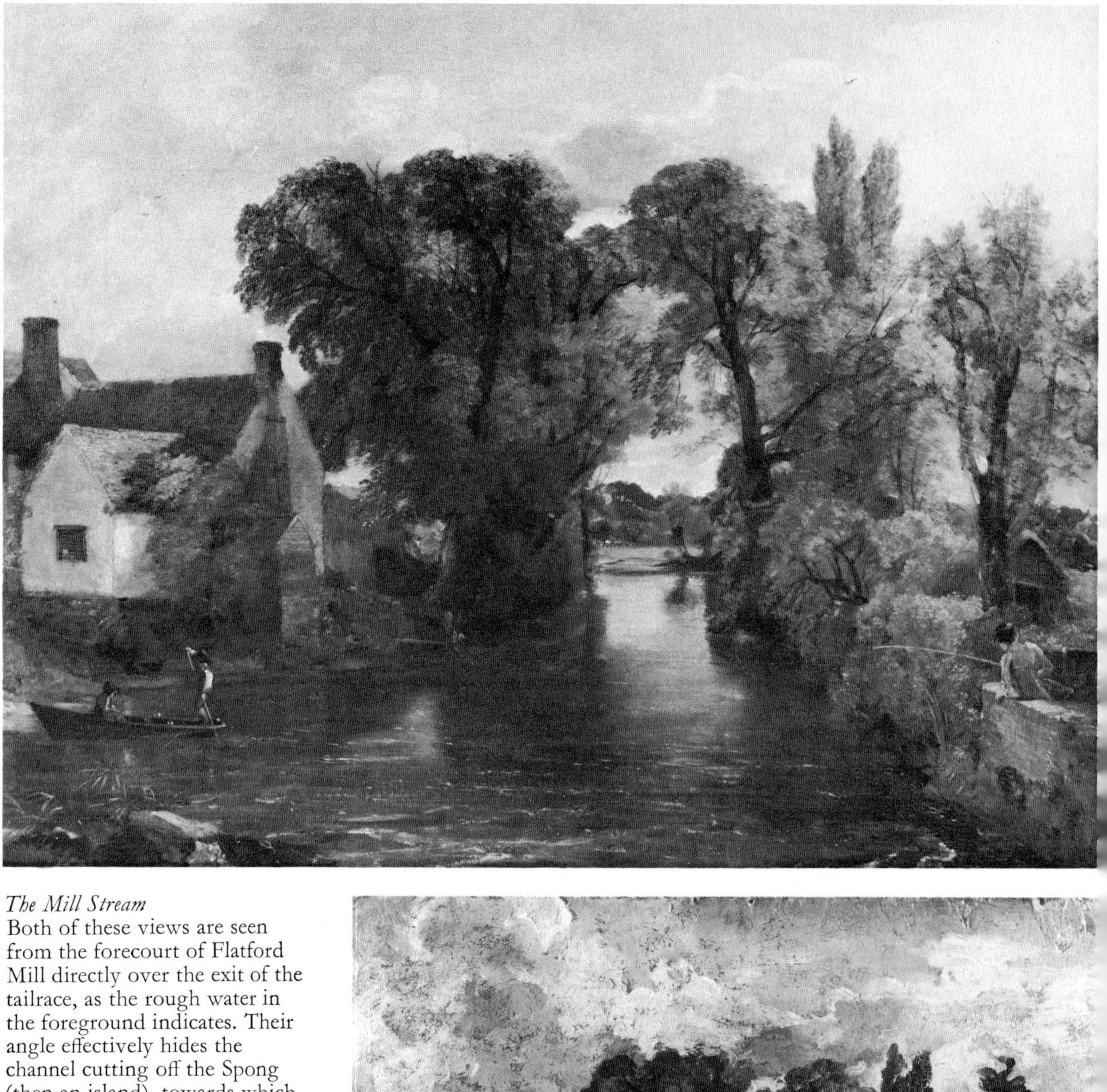

31

The Mill Stream
Both of these views are seen from the forecourt of Flatford Mill directly over the exit of the tailrace, as the rough water in the foreground indicates. Their angle effectively hides the channel cutting off the Spong (then an island), towards which the waggon in *The Hay Wain* is heading. As the colour photograph shows (II), Constable has portrayed this scene very accurately.
There are, of course, many other studies of Willy Lott's Cottage from this and other viewpoints which Constable later portrayed in *The Hay Wain* and *The Valley Farm* (see Appendix). His practice of making an oil sketch which was very close to the final painting and yet which obviously inspired him to make certain compositional changes seems to start around this time.

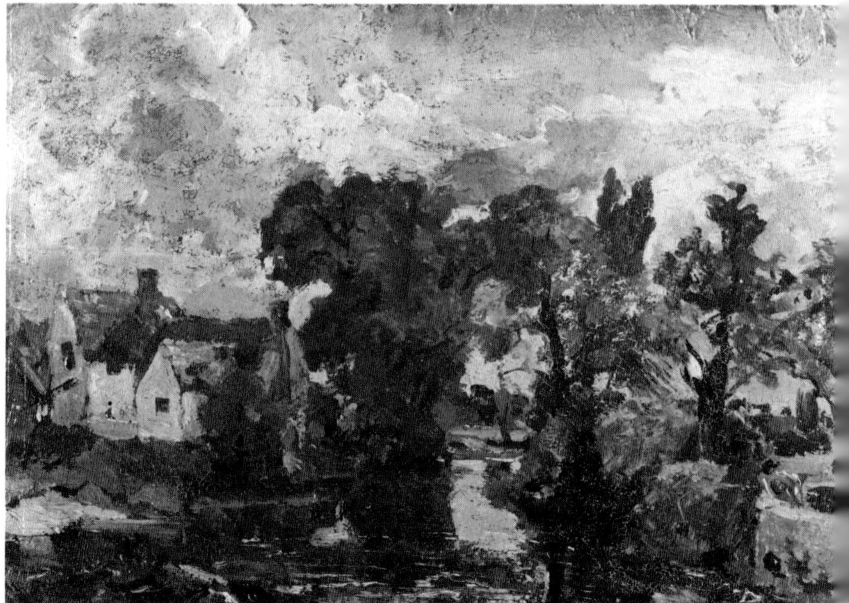

32

The climax of this development is to be seen in the oil-sketch in the Tate 32
Gallery for *The Mill Stream* of 1814. Apart from its small scale (8in × $11\frac{1}{4}$in), this little panel has much of the function of the full-size oil-sketches which were to precede the six-foot Stour scenes, in the sense that here the essentials of the final composition are worked out in broad masses of tone. Moreover, the use of a dark ground survives both in the full-size sketches and in the finished Academy pictures: a close inspection of *The Hay Wain*, for instance, will reveal numerous passages where this brown ground is clearly visible; and in *The Cornfield* they are still more numerous: for example, much of the foliage of the principal tree on the right, where it is silhouetted against the meadow, has simply been omitted, so that what, at a distance, the eye reads as a shadowed clump of leaves is in reality no more than the reddish-brown IV
preparation.

Accordingly, by the year 1814, when *The Mill Stream* was exhibited at the Academy, Constable had already progressed far along the road which was to lead to *The Hay Wain*. Yet it seems that this development was temporarily interrupted, in that year precisely, by his concern over the problem of finishing. In February 1814, at the time when he was completing *The Mill Stream*, he wrote to John Dunthorne about the progress of the picture: "I am anxious about the large picture of Willy Lott's house, which Mr Nursey says promises uncommonly well in masses, etc., and tones—but I am determined to detail but not retail it out." As Michael Kitson has put it, we may interpret this last expressive phrase "as a determination to particularize forms as much as possible without at the same time sacrificing unity of tone, colour and atmosphere; he wanted to hold a big picture together while keeping in it the qualities he had been accustomed to express only in small sketches". In the same letter Constable went on to announce that he had made a resolution:

> I am determined to finish a small picture on the spot for every one I intend to make in future. But this I have always talked about but have never yet done—I think however my mind is more settled and determined than ever on this point. Hitherto (as Shakespeare says) "I have been too infirm of purpose."

A certain discipline was indeed forced upon him by his awareness, in the period spanned by *The Mill Stream* and *Flatford Mill, on the River Stour,* of the need to reconcile his aim of breadth of composition with his concern with particularized Nature; and *Flatford Mill* marks his successful resolution of the problem.

Constable had long been criticized in England for his want of finish. In July 1814, after the exhibition of *The Mill Stream*, he had called upon Joseph Farington, the Academician and diarist, who was the friend to many aspiring artists, whom he advised and encouraged. Constable wished to learn from him what his chances were of election that November to an Associateship of the Royal Academy; and Farington gave him to understand, citing the views of one Academician in particular, Henry Thomson, that in the opinion of his colleagues his pictures lacked proper attention to finish, and recommended a study of the work of Claude before his return to Suffolk. Constable took this advice, and at once went to look again at the five splendid Claudes in the marvellous collection (now in the National Gallery) which John Julius Angerstein, a Russian émigré, had formed at his house at 100 Pall Mall, and which he always made available to visitors. And it was with Claude in mind that, on his return to East Bergholt, Constable set about the painting of a picture which would not only meet the objections of his critics but enable him to grapple with a problem whose solution had hitherto eluded him. This was the *Boat-building near Flatford Mill* (in the Victoria and Albert 33
Museum), which was exhibited at the Royal Academy in the following year (1815). Nevertheless, it was to be another five years, from the time of his discussion with Farington, before Constable was elected an Associate Member of the Academy, at the age of forty-three.

Boat-building and the slightly earlier *Mill Stream* (shown, as we have seen, at the Academy in 1814) mark, in their different ways, an important stage in the development which culminated in the six-foot Stour scenes. In the latter picture, Constable had chosen as his subject-matter a familiar view of Willy II
Lott's House, seen from his father's mill at Flatford; and some seven years later, by taking a slightly different viewpoint, a little way to the left, he used the same *motif* again for *The Hay Wain.* When he painted *Boat-building*, he took up his stance behind Flatford Mill—at a point between the mill and the bridge—and looked out, across the River Stour, towards the meadows which fill the right half of *The Hay Wain.* The deep trench used for building the boats is still there to this day, though difficult to see. Both pictures, therefore, anticipate *The Hay Wain*, and the Stour scenes generally, in their subject-matter. There is, however, a difference. Constable told Leslie that he had painted *Boat-building* entirely in the open air. Moreover, this was a picture in which he was attempting to solve the problem of 'finishing' by applying the lessons of Claude to the direct study of Nature. Other paintings of Suffolk scenes from this period show a precision of detail similar to that

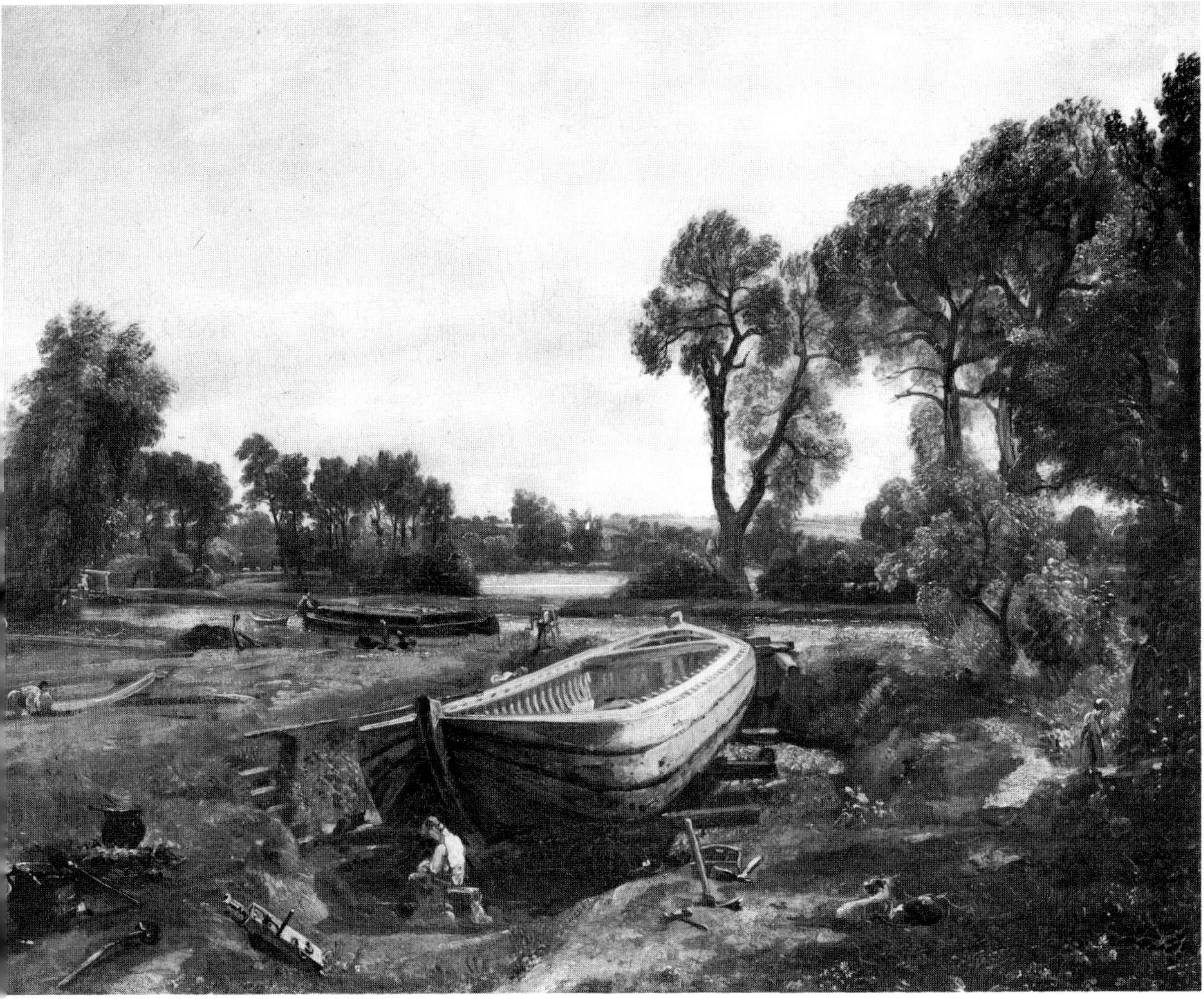

33

Boat-building near Flatford Mill
This canvas—painted in the open air—portrays the scene of one of the barges being built in a little dry dock opposite and a little above Flatford Lock. What was the dock is now flooded, and its entrance from the river is spanned by a little rustic bridge leading from the tea garden behind Bridge Cottage. No access is allowed to the public and regrettably the site is now marred by untidy outbuildings. The busy scene of the barge under construction is full of authentic detail, showing many tools which are still in use by craftsmen and shipwrights even today. The view across the meadows on the far side of the river appears again from a different angle in *The Hay Wain.*

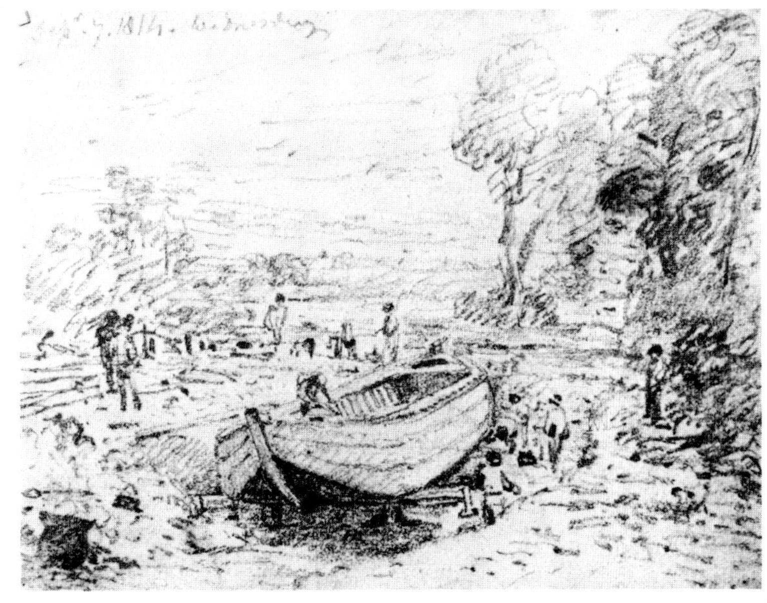

34

evinced in *Boat-building*: I refer to such pictures as the views of Golding Constable's gardens, the *Dedham Vale with a Ploughman* (Collection of Mr and Mrs Paul Mellon) and the superb *Stour Valley and Dedham Church* (Museum of Fine Arts, Boston). The development in Constable's art represented by all these exquisitely handled works reaches its climax in a major composition which is intimately connected with the six-foot Stour scenes—the famous *Flatford Mill, on the River Stour* (Tate Gallery), which is signed and dated 1817. 35
This picture—perhaps begun in Suffolk—combines a close attention to detail and finish with the characteristic subject-matter of the six-foot canvases.

Two pencil drawings in the 1814 sketchbook are related to *Boat-building*. One of these is a study of workmen engaged on the construction of a boat, together with a seated boy, two cauldrons and a ladle—these latter details, including the figure of the boy, being incorporated in the finished picture. The other is a compositional sketch, and is dated *Sept. 7. 1814, Wednesday.* 34
Although the date of the picture is often said to be 1815—the year, certainly, of its exhibition at the Academy—it must have been painted in 1814. While Constable's statement that the picture was painted out of doors cannot be doubted, allowance must be made for the introduction of details from his sketchbook, such as the boy in the white shirt who is seated in the foreground of the painting.

Flatford Mill, on the River Stour

The resources of the 1814 sketchbook, and of the similar sketchbook used by Constable in the previous year, were to prove virtually endless. Many of the tiny pencil drawings in these sketchbooks became the basis for later compositions on a large scale, including several of the six-foot Stour scenes; and in this context the connection between the *Flatford Mill, on the River Stour,* of 1817, and the six-foot canvases is all the closer; for the genesis of the composition can be seen in a drawing of the towpath in the 1814 sketchbook, 37
showing the two trees on the right, the lock and Flatford Mill in the distance. The drawing was made from Flatford Old Bridge—which appears in a number of Constable's sketches, and which has since been replaced by a modern reconstruction—and one can still stand on the rising ground near the bridge where Constable himself stood when he made this drawing. A line of willows along the bank, by the river's edge, now obscures the view 36
of Flatford Mill and the little island in front of it, where the river divides; but even the stream seen on the very right in Constable's picture still survives.

It was from the same bridge that Constable made two other studies that relate to *Flatford Mill.* The first is an oil-sketch, very free in style, in a private collection in Toronto, which was first published by Charles Rhyne. As Rhyne has pointed out, this sketch is still more closely connected with the background of the Tate picture than the little drawing in the 1814 sketch-book; and indeed it already provides a general basis for the design as a whole.
The second is a pencil drawing, of considerable size, of the two trees in the 38
right foreground. It is inscribed, in Constable's hand: *Octr. 17th. 1817. E. Bergholt.* Flatford Mill, although separated from the village itself by more than half a mile of farmlands, is in the parish of East Bergholt, and there is no doubt that Constable made this drawing by Flatford Bridge. Nevertheless the drawing presents something of a puzzle, until we consider Constable's working methods; for it was made after the Tate picture, as it seems, was sent to the Academy exhibition of 1817. Because it postdates the exhibition of the picture at the Academy it has been assumed that it cannot, in any sense, be a study for the painting. Yet unless it relates in some way to the painting it is hard to account for it. The painting is signed and dated 1817, and we must ask why Constable went back, in the same year, to the same spot by the cattle-bridge at Flatford, and drew the same trees, having already depicted them in his Academy picture. The circumstance is all the more interesting because, as Graham Reynolds has pointed out in the context of Constable's naturalism ("the particularisation, the concern with individual form, which Constable opposed to the generalization, the abstraction towards an ideal tree, of eighteenth-century theory"), the drawing of 1817 records the fact that by that year the foremost tree—which seems, I think, to be an alder—had lost one of its three principal branches, which are all consistently represented in drawings of 1813 and 1814, including the view of the towpath in the 1814 sketchbook; and this change in the appearance of the tree is also shown in the Tate Gallery picture, where (as in the 1817 drawing) its position, in Mr Reynolds's words, is "marked by a bulbous growth from which it had fallen or been cut."

The Tate picture has always been identified with the 'Scene on a Navigable River' which was exhibited at the Academy in 1817, and with the large painting that Farington had seen in Constable's studio the previous January; and it has also been assumed that this was the same work that Constable showed in the following year at the British Institution, under the title 'Scene on the Banks of a River' (the size being given as 4ft 10in × 5ft 8in, including the frame—which would be compatible with the dimensions of the Tate

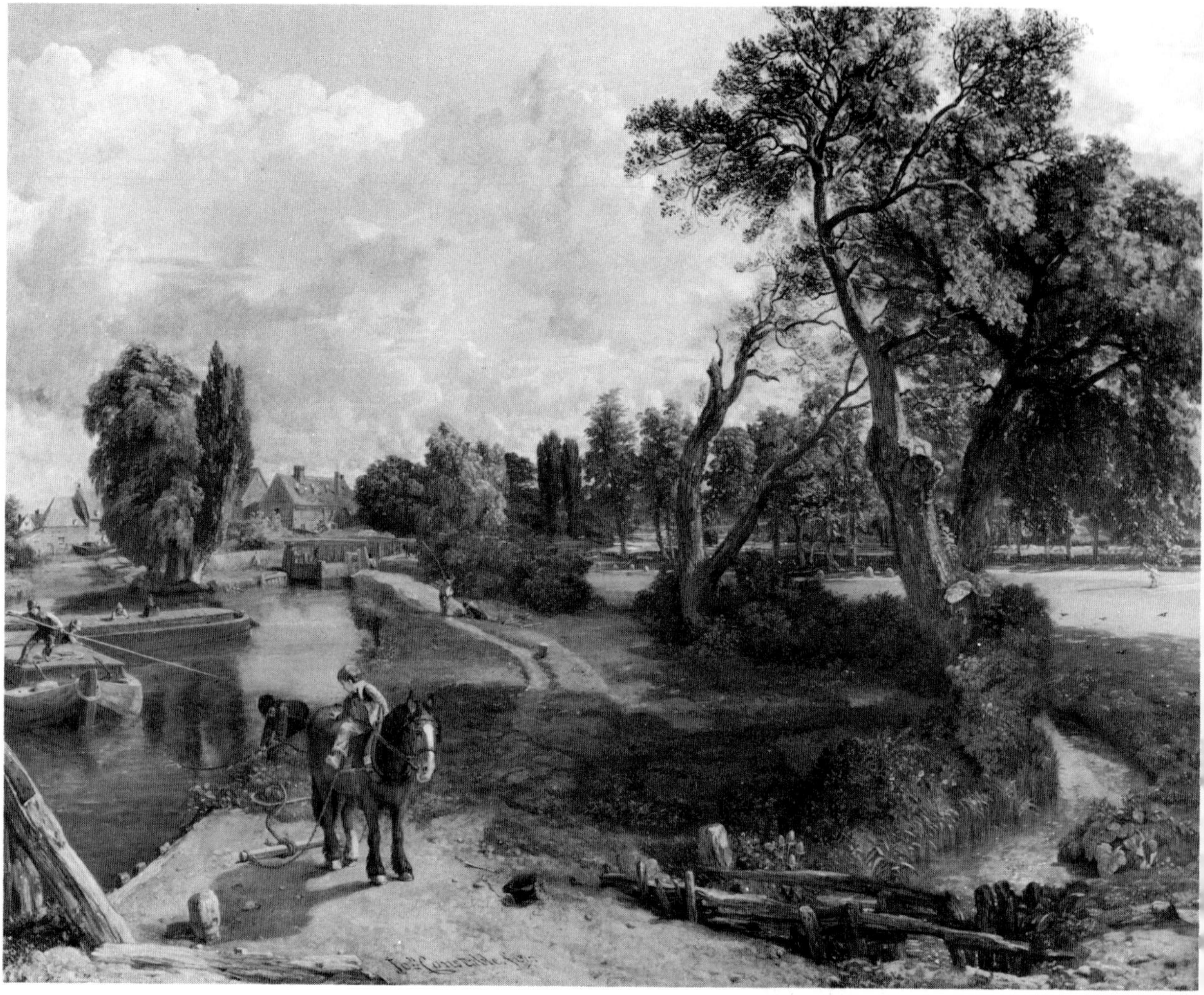

35

Flatford Mill, on the River Stour
A tiny pencil drawing in the 1814 sketchbook (37) became the basis for *Flatford Mill,* painted three years later, just as other sketches formed the basis of the great six-foot canvases. But an oil sketch done even earlier in 1810-11 (now in Toronto), being horizontal, is closer to the final design although it is not painted from the same viewpoint. An oil study (Widener Collection, Philadelphia) also exists, showing the horse without the boy and no barge.

Willows now obscure the view of Flatford Mill from the towpath depicted so meticulously by Constable in his 1817 painting: but the stream at the very right and the rising ground at the very left leading to the bridge can still be seen today.

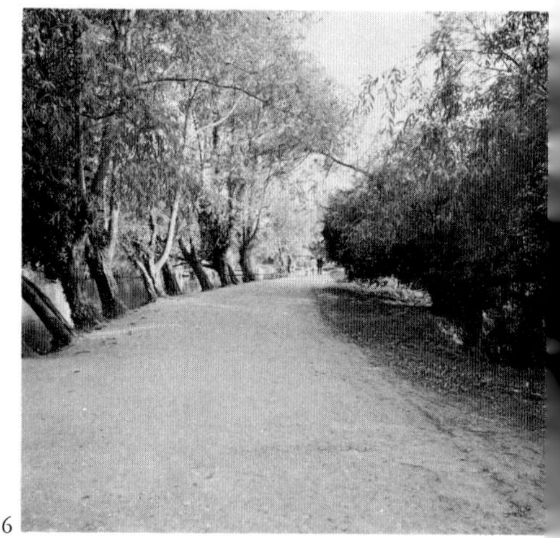

36

37

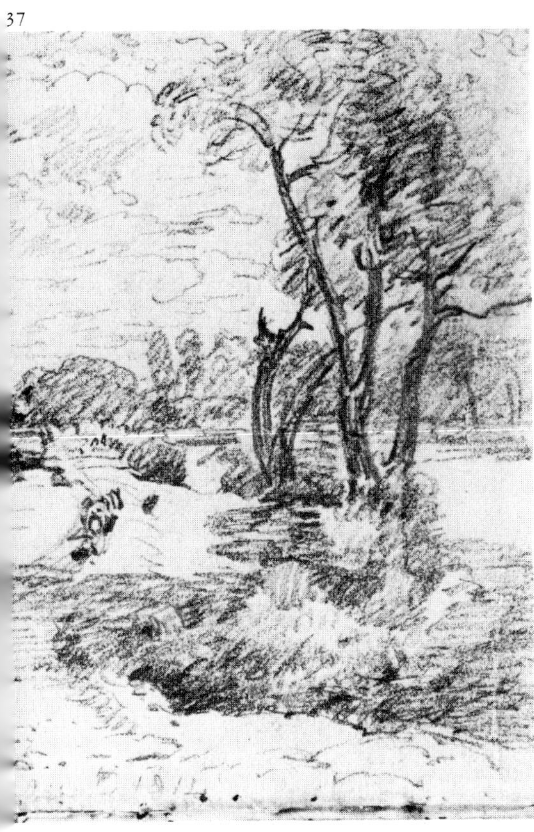

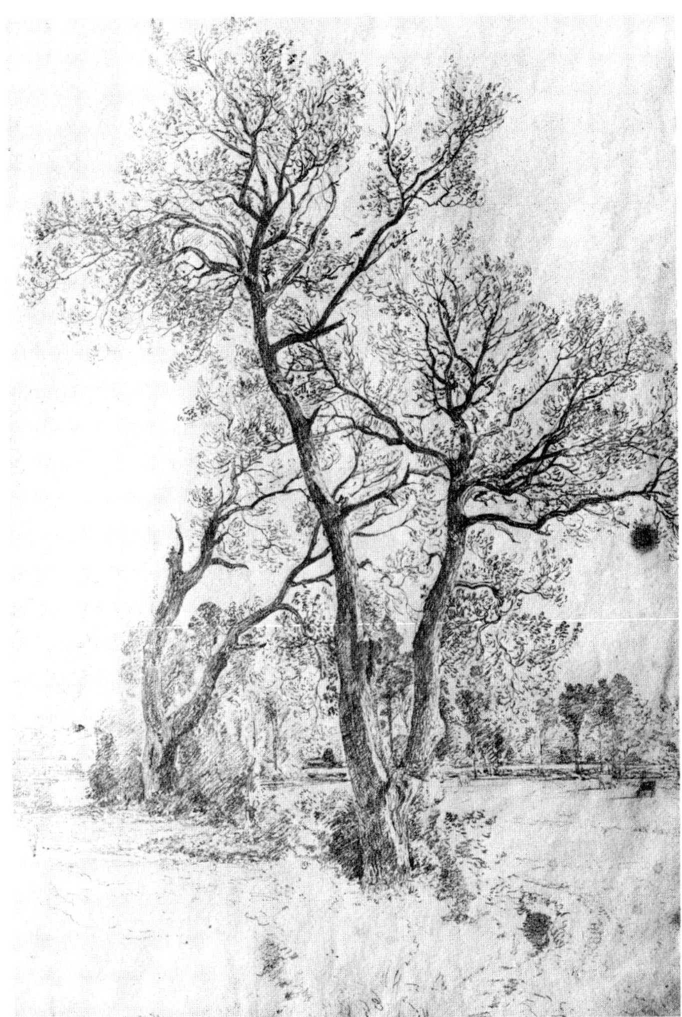

38

Constable gave meticulous attention to the accuracy and finish of this painting which was exhibited at the Academy in January 1817. It is strange, therefore, to find an ambitious pencil sketch of the two most prominent trees of the painting dated *after* the exhibition was over (*Trees at East Bergholt*, 38). A plausible explanation is that he was still not satisfied with the picture and made a further study in front of the trees themselves, later reworking the picture at home in London.

canvas, which are 40in × 50in). Now in subsequent years Constable is known to have made it his practice to get important, unsold pictures back from the Academy and to resume work on them after the close of the exhibition. It looks as though he must have been dissatisfied with his treatment of the trees in the foreground, being sensitive, as we know, to criticisms about his lack of 'finish'.[3] The most plausible explanation of the large drawing that I can offer is that he decided to rework the picture, and prepared himself, during his visit to Suffolk that summer and autumn, by making a detailed study of the two trees from exactly the right spot by the cattle-bridge. Some *pentimenti* in this area of the picture, notably on the top of the left branch of the left-hand tree, seem to confirm the validity of this hypothesis. Moreover, in the finished painting the extremities of the trees in this area correspond so precisely to the branches and leaves seen in the drawing that it seems quite unlikely that the trees could have disposed themselves in exactly this aspect in the previous summer. The drawing of 17 October 1817 demonstrates the accuracy of Constable's rendering of the two trees in the painting: he has clothed them in larger masses of foliage than appear in the drawing, and there are slight differences of other kinds (including the retention in the painting of a bough, shown in the sketchbook drawing of 1814, which had fallen off by 1817); but the attention to detail and to truth of appearances recalls the realism of *Boat-building*, painted from Nature. It is of interest that a critic writing in 1818, when the painting was shown at the British Institution, should have remarked that Constable's work now displayed "the most laboured finish".

With the completion of *Flatford Mill,* Constable was ready to embark, a year or two later, upon the first of his six-foot canvases—those imaginative interpretations of familiar scenes "recollected in tranquillity". In *Flatford Mill* he appears to have aimed at a truthfulness to his subject akin to the careful naturalism of *Boat-building*: to judge from the related studies, his modifications of his subject-matter for pictorial ends were relatively slight; and although they are not to be dismissed as insignificant, they seem to have consisted largely of subtle variations in spacing or, for example, in the tilt of a bough (as in the tree in the right foreground), or in the massing of forms (as in the distant trees to the right of Flatford Mill). But with the six-foot canvases, begun and finished in London, variations and invention play a more fundamental role in Constable's method.

The White Horse

The first of the six-foot canvases, *The White Horse*, was completed in 1819 and exhibited that year at the Royal Academy under the title 'A Scene on the River Stour'. It shows a white horse being ferried in a barge across the river, where the tow-path crosses from one bank to the other, and it soon became known as 'Constable's White Horse'. As has been mentioned, it was this picture, now in the Frick Collection in New York, that secured Constable's 39
election later in the same year as an Associate of the Royal Academy.

Two pencil studies can be related directly to the composition. The first is a small drawing in the 1814 sketchbook, in which the principal landscape features of the finished picture are already established, excluding the area to the right of the thatched boathouse. The second is a study of waterlilies and reeds on a page of the 1813 sketchbook, which seems to have been 82
used for the foreground. Beside the boat-house he introduced a prominent tree which arches over it, and—perhaps from much earlier studies—painted in the rest of the composition to the right. This tree has an important role in the design: providing a point of emphasis which divides the composition laterally into a larger and smaller area, approximately in the manner of the Golden Section (a proportion which artists usually arrive at instinctively), it has the same pictorial function as the similar tree in the corresponding area of *The Hay Wain*.

It is possible that, if we allow for separate studies of the barge, the figures, and the horse and cattle, Constable worked out his composition mainly from the indications given in the tiny pencil drawing in the 1814 sketchbook, although further sketches may well have been used. He had spent much of the previous summer on portrait commissions; in July he had gone to Salisbury to give instruction in oil-painting to the bishop's talented daughter, Dolly Fisher; and at the end of the month he had made a short visit to East Bergholt. His father had died two years earlier, and, towards the end of October, Constable spent a few more days in Suffolk, on business connected with the sale of East Bergholt House. During the winter he devoted his main energies, in London, to the painting of *The White Horse*. Whatever time he may have had to make studies during his short visits to East Bergholt in July and October, the fact remains that the picture was painted far away from the subject, and is the first of a series of large-scale compositions which were worked out and meditated in the studio.

The White Horse was well received at the Academy exhibition of 1819.

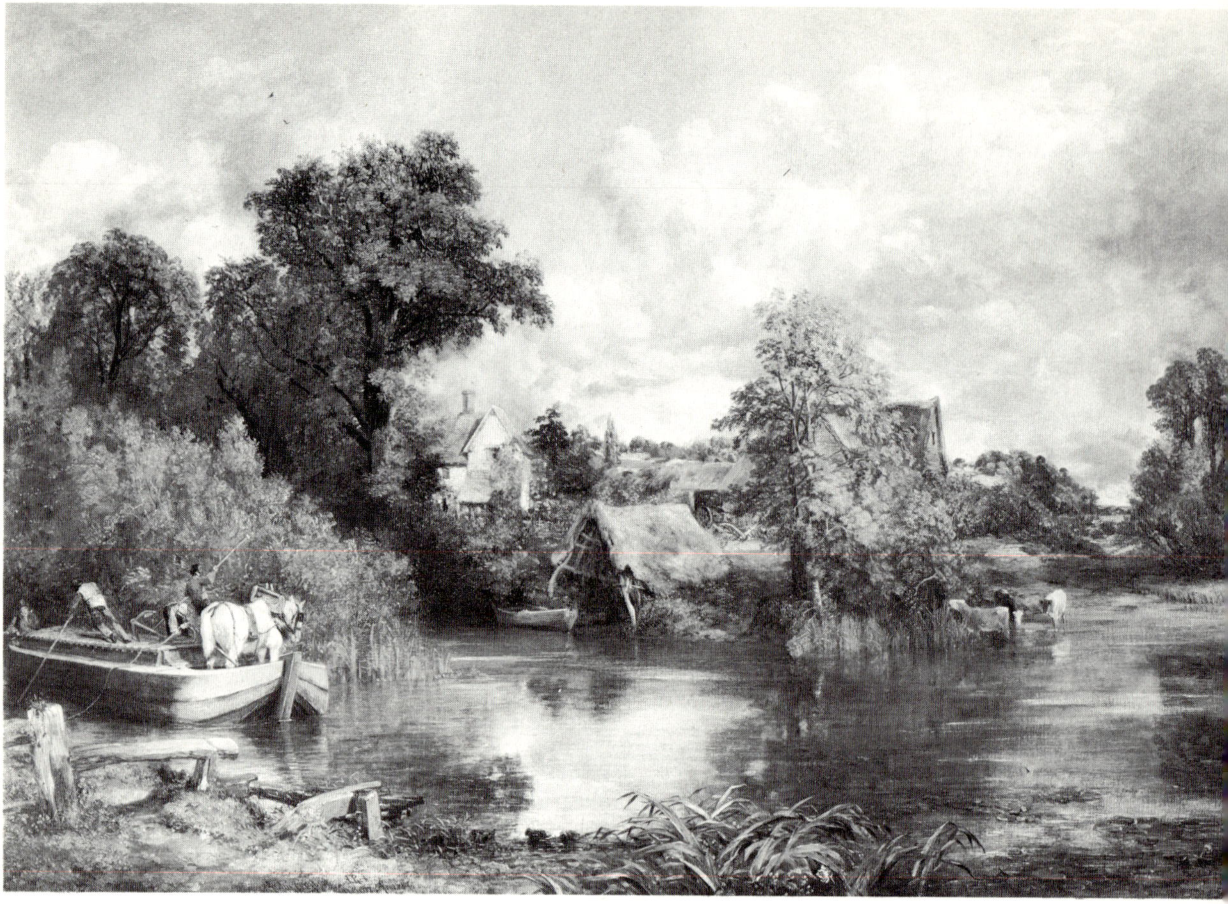

39

The White Horse

This composition appears to be based upon a scene just over a quarter of a mile above Flatford Bridge. The barge at the left of the picture is coming down from Dedham, and the river at this point is joined by a channel which drains the water from the meadows at Stratford St Mary, and is also fed by one or two of the streams coming from the hills to the north. There is a farm up above the river at this point. Going upstream from Flatford the towpath is on the south side of the river, as shown in this painting; but by the time it reaches Dedham it is on the north side of the river. However, the horses used to cross from one side to the other by means of the barge a short distance before coming to the confluence of the tailrace of Dedham Mill. At various points, between Brantham and Sudbury, where the towpath changed from one bank to the other, the towing horses were trained to step on to the barge and to step off again. The photograph taken in 1902 shows this actually happening at a point between Brantham Mill and Flatford Mill. It seems doubtful whether a horse would have been on a barge at the particular spot shown in the painting.

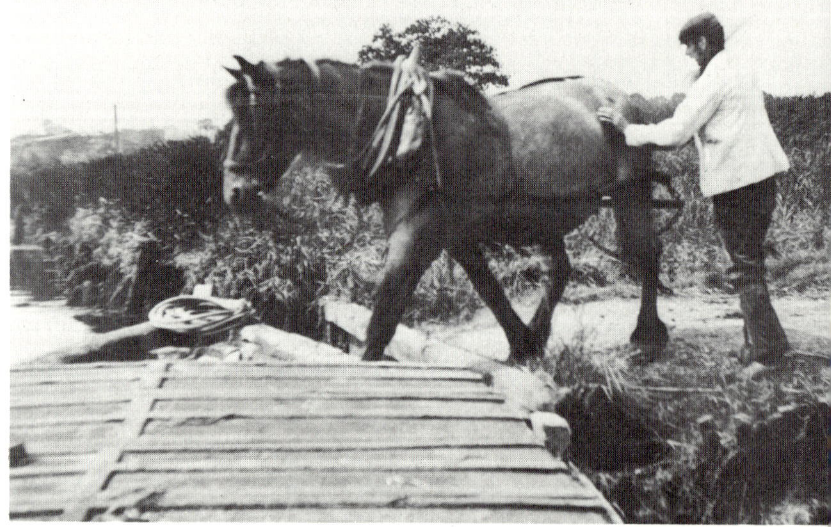

The *Morning Chronicle* critic was particularly warm in his appreciation. "What a grasp of everything beautiful in rural scenery!" he wrote. "This young artist is rising very fast in reputation, and we predict that he soon will be at the very top of that line of art of which the present picture forms so beautiful an ornament." Yet it is a measure of the length of time needed by Constable to make a strong impact upon public taste that, although he was now in his forty-third year, he could be thought of as a 'young artist'. Moreover another ten years were to pass before Constable was elected a full Academician, several artists much inferior to him being preferred in the interval. It is of interest that *The Examiner* should have contrasted the picture with the landscapes of Turner, saying that, unlike Turner, Constable "does not give a sentiment, a soul to the exterior of Nature", but "gives her outward look, her complexion and physical countenance". It may not be coincidental that the second of the six-foot canvases, the *Stratford Mill* of 1820, is more concerned with the expression of the artist's response to Nature's moods.

In July John Fisher, who was now a canon residentiary of Salisbury, and had lately become prebendary of Fordingham with Writhlington, in the diocese of Sarum, wrote to Constable from Salisbury inquiring, on behalf of an imaginary friend, as to the price of the picture, intending to purchase it himself. In allusion to a well-known painting by Benjamin West, entitled *Death on the Pale Horse* (a subject which also attracted Turner), Fisher wrote: "We will call it if you please '*Life* and the pale Horse', in contra-distinction to Mr West's painting. Did you not express a wish to have it on your easel again to subdue a few lights and cool your trees? I think you said so. Because the gentleman who mediates the purchase does not immediately want it." Constable, evidently not suspecting the identity of the intending purchaser, informed Fisher that the price was one hundred guineas exclusive of the frame. The sale of *The White Horse* to Fisher brought Constable the largest sum he had ever received for a landscape; but it was still a sale to a personal friend.

The most interesting part of Fisher's letter is the reference to Constable's wish to continue work on *The White Horse* after its return from the Academy. Constable himself confirmed his intention in his reply to Fisher, in which he wrote of the picture: "It has served a good apprenticeship in the Academy and I shall avail myself of it by working a good deal upon it before it goes on a second to the British Gallery." It was his frequent custom to show some of his Academy pictures again at the British Institution. But *The White Horse* had already found a buyer, and moreover had enjoyed great public success:

it is characteristic of Constable's constant search for perfection that, notwithstanding these circumstances, he should have resolved to work on it "a good deal" before exhibiting it a second time and releasing it to its purchaser. Such conscientiousness is all the more striking when we consider that Constable had been preoccupied with this one composition—his only exhibit at the Academy in 1819—throughout the winter months. Fisher did not receive the picture until the following April, over a year and a half after it had been begun. Constable was to borrow it back in 1825 in order to show it, along with *Stratford Mill*, which Fisher had bought as a present for his friend and solicitor John Perne Tinney, at a special exhibition of "some of the best pictures of living artists" (in Leslie's words) which had been arranged at the British Institution in that year. Then, in the same year, without seeking Fisher's permission, he exhibited *The White Horse* at Lille, where it won him the honour of his second gold medal from France, the first having been awarded him in the previous year when *The Hay Wain* had been shown in Paris. Constable's procedure after the first exhibition of *Stratford Mill* was no less typical: even after its purchase he got it back to his studio so that he could continue work on it. The picture was still in Constable's studio in February 1821, when *The Hay Wain* was well advanced.

Stratford Mill

It was with the success of *The White Horse* behind him, but with that picture still on his easel, that he began making preparations in the following winter
for the next Academy exhibition. *Stratford Mill*, his second six-foot canvas, 41
was the result, and on 1 April 1820 Constable called upon Farington to tell him of its progress. This picture later came to be known as 'The Young Waltonians' from David Lucas's mezzotint engraving of it: Isaak Walton's *Compleat Angler* had become widely popular, and the inclusion of the young boys among the figures seen fishing in the river in the foreground of the picture gave it its new title. An early stage in Constable's development of the composition is shown in a sketch in oils for *Stratford Mill* (in a private collection): it was evidently painted rapidly and is summary, although brilliant, in execution—the intention being to set down a general conception before much in the way of detail was considered. In the final composition a great deal has been changed, during the long process of perfection. Drawings that can definitely be associated with *Stratford Mill* are to be found in the 1813
sketchbook: these are the study of waterlilies and reeds already used for *The* 82

White Horse and a study of a timber fence which Constable adapted, with variations, to the feature in the right foreground.

The only likely occasion on which Constable could conceivably have made other studies on the spot in the summer of 1819 was during a brief visit to East Bergholt in May, in response to a letter from his brother Abram informing him that Dr Rhudde was dying. He arrived there on 6 May, to learn that Dr Rhudde had died that morning; and he was back in London at least by 25 May, when his presence in town is recorded by Farington. There was a further visit to East Bergholt, to see Abram at Flatford Mill, in late October: two letters written to his wife from East Bergholt are dated 26 October (shortly after his arrival) and 28 October; but it seems that two days later he returned to Hampstead, where that autumn he had rented a house called Albion Cottage, for the sake of his wife's health.

An oil-sketch, *Branch Hill Pond, Hampstead,* now in the Victoria and Albert Museum, is inscribed on the stretcher, *End of Octr. 1819;* and this may be one of the 'two pictures, Studies on Hampstead Heath', which Farington says were shown to him by Constable on 2 November. This is a marvellously atmospheric sketch, and it already establishes the general design and something of the detail of a later composition, followed closely in the famous *Heath* mezzotinted by David Lucas. Much of the atmospheric quality of this painting, together with its suggestion of shifting lights and darks, is preserved in *Stratford Mill*; but the drama of the lighting begins to be reflected in the six-foot canvases only with *The Hay Wain*, where the reflection in the water of bright patches of sky and deep shadows is suggested with a comparable intensity.

As Constable looked out over Hampstead Heath from the windows of Albion Cottage, he saw a landscape relatively bare and featureless, but ceaselessly changing under its open skies. His sure eye and hand were now capable of transmitting to canvas, by a few masterly strokes and touches, the generalized forms of the heath, with its isolated clusters of trees and its sudden glints of water: this sombre landscape, illuminated here and there by flashes of sunlight, became for him the vehicle for the expression of a profound meditated emotion. Some of his sketches of the Heath were worked up into finished pictures of exquisite refinement, and nowhere in Constable's work is his subtlety of tonal arrangement more in evidence, or more communicative: notwithstanding the beauty of his colour, it is his mastery of tone in the Hampstead pictures that suggests comparisons with the sublime, storm-ridden, and almost monochromatic landscapes of Rembrandt, and with the

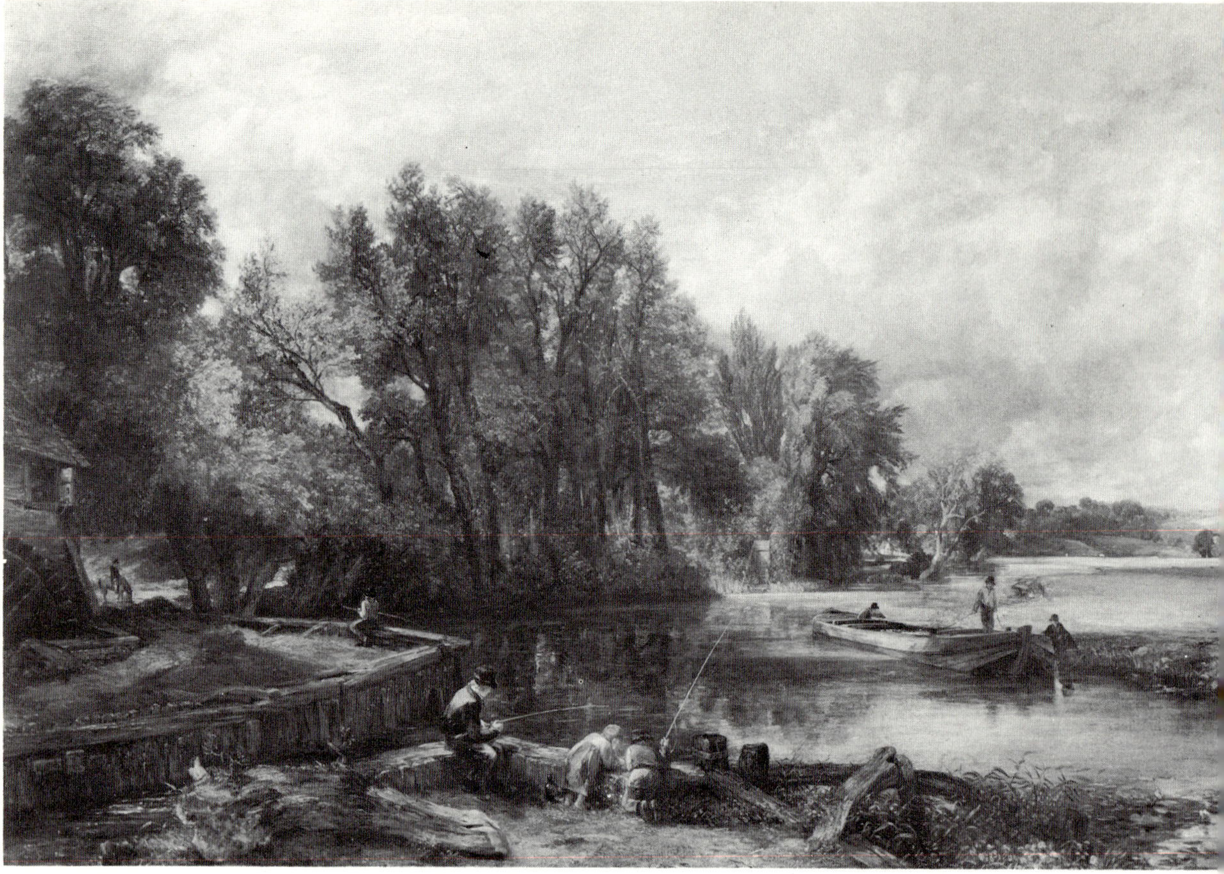

41

Stratford Mill on the Stour
This scene, just by Stratford St Mary village street, is still very recognisable, though the old mill which can just be seen on the left edge of the painting was replaced about 1850 when another mill was erected for the manufacture of macaroni. This venture failed about thirty years later but the mill remained in a dilapidated state until 1947, when its walls were reduced to about six feet in height. The footpath and bridge leading past the north side of the mill across the river to Langham Church were reconstructed and the old timber quay on the west and south was replaced with steel piling and reinforced concrete. The footbridge is rather nearer the point where the young boys

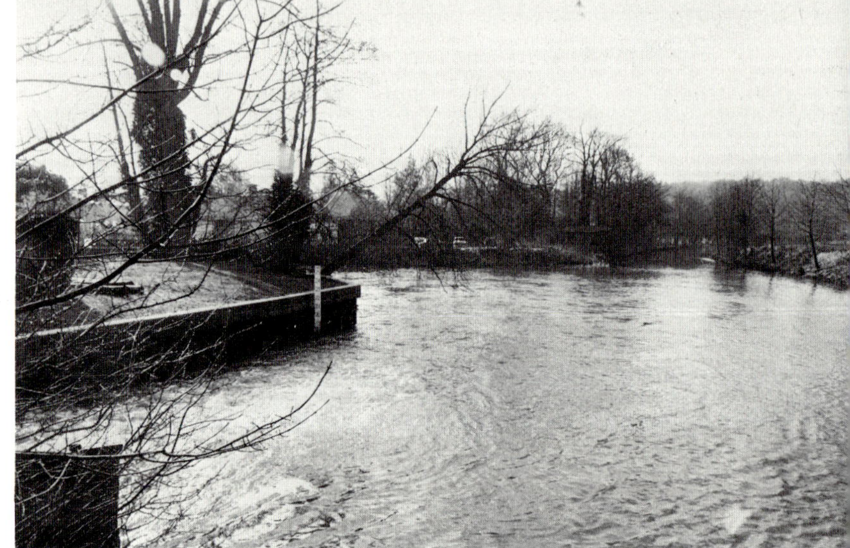

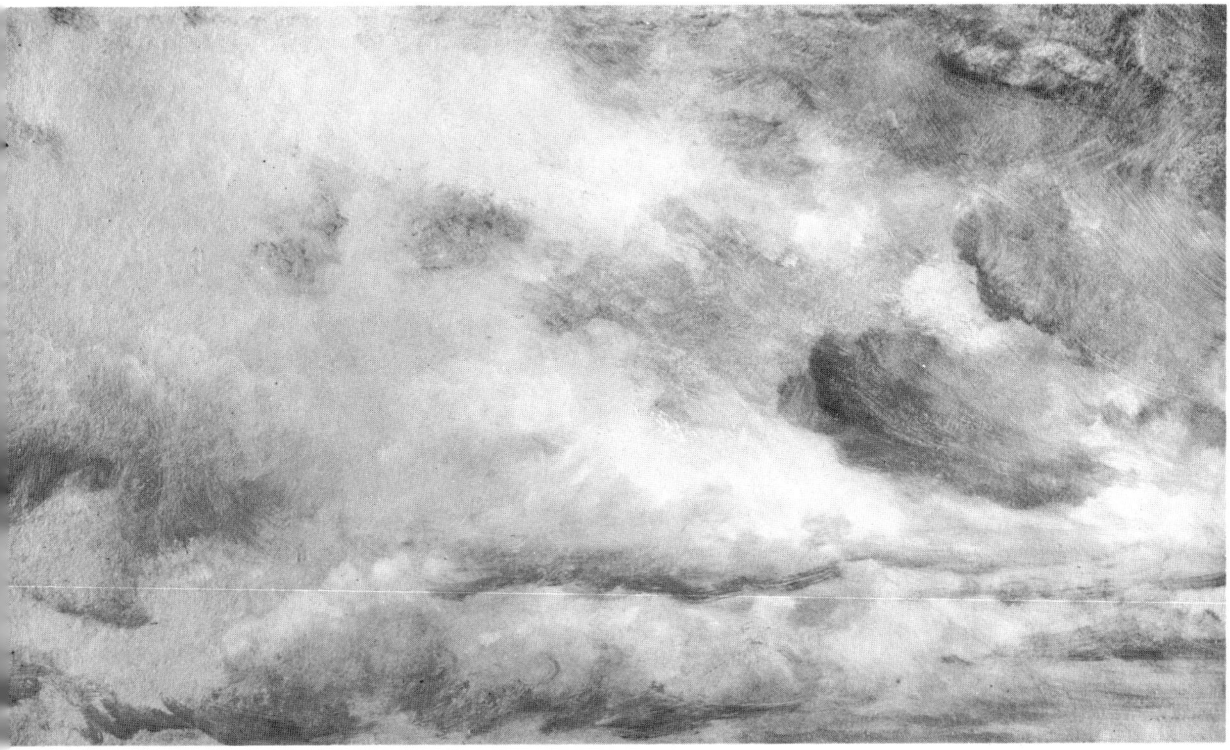

43

are fishing but otherwise the river itself and the scene are very little altered. Willow trees along the west side of the river block out the Langham Hills and so spoil the view to a slight extent. The contrasts of gleaming lights and darks in *Stratford Mill* (41) were a new feature of Constable's art, though its subject matter of the boys fishing made it popular. At the time Constable was working on it he was absorbing new perceptions of atmosphere from his walks on Hampstead Heath, where he became aware of the drama of different cloud effects in the vast skies (43). David Lucas's mezzotint version of the painting *Branch Hill Pond* (Victoria and Albert Museum) exaggerates the quality of Constable's skies (as well as adding some birds).

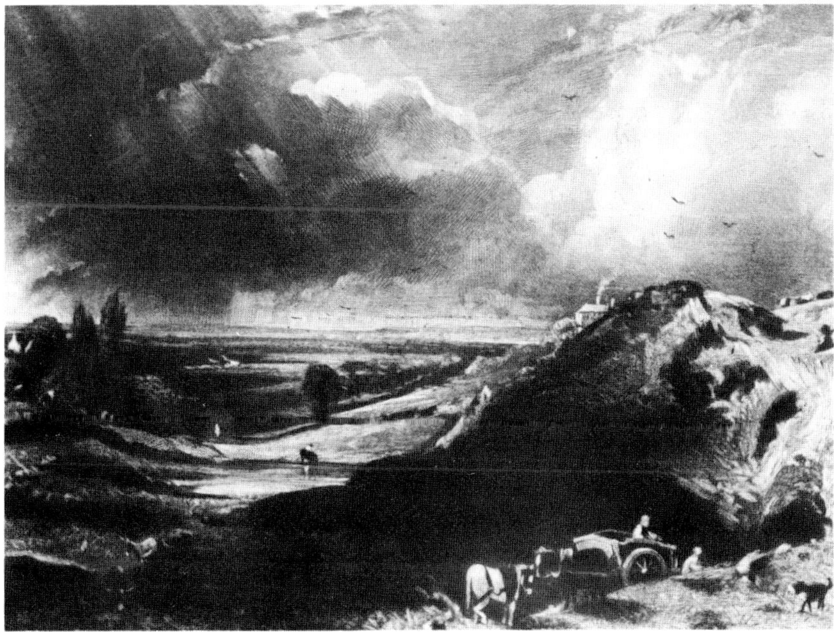

44

gentler landscapes of Ruisdael. The celebrated *Heath*, which Lucas engraved in monochrome and made popular, is the equivalent in Constable's art of Rembrandt's *Mill*, of which he was to speak appreciatively in his lectures. It seems significant that a small landscape by Rembrandt, also of a mill, was presented to Constable by Sir George Beaumont in the summer of 1821. Constable described it to Fisher as "a beautiful little landscape . . . , full of tone and chiaroscuro". Shortly afterwards he wrote again to Fisher to say that at Hampstead he had been making "many *skies* and effects—for I wish it could be said of me as Fuseli says of Rembrandt, 'he followed nature in her calmest abodes and could pluck a flower on every hedge—yet he was born to cast a stedfast eye on the bolder phenomena of nature'." He added: "We have had noble clouds and effects of light and dark and colour. . . ."

Hampstead provided Constable not only with an opportunity to observe and study the skies in a way that no painter before him had done but also with subject-matter peculiarly suited to his meditative genius—a sort of fundamental or universal landscape in whose reflections of Nature's changing moods he could find, as it seems, the outward symbols of his own deepest feelings. In front of such pictures we are conscious first of the melody of inspiration; and then, as though it were a necessary accompaniment, of the sombre chords of Constable's resonant tonalities. We seem to be in touch not simply with a unique, poetic sensibility but also with a mind filled with alternate hopes, joys and anxious griefs. For all those who understand Constable, the Hampstead pictures must hold a special place: family circumstance, which was to end in tragedy, had taken him to Albion Cottage, as it took him later to his other residences there in Downshire Hill and Well Walk; and he appears to have formed an attachment to the Heath which alone could be said, in any sense, to have vied with his feelings towards East Bergholt—of which he once remarked, "I should paint my own places best".

The Hay Wain

He did so pre-eminently in *The Hay Wain*, which bears the imprint, nevertheless, of his Hampstead experience. The sumptuous sky of *The Hay Wain*, II
laden with cumulus, reflects that increasing preoccupation with the role of the
sky in Nature, and its consequent role in landscape painting, which marks the
Hampstead period. By October 1822 he could write to Fisher, "I have made 43
about 50 careful studies of *skies*"; and *The Hay Wain*, painted in the winter of
1820–1, already demonstrates the value to Constable of a study which was

virtually scientific in its attention to strict observation.[4] In this sense we may truly say that *The Hay Wain* is a Suffolk scene under a Hampstead sky. It is, of course, much more than that—and most essentially a recollection of one of the artist's favourite places, the ford and river by Flatford Mill, which there is no reason to think he had need to revisit before embarking upon what was to become his most famous and most influential composition.

Between January and July of 1820 Constable is recorded in London in various entries in Farington's diary. On 5 July he left with his wife and children on a visit to Salisbury, where he spent nearly two months, before returning to London towards the end of August. On 1 September he wrote to Fisher to say that he had settled his wife and his two children, John and Maria (the first of six), at Hampstead, adding, "I am glad to get them out of London for every reason". In September he visited his old friend and patron Henry Greswolde Lewis at Malvern Hall in Warwickshire, and then rejoined his family in Hampstead. In November he returned to his house in London, which was then in Keppel Street—before his removal two years later to Charlotte Street,—and there eventually began work upon the great painting which was to become known as *The Hay Wain*. We already learn of its existence from a letter written by John Fisher on 14 February 1821, in which the archdeacon took the opportunity to prod the artist on the subject of *Stratford Mill*, which was still in his studio: "When will Tinney receive his picture? And how thrives the 'hay wain'?"

By this time, presumably, Constable would already have executed the full-size oil-sketch of the composition (now in the Victoria and Albert Museum), 51
and work on the final painting would have been well advanced. Constable's practice of making such full-size sketches is a well-known aspect of his procedure in this period of his maturity as an artist, although he did not invariably adopt it. It is particularly relevant to the theme of the present book to discuss these large sketches in relation to three of the Stour scenes—*The Hay Wain*, *A View on the Stour* and *The Leaping Horse*.

The Hay Wain is *The Mill Stream* 'writ large', Constable's final and perfected statement of a theme which had long attracted him, although Willy Lott's House, seen from a different angle, was still to be the subject of another major composition, *The Valley Farm* of 1835. The cottage which is so familiar to us from these pictures has a place in local folklore: it was called Willy Lott's House after a farmer who owned it in Constable's day, and who is said never to have spent more than four days away from home during the eighty years of his life. To Constable it must have been associated with some of his

very earliest memories, for it stands only a stone's throw away from Flatford Mill, which, as one of his father's principal properties, he had known intimately from boyhood. When he began work on *The Hay Wain* in the winter of 1820–1 he had, therefore, a subject which he would have known by heart; and in addition to *The Mill Stream* (Christchurch Mansion, Ipswich) and the prepara- 31
tory oil-sketch for it (Tate Gallery), Constable had at his disposal at least three 32
other oil-sketches of Willy Lott's House. The first two of these, painted on two sides of a sheet of paper, are in the Victoria and Albert Museum, and can be dated, on stylistic grounds, about 1811–14. The third, at Ipswich, is dated on the back 29 July 1816.

The sketch of July 1816 is of considerable interest, for the viewpoint differs from that of *The Mill Stream*, exhibited at the Royal Academy two years earlier, and is substantially the same as it is in *The Hay Wain*. Constable has 49
moved a few yards along the path which skirts the pond and leads up to Willy Lott's House. In other words, soon after completing *The Mill Stream* he was already working towards the conception which he was to realize in *The Hay Wain*. The 1816 sketch at Ipswich contains, in fact, the basic landscape elements of the main, left-hand area of *The Hay Wain*, up to the tree behind the hay-wagon. A quite early stage in the development of the composition of *The Hay Wain* can also be seen in a tiny oil-sketch in the Mellon Collection. This retains the general pattern of the 1816 sketch, but extends the design to the right, opening up the landscape at this point, where in *The Mill Stream* it was still obscured by trees, and introducing the sail of a passing boat. Evidently for compositional reasons, he also moved the chimney of Willy Lott's House to the right, shortening the length of the roof, as indeed we find in the completed *Hay Wain* although not in the full-size oil-sketch in the Victoria and Albert Museum.

The figure of a woman with a pitcher beside the house is common to *The Mill Stream*, the Ipswich sketch and the Mellon sketch. It was already present in one of the little sketches of about 1811–14 in the Victoria and Albert 45
Museum; and it was retained in the full-size sketch for *The Hay Wain* and in the completed picture. To this figure Constable added the image of the horse and wagon fording the stream, as is shown, in a summary manner, by the little Mellon sketch. In the area to the right, for which none of the earlier studies provided any information, he painted in some low trees or scrub, with a glimpse of the meadows beyond. Originally, as we see from this sketch, the main feature of interest here was to have been the sail of a boat passing down the river, such as Constable was later to include in the background of

his next six-foot canvas, the *View on the Stour near Dedham*, exhibited at the
Academy in 1822: a similar boat with a sail had already figured prominently
in the left foreground of the *Dedham Mill and Lock* (Victoria and Albert 22
Museum), painted in 1820. But by the time that Constable developed the full-
size oil-sketch for *The Hay Wain*, he had abandoned this feature and had 51
decided to open up the meadows on the right to create a distant vista: there
can be little doubt that Constable was influenced here by his recollection of
Rubens's *Château de Steen* (National Gallery), owned by his friend Sir George 50
Beaumont.

The full-size oil-sketch, together with a further sketch in oils in the
Mellon Collection, contains almost all the principal elements of the picture
as it was first exhibited. The horse, whose rider is said to have been a
portrait of Golding Constable, was derived from the *verso* of the sheet of
about 1810–14 in the Victoria and Albert Museum. Both the horse and its 46
rider were retained in the final picture, but Constable later removed them—
probably after he had got *The Hay Wain* back from the Academy—and substituted a barrel, which was in turn painted out. With the passage of time
the shadowy forms of these details have become visible again under the 48
surface paint. Clearly Constable felt (and with justice) that so much incident in the foreground was unnecessary and distracting. The interest at this
point had to be subsumed by the little dog, which appears now farther to the
right than its original position, as shown by the full-size sketch. This dog,
however, was already well trained (so to speak) to obey the artist's bidding.
When Constable painted *The Hay Wain* the dog was probably no longer
alive; or, at best, it must have been full of years: for Constable had first
recorded its frisky motion when he painted the sketch on the *recto* of the 45
early sheet of studies in the Victoria and Albert Museum, where the dog
appears still farther back towards Willy Lott's House. The attitude of the
dog in *The Hay Wain* suggests that Constable now used another model; but
the conception goes back some seven to ten years. Meanwhile, in his desire
for truth of detail, he wrote to John Dunthorne at East Bergholt, requesting
a drawing of a hay-waggon.

The two early oil-sketches of Willy Lott's House had, then, supplied Constable with the *motifs* of the dog and the horse which it approaches. Both sketches and the Ipswich sketch of 1816 also became the basis for his representation of the house and the neighbouring trees. As we have seen, the two early sketches were made from different points on the bank of the pool. The difference can be measured by a comparison between the strong

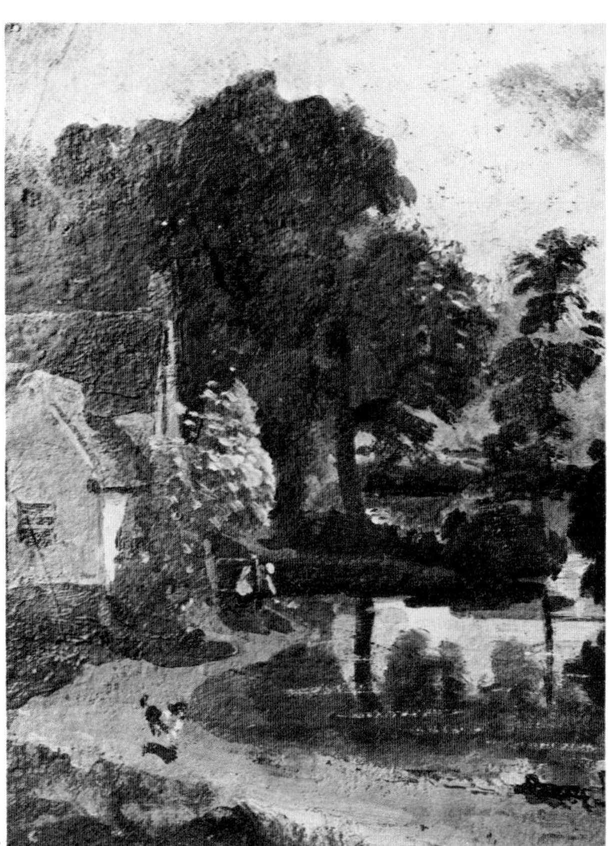

45

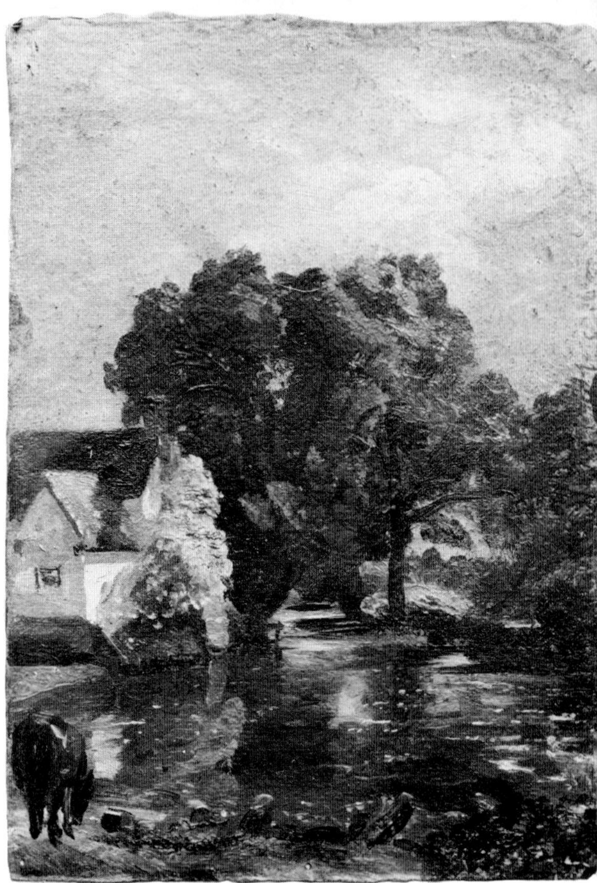

Studies for *The Hay Wain*
There are four oil sketches or studies of Willy Lott's Cottage—in addition to those for *The Mill Stream* viewed from a different angle—which are all taken from the same general position a few yards inside the present gate to the cottage and its farm. Only one of these (49) is actually dated. The others have been assigned to different years according to their style. The water level varies and in two studies is low enough for the shore of the pool to be exposed and a girl to appear beyond the post and rail beside the cottage. Two show the river very much in flood. There are also differences between these and those for *The Mill Stream* (31) in respect of the bushes which in some cases mask the far meadows and in others reveal them. These differences are fully discussed in the Appendix.

There are also two compositional studies now in the Mellon Collection; a tiny one incorporates a barge with a sail and the other, larger but still much smaller than the finished work, shows a development towards the final composition. In the composition of this study, as in the full-size study and the finished work, Constable was undoubtedly influenced by Rubens's *Château de Steen* with its architectural feature on the left and the flat Flemish agricultural landscape stretching away to the right (50). The full-size sketch includes a figure on horseback said to be Constable's father (51). Quite rightly Constable decided that this would distract from the chief element of the composition and so the figure was painted out of the exhibited *Hay Wain*, as an x-ray photograph shows (48). Constable certainly shortened the roof of the cottage so as to include the second chimney and back it with trees—possibly too he widened the stream. Other questions of fact and topography, such as whether the waggon would really have gone into the pool, are also fully dealt with in the Appendix.

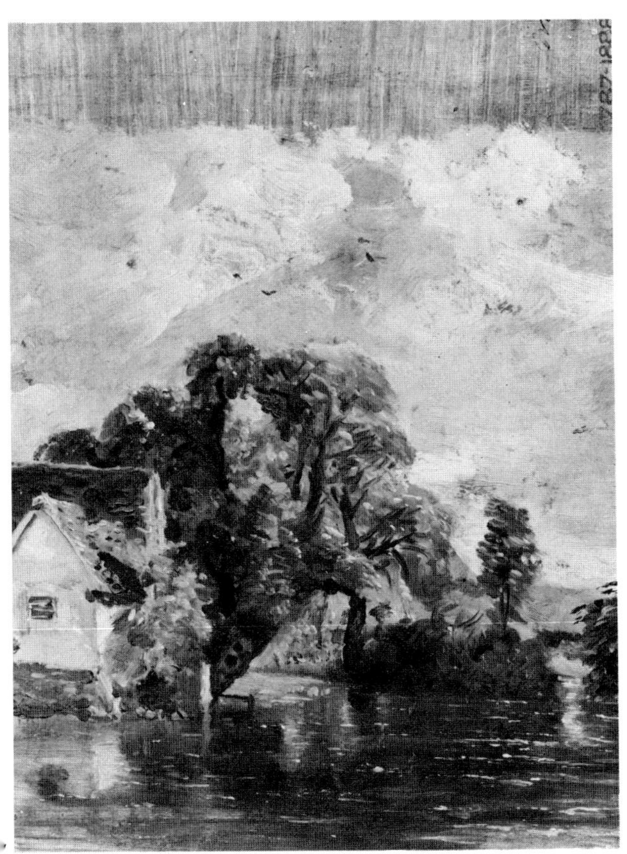

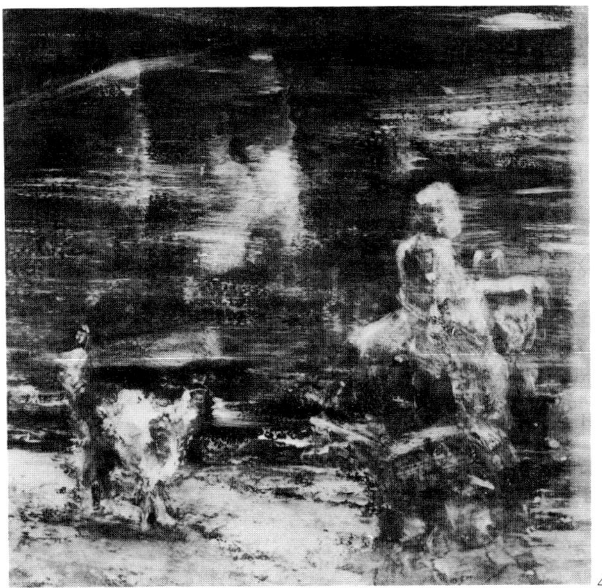

48

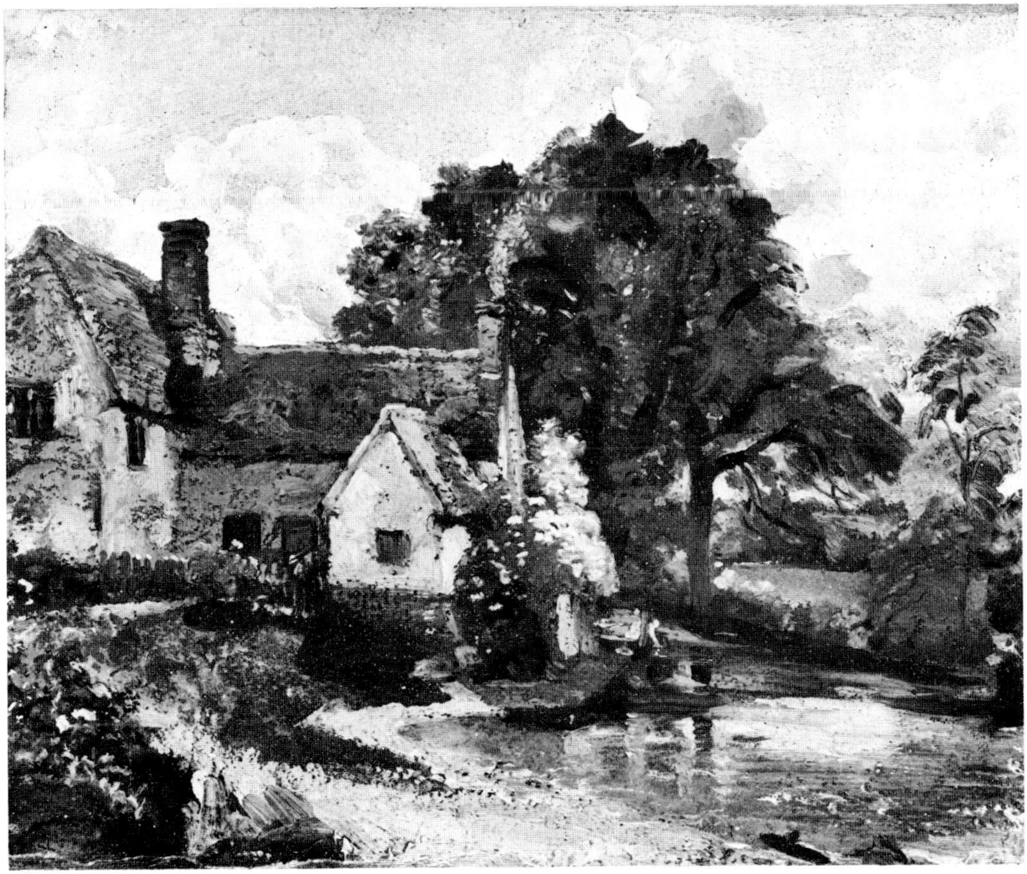

49

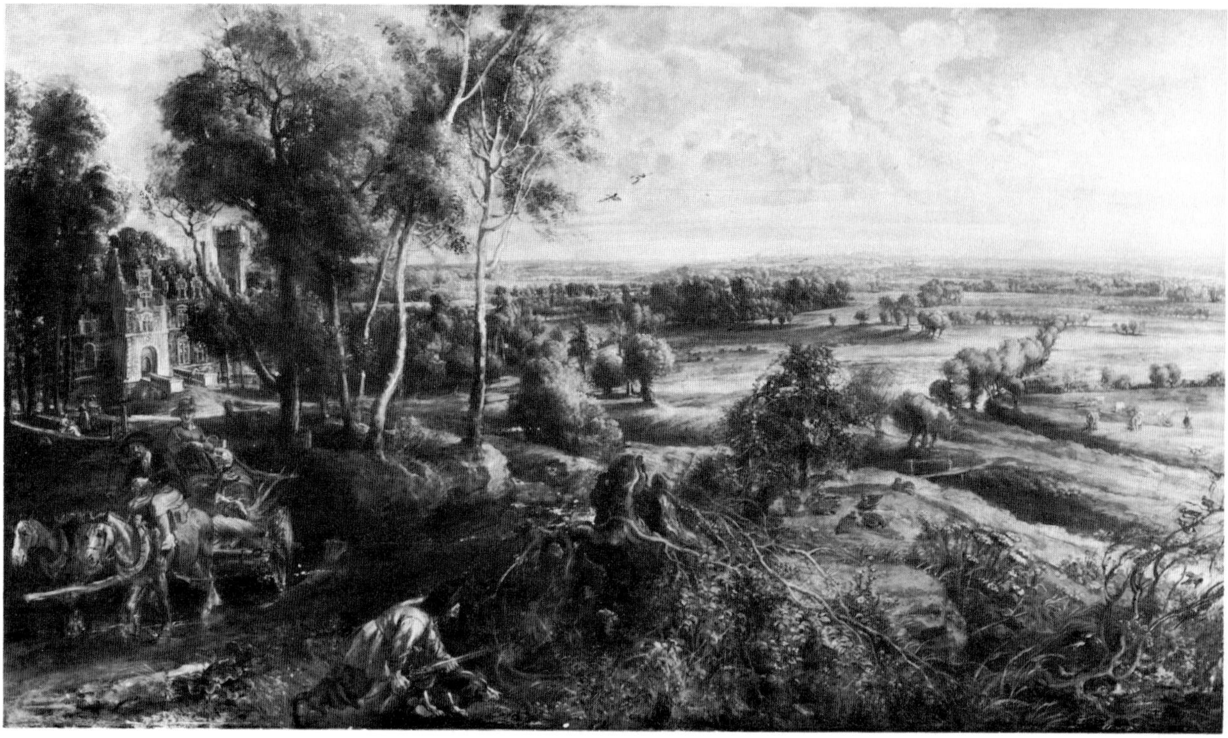

50

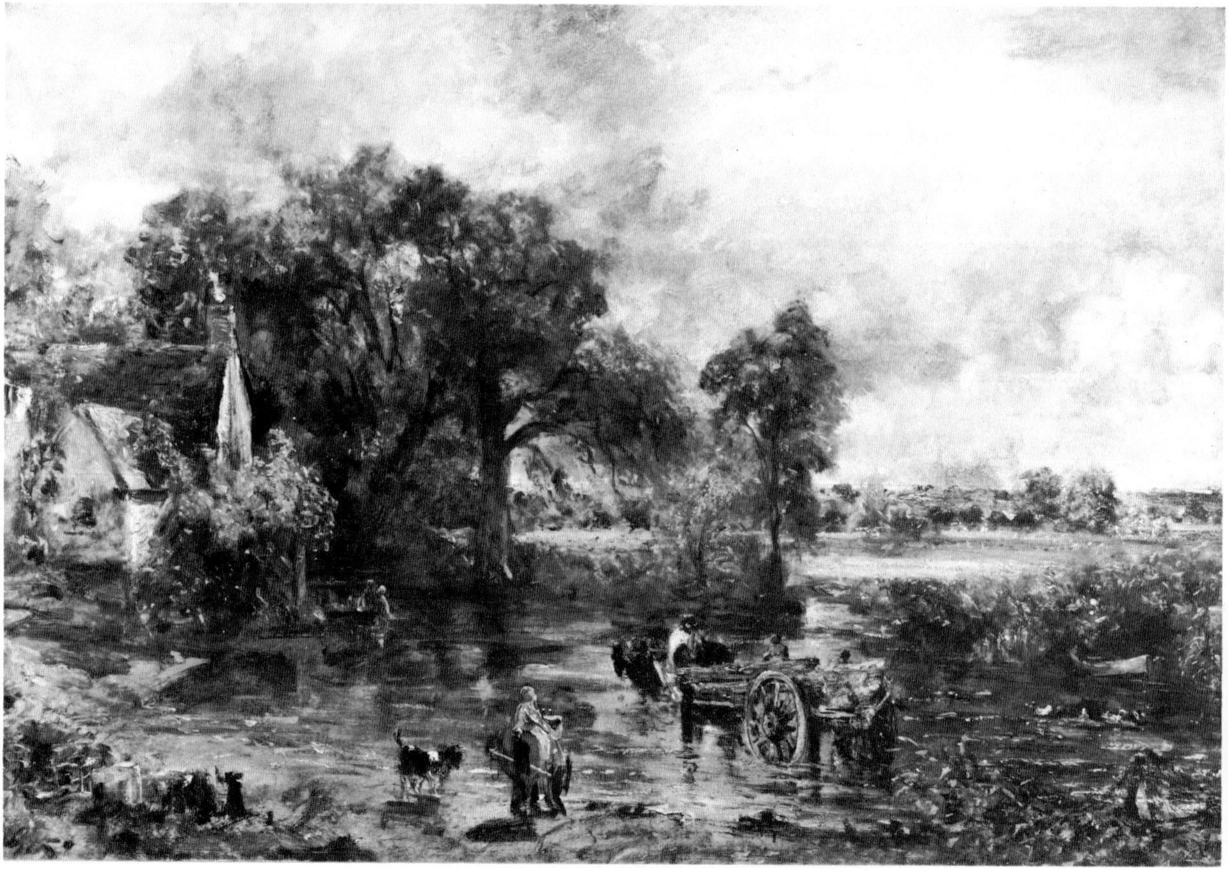

51

foreshortening of the side wall of the house, in the sketch on the *recto*, and the wider angle of foreshortening in the sketch on the *verso*. In the former, the house and the mass of elm trees next to it are more closed up together: in the latter, the view opens out to disclose much more of the group of trees, together with the stretch of water which leads to the ford across the river. But in *The Hay Wain* we are not looking in quite the same direction as in *The Mill Stream*. The viewpoint is farther to the left, closer to Willy Lott's House, and we are not looking so directly at the house, but past it, towards the fields that stretch out to the right of the channel (and beyond the Stour). It is an extended view, appropriate to a horizontal composition—markedly more horizontal in format than *The Mill Stream*. Hence the strong foreshortening of the side of Willy Lott's House in *The Hay Wain*, in contrast to the more frontal perspective in *The Mill Stream* and the almost equally frontal perspective in the sketch on the *verso* of the sheet in the Victoria and Albert Museum. In fact the viewpoint of *The Hay Wain* is essentially that of the sketch on the *recto* of the same sheet and of the more complete sketch at Ipswich.

Nevertheless, in designing a horizontal composition from this viewpoint, Constable clearly preferred one element of the *verso* sketch—the open dis-
position of house and trees,—and he seems to have arrived at a compromise 46
between the perspectival treatment of Willy Lott's House given in the
Ipswich sketch, with its marked foreshortening, and that of the *verso* sketch 49
in the Victoria and Albert Museum, in which the single-storey extension to the house is viewed more frontally. This viewpoint, however, left a bare patch of sky above the roof of the house, at the very left of the composition (as in the *recto* sketch). It is apparent from the full-size sketch for *The Hay Wain* that Constable soon decided to introduce further trees in order to break the abrupt edge formed by the roof against the sky. The tall chimney was still absent, although Constable's sense that a vertical form of this kind was needed at the left edge of his composition is evident from the tiny Mellon sketch, where, as we have seen, Constable included the chimney by the device of 'moving' it to the right. This was the solution which he finally accepted; and a comparison between the house as it is represented in *The Hay Wain* and its actual aspect, as recorded by the Ipswich sketch, or by *The Mill
Stream,* or by a modern photograph, shows that Constable took several 11
feet from the length of the roof in order to accommodate the chimney.

Much information about the appearance of the trees beside the house would have been available from the Victoria and Albert Museum sketches, the Ipswich sketch, and, although the angle was very different, *The Mill*

Stream. But it is clear that Constable must have deliberately made the trunks of the two principal elms rather thicker and more imposing; at the same time the young tree seen on the very right in the *recto* sketch and in the Ipswich sketch has been increased in scale and significance: this tree, as we have observed, performs an important function in the design of *The Hay Wain* as a whole, establishing a vertical division, or interval, which is emphasized by the wheel of the hay-waggon. Whether or not it is the same tree that is depicted in *The Mill Stream*, beyond the young fisherman who leans over the wall by Flatford Mill, as it seems to be, it is now solitary; and to its right the level meadows recede, unobscured by intervening trees or bushes. Was there such a clear view of the meadows in Constable's time? When we reconsider in this context the tiny Mellon sketch, in which small trees and bushes obscure the view of the meadows, as they still obscure it today, we may perhaps incline to the hypothesis that this important feature of *The Hay Wain*,
corresponding to the similar expanse of fields in Rubens's *Château de Steen*, 50
was a compositional device invented by Constable in the studio, rather than a literal interpretation of the actual prospect from his father's mill. New evidence on this question has, however, been adduced by Attfield Brooks, which provides cogent arguments against the necessity of such a hypothesis, although it does not lessen the probability that Constable was also inspired by the example of Rubens's great picture. (See Appendix.)

There is no need, perhaps, to analyse the balanced harmony of *The Hay Wain*, or the art whereby its measured intervals and its weighting of form against form, of darks against lights, cohere within a perfected whole, or to suggest in words its evocation of domesticated Nature in all its glistening, sun-drenched charm; but what might, possibly, be missed is its spatial harmony: Constable was very much concerned in *The Hay Wain* with perspective and with the manipulation of his forms and planes in space; the whole treatment of the composition is more *sculptural* than in the two earlier six-foot canvases—a development consummated in such later works as *The Cornfield* and the Edinburgh *Dedham Vale*. We see this, for example, in the handling of forms which thrust into space, such as the broadly treated horses, waggon and white-coated driver, or Willy Lott's House itself, or in the pictorial function given to the dog in the foreground, its turning movement drawing the eye forward and then back towards the hay-waggon and beyond it to the distant meadows. The spaces of the composition open out as never before, and in the next of his 'six-footers', the *View on the Stour near Dedham,* painted a year later, Constable was to increase still further the difference in scale between near and distant forms. And dominating the spacious, and indeed spatial, landscape of *The Hay Wain*, there move in banks the massy *cumuli* which he seems to have preferred to all other cloud-forms, and whose rounded shapes he was studying on Hampstead Heath as he went 'skying', as he called it. These set the silvery tone which runs through the quiet art of Constable. The sky is very similar in character to those found in two pictures of Hampstead Heath of about 1820 in the Tate Gallery and the Fitzwilliam Museum at Cambridge. There is surely significance in the fact that when Constable showed *The Hay Wain* at the Academy in 1821, one of his other exhibits was a view of Hampstead Heath.

Much nonsense has been written about Constable's practice—as in the case of *The Hay Wain*—of making full-size oil-sketches for his great Stour scenes. It has been suggested that his artistic intentions were fully realized in these sketches, and that the final pictures were intended merely to satisfy public taste and the conventional insistence upon 'finish'. There is nothing in Constable's prolific correspondence to justify this view. Certainly it is fantastic to suppose that Constable ever considered the brown and yellow meadows and blue-grey skies of the full-size sketch for *The Hay Wain* as in any sense a realization of his deepest feelings in front of Nature.

At the time that Constable was putting the finishing touches to *The Hay Wain*, Fisher chanced to recommend him to read Henry Matthews's *Diary of an Invalid,* in which the author supports the eighteenth-century tradition of representing Nature's greens by browns:

> Gaspar Poussin's green landscapes have no charms for me. The fact seems to be, that the delightful green of nature cannot be represented in a picture. Our own Glover had, perhaps, made the greatest possible exertions to surmount the difficulty, and give with fidelity the real colours of nature; but I believe the beauty of his pictures is in an inverse ratio to their fidelity; and that nature must be stripped of her green livery, and dressed in the browns of the painters, or confined to her own autumnal tints in order to be transferred to canvas.

Constable, having perused the book, at once protested at this ignorance, and not least at the criticism of Gaspard Poussin, "whose works contain the highest feeling of Landscape painting yet seen—such an union of patient study with a poetical mind", and continued: "This is too bad and one would throw the book out of the window—but that its grossness is its own cure."

A glance at the full-size sketch for *The Hay Wain* will show how very 51 summary is the treatment of the sky—one of Constable's central preoccupations in these years. A comparison with the completed painting, or for that matter with the sketches of skies made at Hampstead, will demonstrate what Constable meant when he wrote to Fisher (in October 1821):

I have done a good deal of skying—I am determined to conquer all difficulties and that most arduous one among the rest. . . .

The passage follows immediately upon his famous remark, "I do not consider myself at work without I am before a six-foot canvas." He goes on to make it clear that the "arduous" difficulty to which he has just referred is a difficulty connected with pictorial composition, with the realization of the completed work of art:

That Landscape painter who does not make his skies a very material part of his composition neglects to avail himself of one of his greatest aids. Sir Joshua Reynolds, speaking of the "Landscape" of Titian and Salvator and Claude, says, "*Even their skies seem to sympathise with the Subject.*" I have often been advised to consider my *Sky* as a "*White Sheet drawn behind the Objects*". Certainly if the Sky is obtrusive (as mine are) it is bad, but if they are *evaded* (as mine are not) it is worse; they must and always shall with me make an effectual part of the composition. It will be difficult to name a class of Landscape, in which the sky is not the "*key note*", the *standard of* "*Scale*", and the chief "*Organ of Sentiment*". You may conceive then what a "*white sheet*" would do for me, impressed as I am with these notions, and they cannot be erroneous. The sky is the "*source of light*" in nature—and governs every thing. Even our common observations on the weather of every day are suggested by them, but it does not occur to us. Their difficulty in painting, both as to composition and execution, is very great, because with all their brilliancy and consequence, they ought not to come forward or be hardly thought about in a picture—any more than extreme distances are.

The pictorial problems to which Constable here alludes were not completely 51
solved in the preliminary full-size sketches, but on the final canvases themselves. In the sketch for *The Hay Wain* the treatment of the sky shows that Constable was thinking in terms of general effects of chiaroscuro and of the distribution of his lights and darks; but even here his ideas changed and developed as he proceeded to the execution of the Academy picture.

A point of interest in the passage from his letter to Fisher, quoted above, is his consciousness that by this date his skies were too "obtrusive". If he felt this of *The Hay Wain*, where the white clouds are radiant with sunlight, he certainly proceeded to calm his sky, and to subdue it, in his next six-foot canvas.

A *View on the Stour near Dedham*

This picture, which Constable refers to in his letters as 'The Bridge', was begun in Hampstead in the summer of 1821, and then continued in London in his new house in Charlotte Street. In April, after sending his *Hay Wain* and other pictures to the Academy, he took a short holiday with his brother Abram at Flatford Mill. His happy memories of his early years at East Bergholt were mingled with sad thoughts of the "solemn changes" which had supervened, by which he meant especially the death of his parents. He wrote that month to his wife:

> How sweet and beautiful is every place, and I visit my old haunts with renewed delight but filled with many regrets and not without many sad and melancholy reflections on the various and solemn changes since the days of my youth. Nothing can exceed the beautiful green of the meadows, which are beginning to fill with buttercups, and various flowers—the birds are singing from morning till night but most of all the skylarks. How delightful is the country, but I long to get back to what is still more dear to me.

If, that spring, Constable made any sketches in Suffolk with his next large Academy picture in mind, they are not known to have survived with the
contents of his studio. Constable's 'Bridge', or *View on the Stour near Dedham*, 56
which in any case is a summer landscape, seems to have been based initially
upon three small pencil drawings in his old 1814 sketchbook (although the 53–55
existence of other sketches must be allowed for), while a drawing of a boy propelling a barge in the 1813 sketchbook was used for the nearest of the two barges, at the centre of the picture, and for the figure standing on it with a pole. Such figures, caught at the moment of strenuous action, were favourites with Constable: they also occur, for instance, in *The Mill Stream*, the *Flatford Mill* of 1817, *The White Horse* and *The Valley Farm*, and contribute greatly to the sense of the flow of normal rustic life which is an important aspect of his intentions as a landscape painter. We recall the advice which 'Antiquity' Smith had given him in his early days, and which he always remembered: "Do not set about inventing figures for a landscape taken from

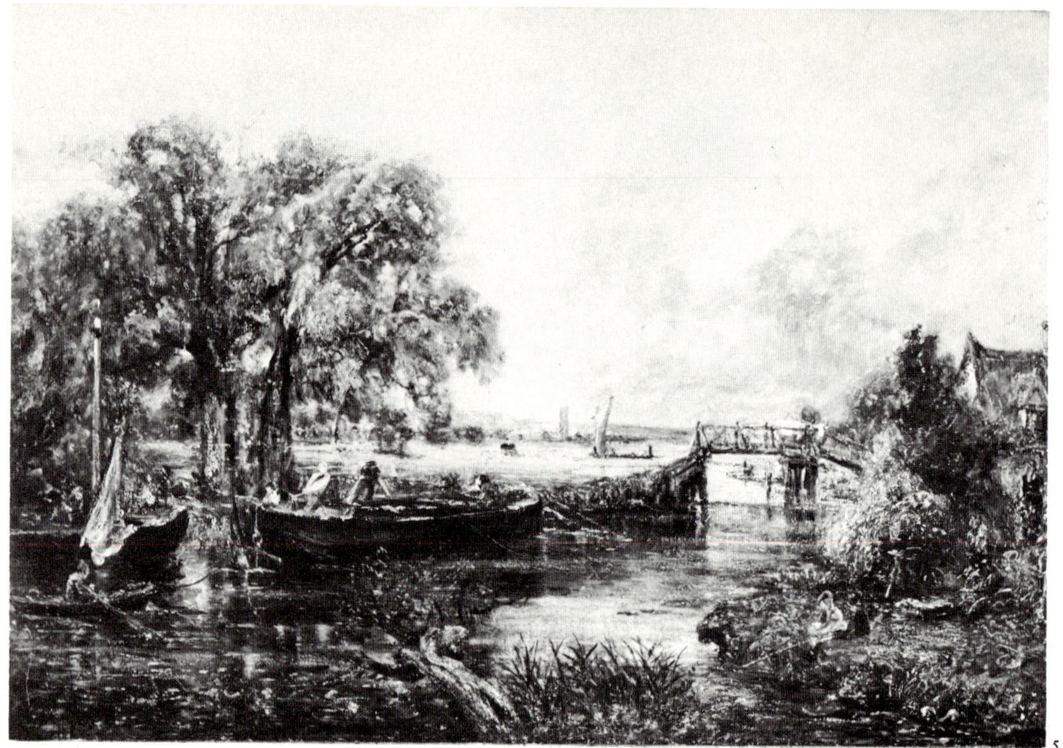

52

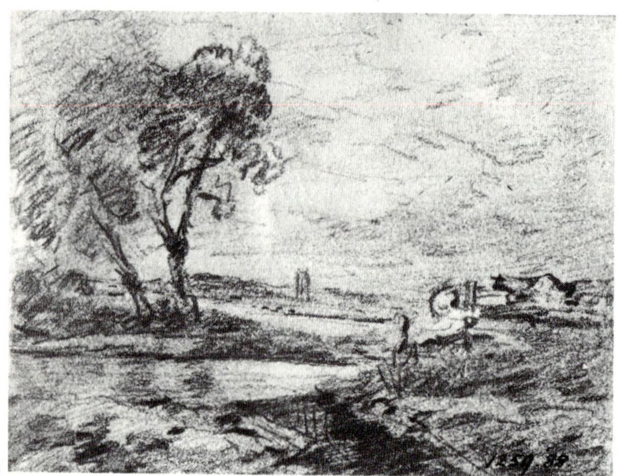

53

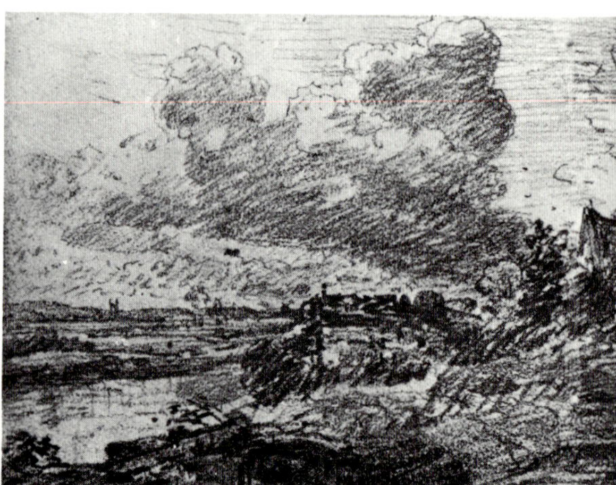

View on the Stour near Dedham
Despite its generalised name, this scene is a highly localised view towards Dedham from Flatford, with the cattle-bridge and Bridge Cottage on the right. The sketches from the little sketchbooks of 1813 and 1814 make clear the exact viewpoint Constable used, which was just by the barrier erected to keep water out of the dock in which barge-building took place. In one of the sketches of the 1814 book (55) the bow of that barge clearly appears with the bridge behind. The painting was

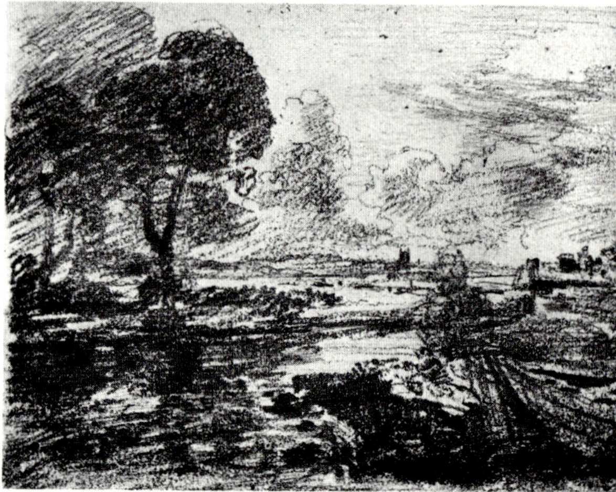

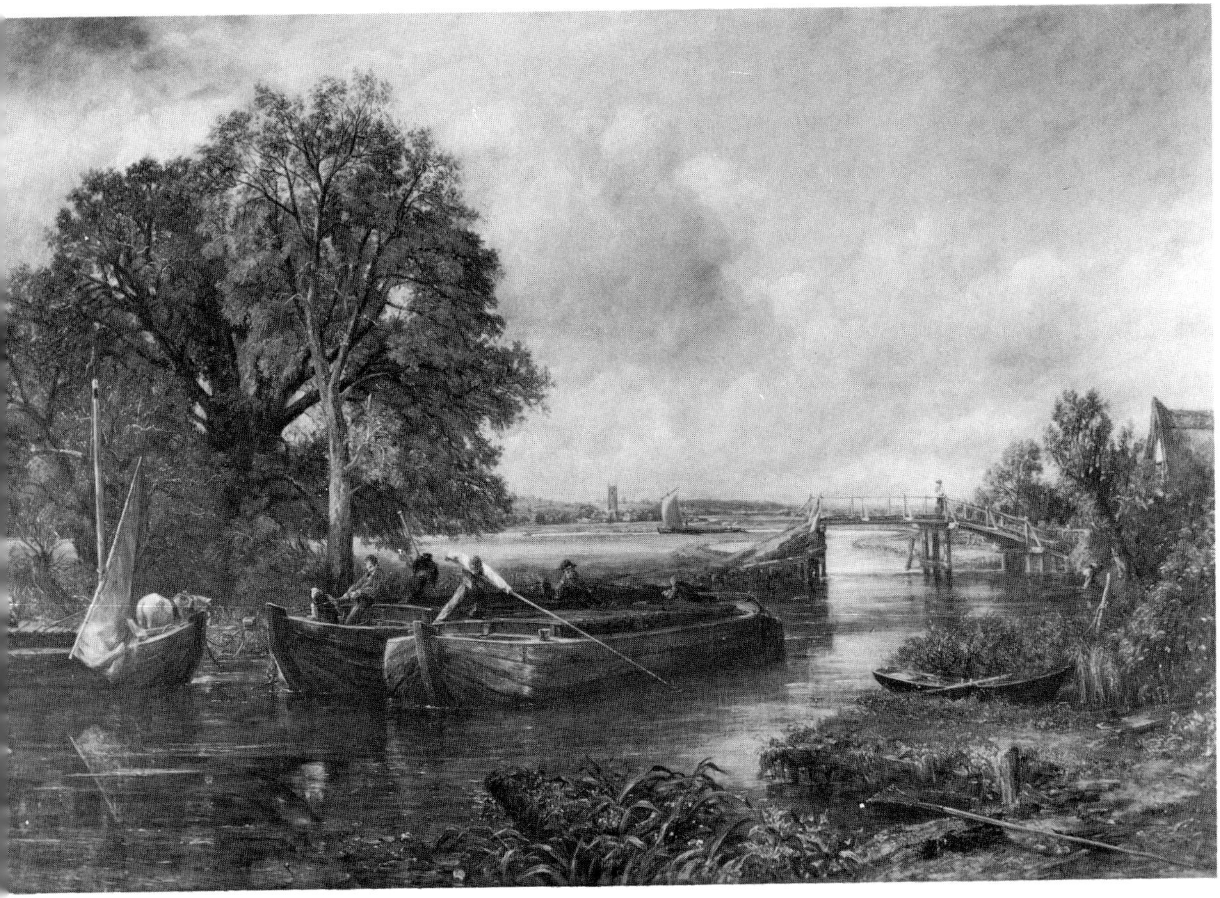

56

xhibited in 1822 but over five ears later, while spending a oliday at Flatford in October 827, Constable made another encil drawing of the scene (57) vhich shows that apart from ariable details he had made a ery accurate portrayal of the ssential features of the landscape n the full-scale oil painting. See he Appendix.

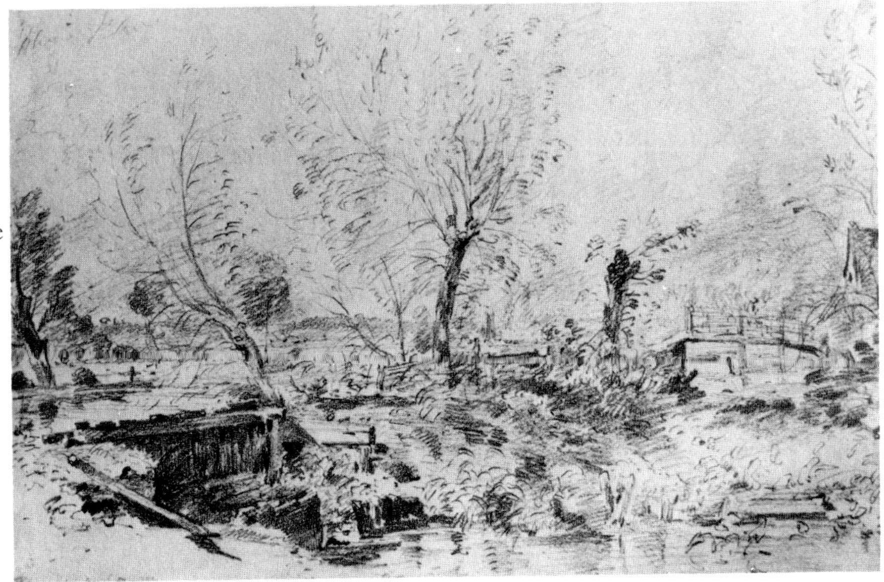

57

\s in *The Hay Wain*, Constable arried out a full-size oil sketch rom which he later removed istractions (52): in this case by educing the large sail on the istant boat which formerly vershadowed the church; by aking out the child fishing in he foreground; and by making he youth with the pole a key gure in the composition. The ree lit up by sunlight growing lose to the water behind him ould never have existed, as we an see from *Flatford Mill* (35), nd the bridge is much more elicate in the painting than it vas in reality.

nature; for you cannot remain an hour in any spot, however solitary, without
the appearance of some living thing that will in all probability accord better
with the scene and the time of day than will any invention of your own."
The same advice could be applied to a landscape 'recollected in tranquillity'.
No other landscape painter of the period ever approached Constable's skill
in the rendering of such figures, which are exquisitely drawn and brilliantly
executed. His draughtsmanship in this respect—so much superior to Turner's,
whose figures often startle by their clumsiness—has never received the full
appreciation due to it. In addition to the early drawings, there has come
down to us Constable's full-size oil-sketch for the picture, now in the Royal 52
Holloway College.

The *View on the Stour near Dedham* (Huntington Library and Art Gallery, 56
Pasadena) might more satisfactorily be called 'The Bridge', the title used by
Constable in his letters to Fisher: for Dedham Church appears only in the
far distance, while the bridge in the foreground is the same cattle-bridge near
Flatford Mill from whose vicinity Constable had taken his viewpoint for the
Flatford Mill, on the River Stour of 1817; and to the right of the bridge we see
the picturesque old cottage, with its unmistakable, prow-like roof, which
still stands almost unaltered today. The 'domestic' aspect of Constable's
great Stour scenes is as apparent as ever, although his eyes now look west
across the fields towards Dedham Church, as they will also look when he
comes to paint *The Lock*; and its function as a focal point in a composition will
be retained in the Edinburgh *Dedham Vale*, in which the view is in the
opposite direction—eastwards from the hill at Langham, beyond Dedham,
with the estuary and the sea in the distance. 74

Constable made several drawings of the old bridge, at various times in his
life, and from various angles; but the drawings in the 1814 sketchbook,
already mentioned, are the only ones that can be directly connected with the
View on the Stour near Dedham. Like the painting, they show a prospect of the
valley of the Stour, with Dedham Church in the distance. Only one of these
drawings shows the sixteenth-century cottage beside the bridge. The portion 54
of it which is included in the drawing is identical with that in the finished
picture, a circumstance which in itself would be sufficient to establish the connection between this drawing and the Academy picture, although in the full- 52
size oil-sketch Constable introduced the tall chimney—a procedure akin to his
hesitation about the chimney of Willy Lott's Cottage in *The Hay Wain*, and
having its source in the same kind of compositional thinking. But, just as
the studies known to have been at Constable's disposal when he composed

The Hay Wain omitted the meadowlands to the right, so this drawing of the footbridge in the 1814 sketchbook stopped short of the trees which appear on the left in the *View on the Stour near Dedham*. These trees were to be altered considerably, as we shall see, when Constable gave his composition its ultimate form; but in the full-size oil-sketch they relate to the trees which appear in the two other drawings in the 1814 sketchbook, which also show a 53
prospect of the meadows towards Dedham Church. In one of them the 55
church occupies the central point, as it does in the painting.

These, then, seem to have been the basic materials used by Constable when he began his composition in the summer of 1821. On a visit to London in January 1822, John Fisher saw it at a fairly early stage. What he saw was very possibly, although not necessarily, the full-size sketch. It is instructive, in the general context of his working methods in this period, that Constable should have felt free to improvise as much as he did as he gradually brought this exciting composition to completion. Of this improvisation we have direct evidence in the form of a note attached to a letter written by Constable to Fisher on 13 April 1822, which was accompanied by a pen-sketch known to Leslie, indicating the changes which he had made in the design:

> The composition is almost totally changed from what you saw. I have taken away the sail, and added another barge in the middle of the picture, with a principal figure, altered the group of trees, and made the bridge entire. The picture has now a rich centre, and the right-hand side becomes only an accessory.

By this time Constable was certainly completing work on the final painting, for the Academy exhibition was upon him. The letter shows that he had not included, until a quite advanced stage in his work, the principal barge and the important figure with the pole engaged in managing it. This addition has much of the function of the black and white dog in *The Hay Wain*; for the illuminated and shadowed sides of the barge establish planar movements directed outwards from the foreground.

In the final form of *The Hay Wain*, if we exclude the labourers in the distant fields, there were only four human figures, of whom two—the woman at the left and the fisherman at the right of the pond—were placed outside the central area. In the *View on the Stour* the number has been greatly increased, and six men and boys—if they are not all boys—manoeuvre the barges at the centre; a further figure appears on the left, near the white horse; farther back, on the near bank, a woman has come to the river's edge from her cottage,

like the woman by Willy Lott's House in *The Hay Wain*; while a young girl
stands on the bridge looking at the young bargemen. Further figures can
be made out on the long barge which is moving up the river in the distance,
its sail reinforcing the vertical emphasis created by the tower of Dedham
Church, and establishing a middle point in space which helps to relate
distance to foreground. But, as in *The Hay Wain*, Constable took care to
allow his "principal figure" to dominate all the others: this is the figure which 56
he had observed some nine years earlier during his stay at East Bergholt
in the summer months of 1813, long before the series of Stour scenes was
begun. The boy with the pole sets up a diagonal movement across the
picture-plane, which is supported by a long-handled eel-spear lying by the
water's edge in the foreground and by a rowing-boat farther back, while
the thrust of his outstretched right leg directs attention inwards to Dedham
Church, the focal point of the picture; but he is also conceived as a form in
space, and unites with his fellows in a circular group which extends back to
the far bank of the river. The treatment of space in the *View on the Stour* is
even subtler than in *The Hay Wain*.

Constable told Fisher that he had "altered the group of trees", and completed the bridge. The differences between the group of trees on the left and the
corresponding group as represented in the full-size sketch are considerable; 52
and among them we may especially note the introduction in the final picture 56
of a contrast between the dark trunk and boughs of the central tree in the
group and the light-toned, sun-receptive trunk and branches of the tree to
the right, which in the preliminary sketch was virtually a repetition of the
dominant elm-tree in *The Hay Wain*; there is also an effective contrast of
shape—between the thick forms of the dark tree and the more delicate lines
of its neighbour. But what are these trees? They are certainly not the trees
which, years earlier, Constable had studied from the bridge, looking along
the tow-path on the far side of the river towards Flatford Mill, and which
form so prominent a feature of the Tate Gallery picture of 1817: perhaps 35
these are present on the very left of the composition; but the light-coloured
tree in the *View on the Stour,* which is clearly an elm, grows from near the
river's edge, and, as is demonstrated by the *Flatford Mill* of 1817, and by
Constable's drawings, it cannot have existed there. Yet this tree has now
assumed a more important role in the design than the little trees by the
cottage recorded in the drawing in the 1814 sketchbook, which was the very 54
starting-point of the composition, the original source of Constable's idea.
Moreover, the trees seen on the left in the two other related drawings in the

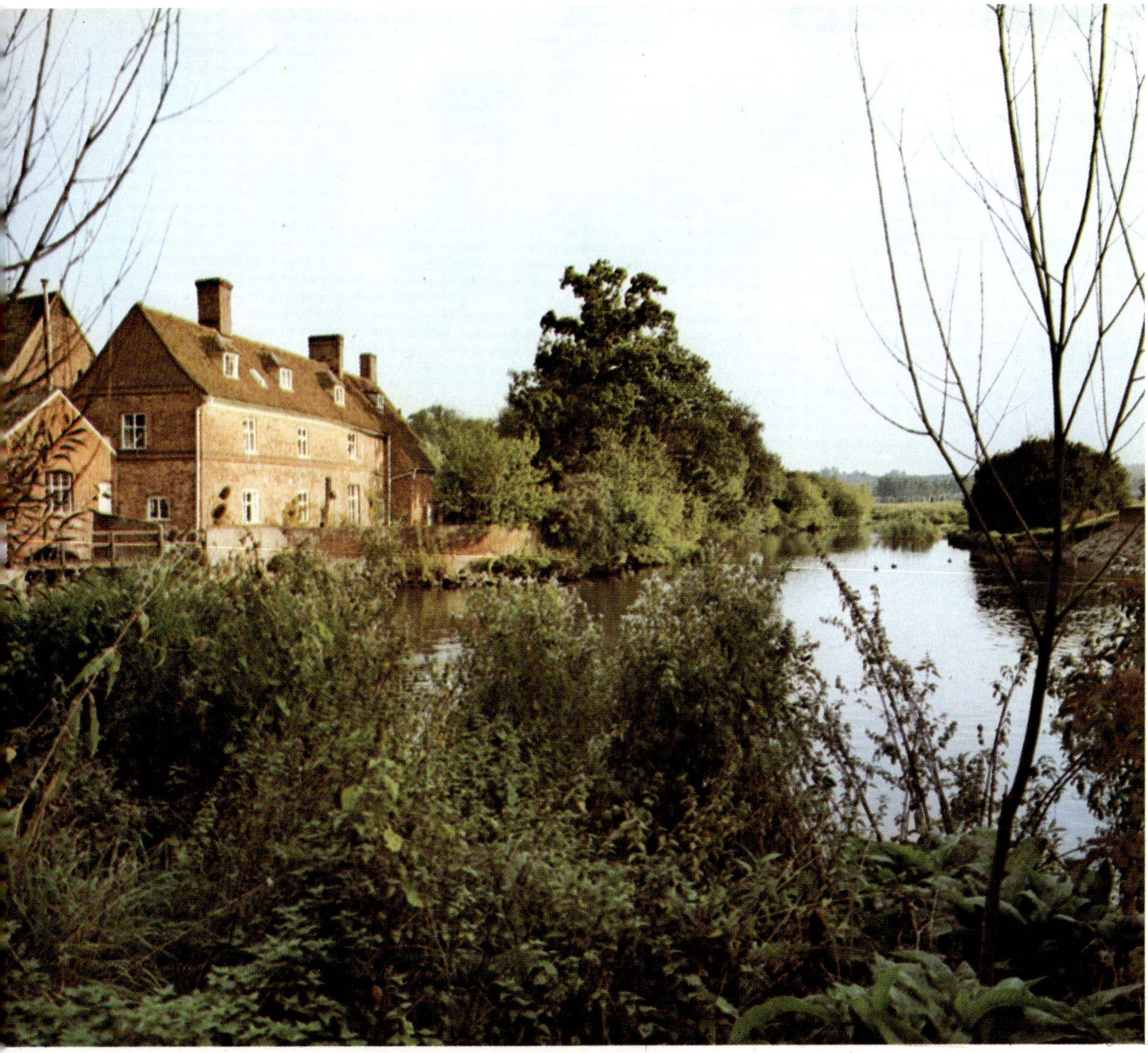

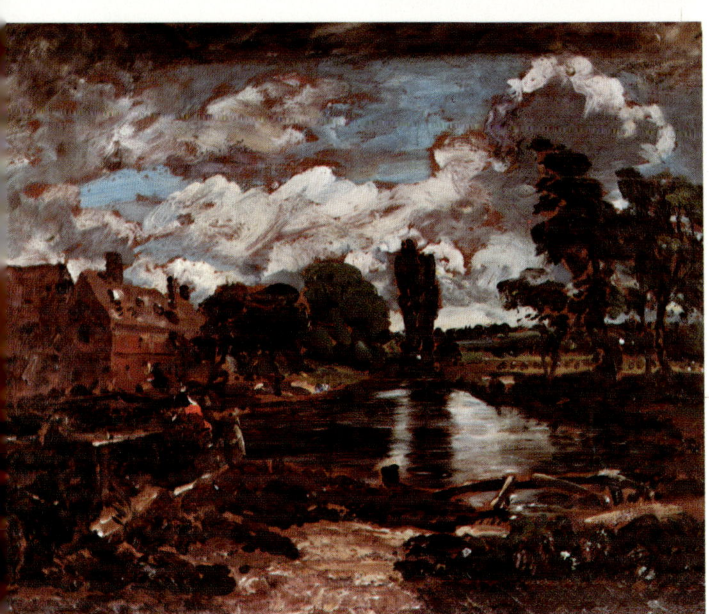

I *Flatford Mill from a Lock on the Stour*
This rapid oil sketch is one of the earliest among Constable's works to take the river as its subject. The viewpoint includes the old lock, but the view is now obscured by a hedge and bushes on the far side of the lock, so that the photograph had to be taken from the private garden on the island between the lock and the Mill.

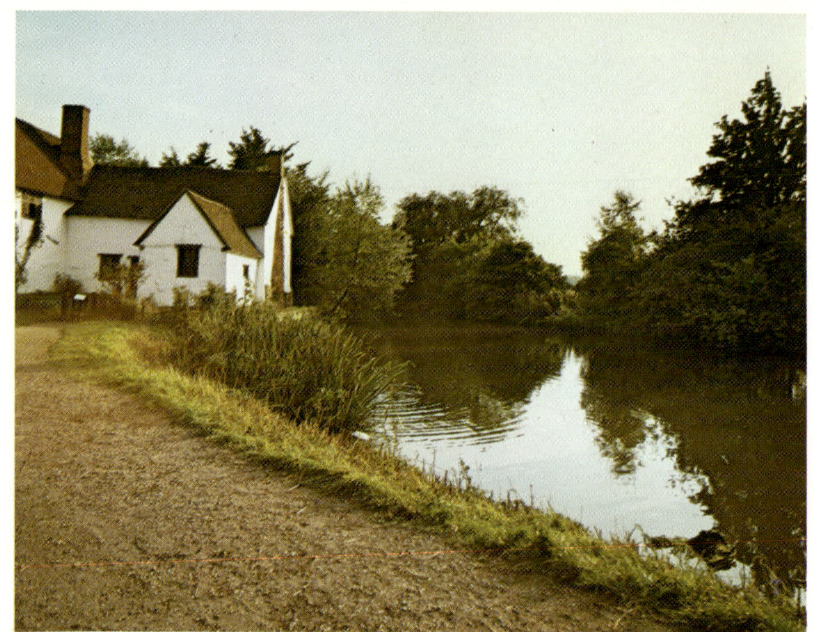

II *The Hay Wain*
Willy Lott's Cottage, a humble building which still stands today (named after a farmer who only left it for four days in his long life) was painted by Constable from different angles on many occasions. Its most famous appearance is on the edge of this magnificent vista, which cannot be captured by any photograph.

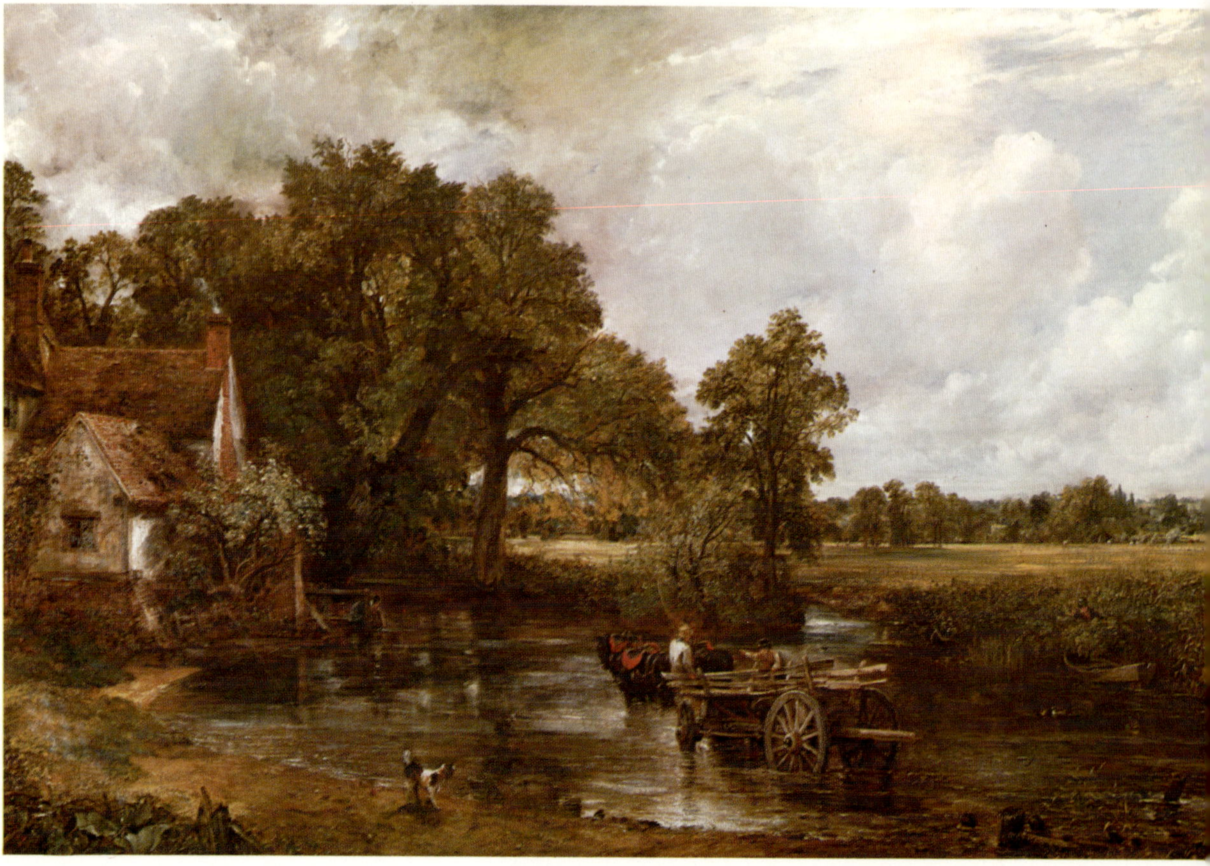

sketchbook must surely be the same trees that occupy the right foreground of the *Flatford Mill* of 1817. If that is so, they were now transformed by Constable into an imposing and dense group. Whatever the composition may have looked like when Fisher saw it, Constable's decision to concentrate attention upon this group of trees and the extra barge, with its figure, transformed the design. As he himself recognized, "the picture has now a rich centre, and the right-hand side becomes only an accessory".

Constable would seem also to have given the rather clumsy wooden bridge a certain refinement: its beams and railings, as recorded in his drawings of it, are thicker, more irregular, and less elegant. His purpose must have been not merely to reduce the emphasis at this point, but also to allow the eye easier passage to the open vista beyond. This is a lovely piece of drawing, and—as in other passages in the picture—we observe an increased nicety in the play of delicate forms against weightier masses. The final effect is one of serenity and harmony, and the bolder contrasts of *The Hay Wain* have been eschewed. Constable told Fisher: "I have endeavoured to paint with more delicacy." In the *View on the Stour* delicate brushwork replaces the broad treatment of *The Hay Wain*. Constable was taking serious note of contemporary criticisms; but in his next Stour scene—*The Lock*—he was to resume that boldness of technique which was appropriate both to the scale and to the expressive content of these canvases, even though *The Lock* itself was of smaller size than the other pictures in the series.

As in *The Hay Wain*, the viewpoint of *A View on the Stour near Dedham* is very near Flatford Mill, and the rather misleading title which has been given to the composition disguises its domestic character: the viewpoint in *The Hay Wain* can be located a few yards from the front door of Flatford Mill;
in order to make the pencil drawings in the 1814 sketchbook, upon which the 54
View on the Stour was to be based, Constable had only to walk round to the back of the mill and stand by the barge-building dock, the barrier of which can be seen in the foreground. As we have seen, in the *Flatford Mill, on the*
River Stour of 1817 we look the other way—towards Flatford Mill from a 35
point near the bridge on the south side of the Stour—and the two gates of the lock at Flatford, which is still in existence today, appear in the background of the picture.

The Lock

The viewpoint for Constable's next great Stour scene, *The Lock* of 1824 (private collection), was just to the other side of the farther of the two locks; and we look back towards the bridge along the south bank of the river. Constable painted two main versions of this composition, the first on an upright canvas, which was shown at the Royal Academy in 1824, and the second on a horizontal canvas, which he presented to the Academy, according to the usual custom, on his election to full membership in 1829. This second version was painted in 1826, and the close relationship of the composition to that 58
of the *View on the Stour near Dedham,* of four years earlier, is very evident: Dedham Church again appears in the distance at the centre; a similar boat with a little sail slung athwart its mast moves into the picture on the left; and on the far right we see the familiar cattle-bridge, now restored to its picturesque roughness of aspect. In the right foreground, almost as though it had wandered in from *The Hay Wain,* is a black and white dog, turning back into the picture, like the similar dog in *The Hay Wain,* or its close relation in *The Cornfield.* The dog is not yet present in the oil-sketch (National Gallery of Art, Melbourne). The subject of *The Lock* appealed to popular taste and Constable painted other variants of the composition.

Constable had evidently intended to show the first version of *The Lock* in 1823, but circumstances had prevented him from completing it in time for the Academy exhibition that April. He had been ill and depressed, and his wife and children had been seriously unwell. In February he told Fisher: "With anxiety—watching—and nursing—and my own present indisposition, I have not seen the full face of my easel since Christmas." One of his anxieties was that he had not been able to finish a painting of *Salisbury Cathedral* for the Bishop; there had been difficulties attending his move to his new house in Charlotte Street—the former residence of his old friend Farington, who had died in 1821; and that February Constable was depressed still further by the news that he had failed again to secure election as a Royal Academician, the one vacancy being filled by his companion of his early London days, Ramsay Richard Reinagle, a painter of a wholly inferior stamp.[5]

At the Academy exhibition of 1823, therefore, Constable was represented by no large composition; but Bishop Fisher's picture, *Salisbury Cathedral from* 25
the Bishop's Grounds (Victoria and Albert Museum), was ready in time, and made a favourable impression. It is of interest that this composition was based upon a drawing made by Constable in 1811—some twelve years earlier.

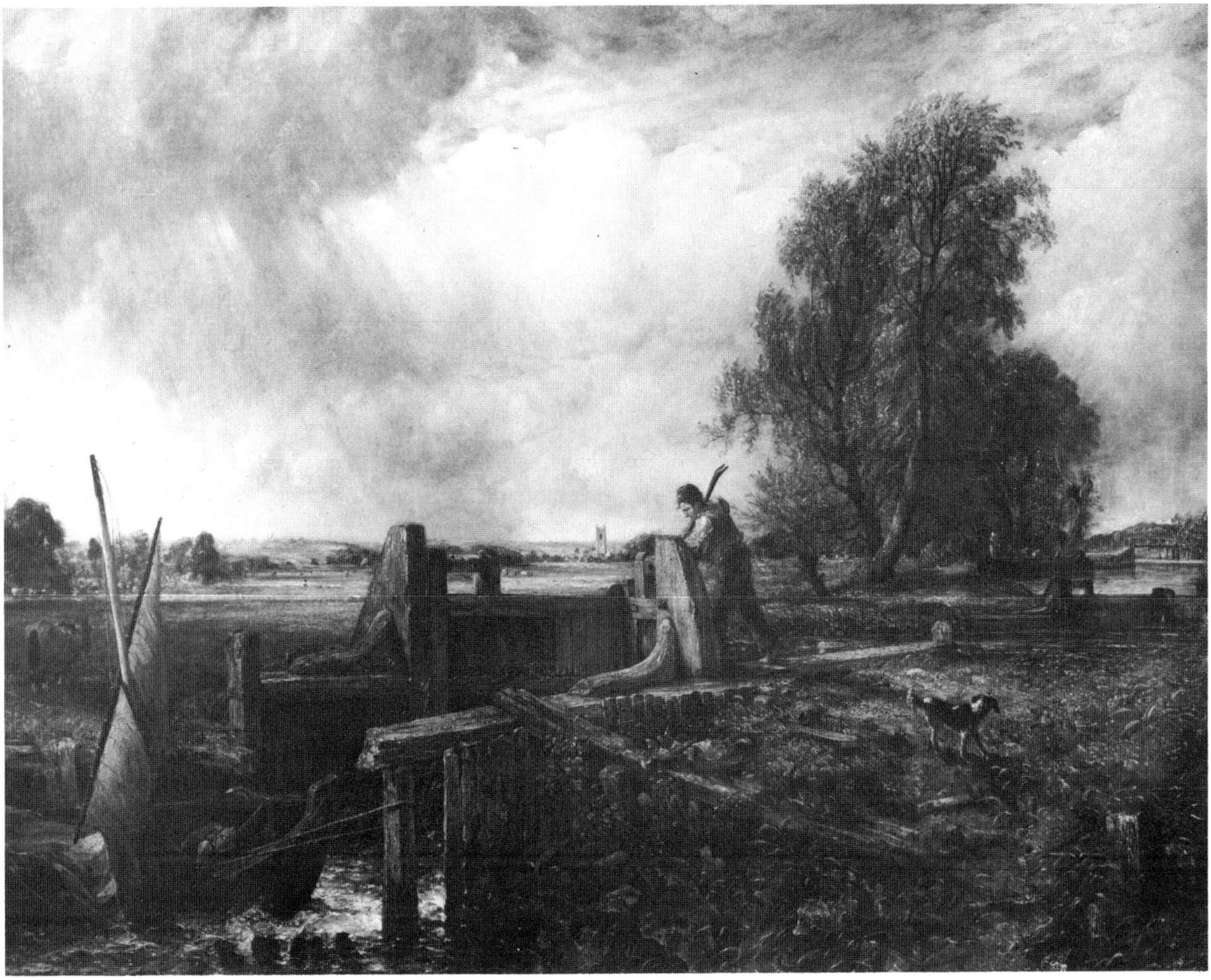

58

The Lock

The scene is Flatford Lock and the viewpoint is the little strip of garden between the mill-pool and the mill house, or possibly one of the windows in the house. The gable of Bridge Cottage and the bridge appear on the extreme right hand of the painting, which shows the lock, and above the nearer lock gate the meadows across to Dedham Church tower. Again the viewpoint is now in private grounds and in any case obstructed by numerous poplar trees which have been planted in the fields beyond the river. In this canvas, slightly smaller than the other Stour scenes, Constable records his delight in ". . . the sound of water escaping from mill dams, . . . willows, old rotten planks, slimy posts, and brickwork—I love such things". He made several versions of this subject. The first *Lock* was sold at the Royal Academy Exhibition of 1824 and still remains with a descendant of the purchaser. This more famous one was presented to the Royal Academy on Constable's election as R.A. in 1829.

When on holiday in 1827, he made a delicate pencil drawing of the same scene from a slightly different viewpoint (59). For further discussion see Appendix.

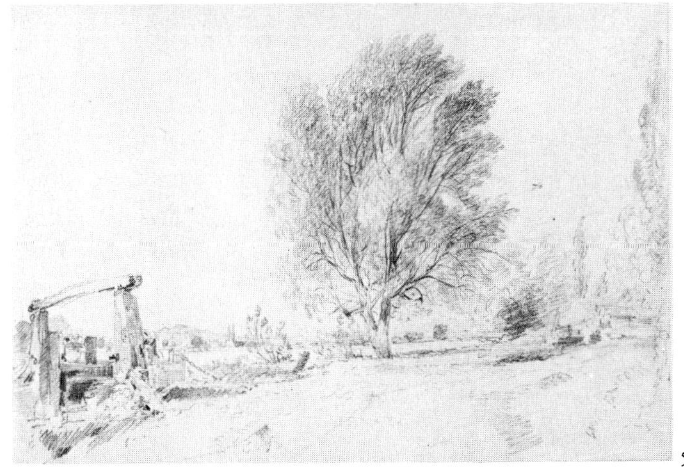

59

With it Constable also showed *A Cottage* and *A Study of Trees, a Sketch*. On 9 May, he conveyed to John Fisher his opinion of the pictures shown by some of his fellow-artists, including Wilkie, whom he much admired, and Turner, whom he now thought "stark mad—with ability"; and he went on to report Fuseli's reaction (which has since become famous) to his own work: "I like de landscape of Constable, but he makes me call for my great-coat." The painting by Turner to which Constable was referring was his large *Bay of Baiae*, now in the Tate Gallery: Constable found its vivid colours excessive, saying of it, "The picture seems painted with saffron and indigo". Such subjects in any case, Constable well knew, were not for him. He had no desire to go to Italy to discover novel subject-matter for his art; and towards the end of his letter to Fisher he touched upon the matter (as though Turner's imaginative composition was still in his mind's eye), beginning with a paraphrase of a passage in Jonathan Richardson's *Theory of Painting*:

"O dear, O dear, I shall never let my longing eyes see that famous country"—are the words of old Richardson. Am I doomed never to see the living scenes which inspired the landscape of Wilson and Claude Lorraine? No! but I was born to paint a happier land, my own dear England—and when I forsake that, or cease to love my country, may I, as Wordsworth says,

> "never more hear
> Her green leaves rustle
> Or her torrents roar."

Constable here quotes, somewhat inaccurately, from Wordsworth's *Thanksgiving Ode*. He had met the poet several times over the years, and although at first he found him too egotistical for his liking, he seems to have come to admire him, and to have responded to his love of simple Nature.

On another occasion Constable was to commend the Dutch painters for being "stay-at-home" people; and he saw a special kinship between his own art and that of Ruisdael, Hobbema and, by the same token, Gainsborough, who had devoted himself to the landscape of his own Suffolk. Constable did not require variety of subject, for, as he once expressed it in a letter to Fisher, "Subject and change of weather and effect will afford variety in landscape. What if Van de Velde had quitted his sea pieces, or Ruisdael his waterfalls, or Hobbema his native woods—would not the world have lost so many features in art?"

In *The Lock*, Constable brought into direct focus, in the immediate fore-

ground, the most ordinary of objects—a lock gate, with its rough boards 58
and slimy planks,—exalting it so that its posts rose up above the green meadows and framed the distant tower of Dedham Church. Here he gave supreme pictorial expression to those boyhood memories of which he had written a few years earlier: "... The sound of water escaping from mill dams ..., willows, old rotten banks, slimy posts, and brickwork—I love such things. Shakespeare could make anything poetical—he mentions 'poor Tom's' haunts among *Sheep cotes—and Mills*. ... As long as I do paint I shall never cease to paint such places." Presumably Constable used an earlier drawing of the lock, which appears much the same, with only slight variations, in both the vertical and the horizontal forms of the composition. Apart from the inclusion in the latter of the old cattle-bridge, the principal differences between the two pictures lie in the transfer of the boat, in the second version, to a position in front of the lock gate, and the very considerable alterations made to the main group of trees—these alterations being quite as radical as those which he had made in evolving the *View on the Stour near Dedham* from the full-size sketch. Once again we are reminded that Constable regarded the great Stour paintings not merely as interpretations of particular views, in the manner of his early pictures, but also as imaginative compositions which yet crystallized his vivid memories of his native scenes. The horizontal version of *The Lock*, which was to be deposited at the Academy as his Diploma work, adds a further element not present in the
upright version: the slanting rays of the sun, sweeping down from dark 58
clouds towards the central area, which by contrast is brightly lit, recall the lighting of some of the Hampstead pictures, and would seem to have their origin both in Constable's cloud studies on the Heath and in the landscapes of Rembrandt, where such slanting rays are often a dominant feature.

The differences between the two pictures in respect of the main group of trees are particularly striking and invite further comment. In October 1827, when Constable revisited Flatford, he made a number of drawings in a now dismembered sketchbook. As Attfield Brooks points out, one of these, in the
British Museum, gives a view of the lock from a similar spot, and near the 59
lock we find an elegant tree, evidently a willow. It would seem, therefore, that in this respect the *Lock* of 1826 related more closely to actuality than the earlier, upright version of the subject. Even so, the drawing and the painting hardly correspond very exactly. The painting of 1826 also includes a further mass of large trees, further back in the distance—nearer, that is to say, to the old cattle-bridge. These trees, which look like grown elms, are of similar

character to the trees with thick trunks that loom up, close by the lock, in the
painting of 1824. Now it is clear from the *Flatford Mill* of 1817, from *Boat-* 35
building, and from the drawing of the towpath in the 1814 sketchbook, that 33
there was at one time a clear view along the towpath from the cattle-bridge to 37
Flatford Lock. A willow-tree could well have grown there in the interval;
but the other trees cannot be so easily explained.

Another piece of evidence may be provided by a further drawing from the
1827 sketchbook, which is in the Victoria and Albert Museum. This gives a 2
view from the boat-building yard which Constable had represented in *Boat-*
building and in *A View on the Stour near Dedham*; but we now look directly towards Flatford Lock (with Flatford Mill represented to the left). The drawing cannot be said to be entirely reliable from a topographical point of view, since Dedham Church appears out of position; but the tree recorded in the British Museum drawing is certainly represented near the lock, although its precise position is hard to determine. To its right, but apparently set back some distance from the towpath, we do find two trees: these could well have been the originals, so to speak, of the more elaborated group of trees in the upright version of *The Lock*. In other words, Constable's ultimate inspiration, according to this interpretation, was a known aspect of a remembered scene.

The Lock was Constable's only exhibit at the Academy in 1824; but this was the year in which *The Hay Wain* and other pictures by him were shown at the Paris Salon, so that it was an eventful year in his public life. Moreover, *The Lock* found a purchaser on the opening day of the exhibition, and after a long period of depression and anxiety Constable began to hope that his struggles might "at last turn towards popularity".

The Leaping Horse

Constable must by now have been emboldened to disregard the criticisms
levelled at his want of finish: certainly *The Leaping Horse* of 1825 is still
broader in treatment than the *Lock* compositions, and the pigment denser in
texture. In this sense there is less difference than before between the full-size 62
sketch, which is preserved in the Victoria and Albert Museum, and the
finished picture, which like *The Lock* belongs to the Royal Academy. Here 60
again, as in *The Lock*, we hear 'the sound of water escaping from mill dams', and the foreground is filled with 'willows, old rotten banks, slimy posts'; but the form that rears up above the receding levels of meadow and river is

now a barge-horse, with its young rider: the horse has been trained to leap the fences by the tow-path which were needed to keep cattle within bounds,

Two wash sketches in the British Museum show the composition at earlier stages of development. In one of these, the horse is not yet represented as
leaping over the fence; in the other, it rears up still more prominently than 63
in the finished picture: we may wonder whether Constable could possibly have been thinking of the rearing horse which dominates Delacroix's great picture of *The Massacre of Chios*, exhibited along with *The Hay Wain* at the Salon of 1824; but no doubt the resemblance, such as it is, must be regarded as fortuitous—although the great animal, especially as rendered in the wash sketch, is perhaps the one image in Constable's art which in any way recalls that preoccupation with the untamed power of animal life which is so characteristic of Delacroix and of much Romantic painting, both in France and in England.

The other wash sketch gives the position of the willow-stump which was retained, in the full-size sketch, to the right of the horse, and for which a drawing (sold at Sotheby's in 1948) is known. An oil-sketch (formerly in the collection of Sir Evan Charteris) shows two willow-stumps—one to the left
and one to the right of the leaping horse. In the finished picture, however, 60
only one stump appears—to the horse's left. The composition has thus been opened up on its right side; and Constable now introduced, at the edge of his canvas, the familiar tower of Dedham Church (not shown in the earlier sketches). It seems probable that at one stage the full-size sketch incorporated both willow-stumps, as Graham Reynolds has surmised. Constable began to work out his composition in the autumn of 1824, and told Fisher on 17 November, "I am planning a large picture", adding that he was not going to take his advice, however much he appreciated it, to vary his subject-matter in an attempt to gain favour with his public. By April he was able to inform his friend that his wife had been delivered of their fifth child, Emily, and that *The Leaping Horse*, as it was later to be known, had been despatched to the Academy. "But," he wrote, "I must say that no picture ever departed from my easel with more anxiety on my part with it. It is a lovely subject, of the canal kind, lively—and soothing—calm and exhilarating, fresh and blowing, but it should have been on my easel a few weeks longer." To stand today before this profoundly expressive composition, which recent cleaning has revealed in all its brilliancy, is an extraordinary experience: for it seems almost incredible that such daring, such emancipation of technique, such slashes of

60

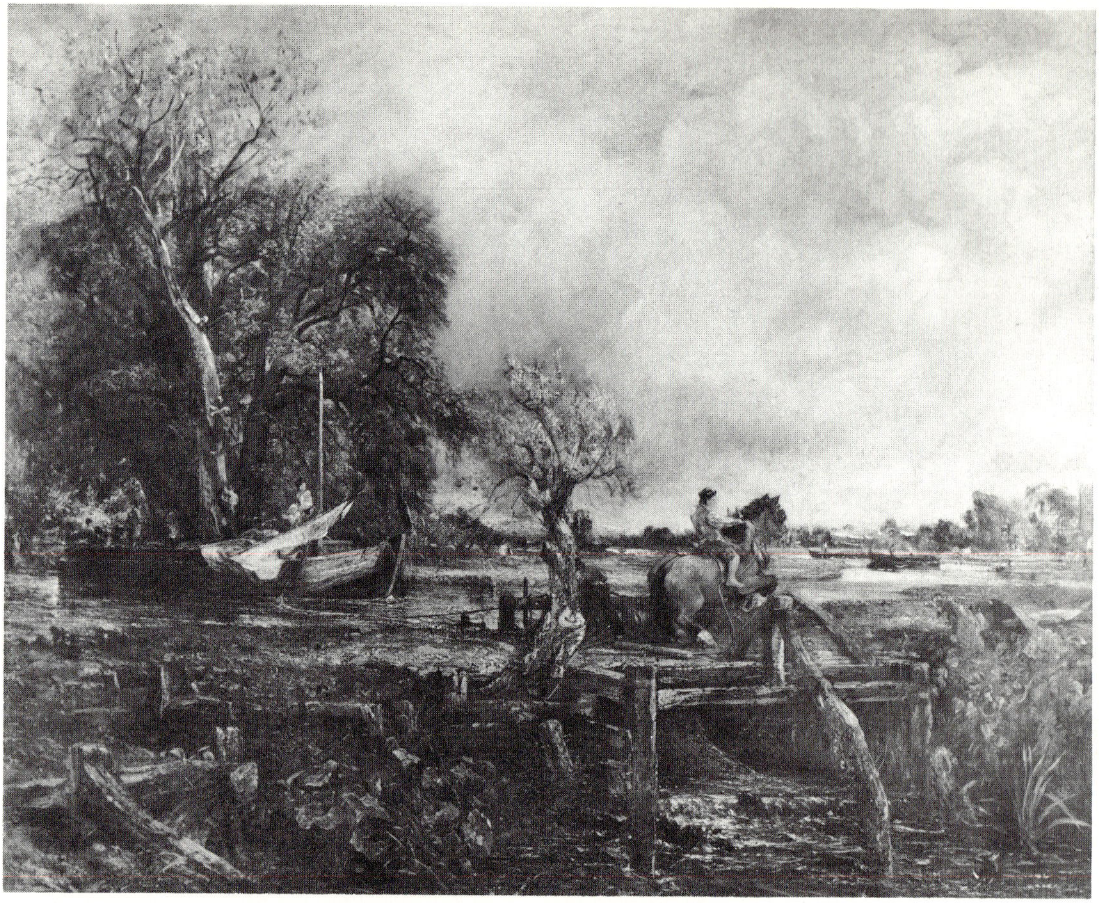

61

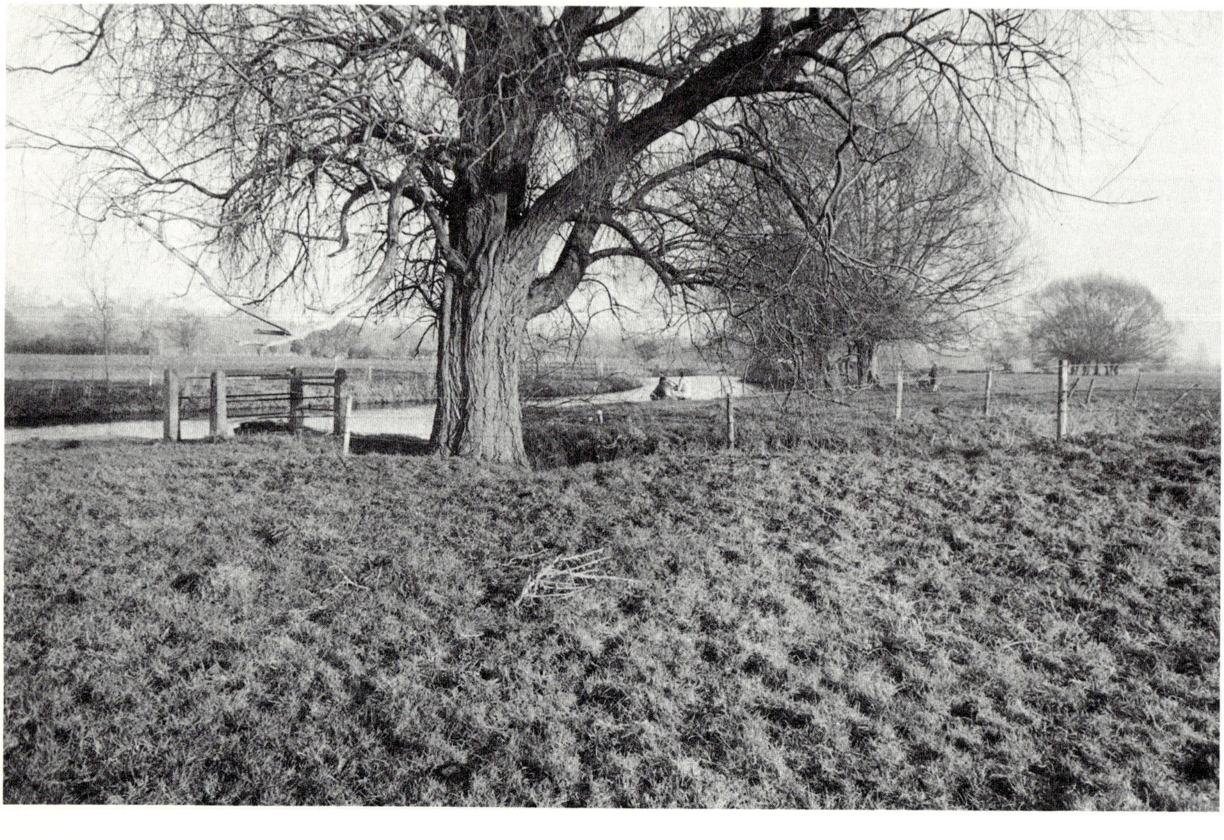

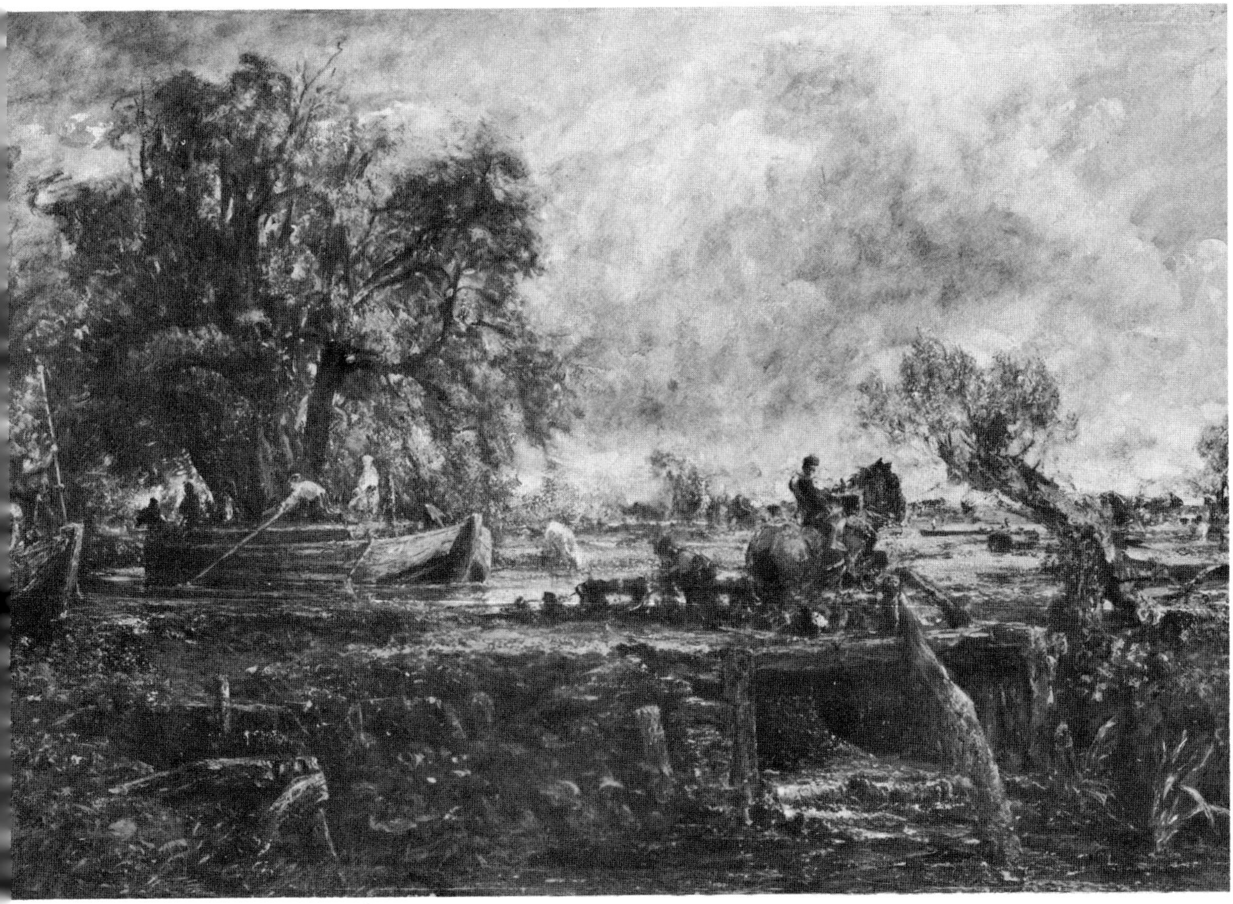

62

The Leaping Horse

The subject of this great painting is almost certainly the sluice—constructed to make the river navigable soon after 1705—on the county boundary between the site of the New Fen Bridge and Dedham. John Constable would have walked across it as a boy on his way to and from Dedham Grammar School, and it is interesting to realise that the horse in the painting is leaping out of Essex into Suffolk! In one of the early wash sketches in the British Museum (63) the New Fen Bridge can be clearly seen, though it is hidden behind the horse in the final work; so the identification of the site is fairly certain. But Dedham Church tower is introduced in the final work in order to aid the composition, in the absence of the willow stump to the right of the horse which appears in all the sketches, and which was painted out before Constable finally relinquished the picture to its buyer. For further details see Appendix.

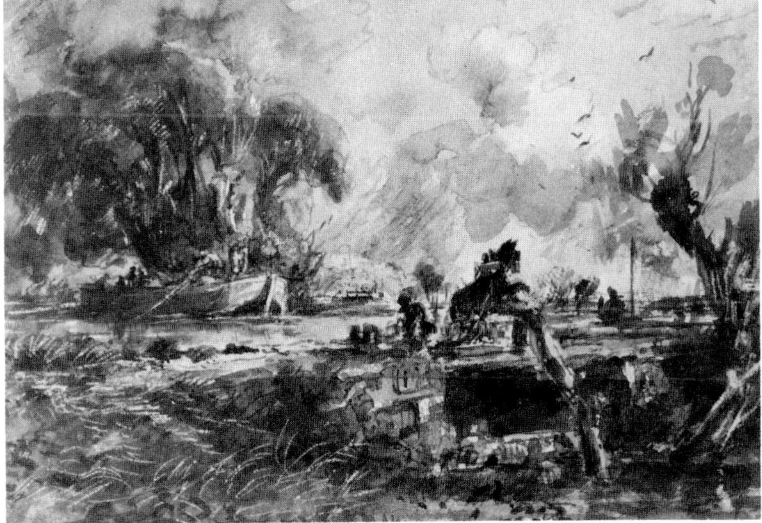

63

brush and palette-knife could have appeared so early in the history of European painting.

Although *The Leaping Horse* (exhibited as 'A Landscape') was surprisingly well received by the critics, Constable still felt that he should have spent longer on it before sending it to the Academy, and got it back on his easel when the exhibition closed. He had been compelled to settle his wife and family at Brighton, for reasons of health, and on 10 September he wrote to Fisher from London: "I am now, thank God, quietly at my easel again. I find it a cure for all ills besides its being the source 'of all my joy and all my woe'." Three days earlier he had noted in the journal which he kept for his wife:

> Set to work on my large picture, took out the old willow stump by my horse, which has improved the picture much; almost finished; made one or two other alterations.

It would appear, then, that the picture, when first exhibited, included the bent willow seen on the right in the full-size sketch. If the second willow-stump—to the horse's left—was not already in being, with the horse bracketed between the two willow trees, this would now have been added: an argument in favour of its having been a late addition is its omission from the two wash sketches in the British Museum and from a little oil-sketch in the Tate Gallery; an argument in favour of the contrary view is the presence of both willow-stumps in the Charteris sketch, and the presence in the full-size sketch, as Graham Reynolds has pointed out, of "a confused area of paint" in the vicinity of the boy immediately to the left of the horse. This figure is engaged in tying the rope of the barge to the fence over which the horse is leaping.

A comparison with the full-size sketch shows the nature of other changes 62
made by Constable—no doubt all or most of them prior to the Academy exhibition. As in the *View on the Stour near Dedham,* a light-toned tree which catches the sun has been introduced to give variety to the main group of trees on the left; and altogether the distribution of lights and darks in this area is far subtler in the finished painting. The strongest lights in the water are now confined to the vista of the winding river on the far right, and a white sail, furled across the barge, assumes the function, given in the sketch to the barge-boy, of catching the light in all its fullness, as well as of preserving—although nearer the centre of the composition—the diagonal originally established by the barge-pole: a diagonally placed beam in the left foreground

reverses this movement, and helps in addition to lead the eye into the spaces of the picture. The sky, in its perfected form, retains its threatening aspect.

The Cornfield

The skies of Constable's personal life continued to be troubled: his eldest child John was delicate; his wife's condition was not improved; and Constable felt it desirable that his family should remain at Brighton during the winter. Meanwhile his old patron the Bishop of Salisbury, John Fisher's uncle, had died, shortly after the opening of the Academy exhibition in the spring of 1825: in previous years he had made a point of attending the Academy on the opening day; and Constable felt keenly the loss of one whose friendship and constant encouragement had meant so much to him. Yet, despite his continued proneness to anxiety and depression, and despite financial worries (some of them occasioned by the vagaries of the French dealers), Constable could now enjoy the satisfactions of his rising reputation. In April he had received from the French Ambassador, at a ceremony which did full honour to his eminence as an artist, the gold medal awarded him for *The Hay Wain*: this was some compensation for his failure to secure election as a Royal Academician; and many further orders for pictures were coming to him from Paris. A large painting of *Waterloo Bridge* was promising well, and although this was to be laid aside and not exhibited until 1832, he soon began
work upon another large Suffolk scene—the famous *Cornfield*, now in the IV
National Gallery. It is one of his most serene compositions, and in this respect, and in its quiet sentiment, its happy evocation of his boyhood memories, it is the counterpart, in terms of a vertical design, of *The Hay Wain* of five years earlier.

A little horizontal landscape of *A Road near Dedham*, in the Mellon collection, which must have been painted at about the same time as the early *Dedham Vale* of 1802 (Victoria and Albert Museum), anticipates *The Cornfield* in a general way; but two oil-sketches are directly related to the composition.
The first is a quite early painting of *A Country Lane*, now in the Tate Gallery, 65
which includes the *motif* of the boy drinking from a stream. The second, in a private collection, would seem to have been made about 1825 or 1826, as a
compositional sketch for *The Cornfield*: we shall return to this sketch presently. 67
It has hitherto been assumed that the first sketch has no connection with the subject of *The Cornfield* apart from the presence in it of the drinking boy. Yet it probably shows the same lane that appears in *The Cornfield*, but from a

different viewpoint. This is the narrow lane leading from East Bergholt to the Vale of Dedham, down which Constable habitually walked as a boy on his way to Dedham Grammar School. In the Tate sketch we would seem to be looking down the lane from a point to the left of the scene represented in *The Cornfield*, where the viewpoint is taken from the fence or gate seen to the right of centre in the sketch; the break in the hedge at this point still exists to this day. The lane turns to the left at this point (as in the Tate sketch), and then to the right, past the plough represented in the National Gallery picture.

The scene represented in *The Cornfield* was identified by the painter's son Captain Charles Constable in a letter published in the *Art Journal* in 1869. In his letter Captain Constable pointed out that the church in the distance never existed, although he seems to have underestimated the extent of his father's practice of changing the literal aspect of a given subject for pictorial purposes:

> The little church in the distance never existed; it is one of the rare instances where my father availed himself of the painter's licence to improve the composition. Dedham Church has a much larger tower and lies to the right hand, outside the limits of the picture. The scene is greatly changed now; all the trees on the left were cut down some years ago.

Yet even today the lane is recognizably the lane that Constable knew; and a III
stream or drain still flows by the bank where Constable introduced his
thirsty boy. On the other hand it is difficult to think that the scene was not
always more ordinary than it became in Constable's powerful imagination.
Even if we discount the evidential value of the Tate sketch (either on the 65
grounds that it cannot be proved to represent the same lane, despite the inclusion of the wooden dam by the stream, or because it was made from a
different viewpoint), the later sketch (in a private collection) shows us a scene 67
that is more charming, and indeed far less sublime, than the majestic composition in the National Gallery. Nor does this second sketch necessarily represent the view as Constable knew it; for it gives the impression of being a study executed in Constable's painting-room; and although on this latter point there can be no absolute certainty, the total evidence at our disposal supports our reading of *The Cornfield* as an imaginative distillation of the artist's memories of his native scenes, and of his feelings about them, inspired by all that one well-remembered scene must have meant to him. This impression is reinforced by other aspects of the picture and of Constable's

procedure in building up his composition, to which we must now turn.

The Victoria and Albert Museum contains two oil-sketches on paper which were used by Constable for details of his composition. The first, dated 2 November 1814, is of a plough (together with part of a further plough), 69
which Constable introduced at the corner of the lane. The same plough is represented also on two pages of the 1814 sketchbook, in one case being seen from the same angle as it is in the oil-sketch. The second oil-sketch is a study of the browsing donkey and its foal which appear on the grassy bank on the left. A similar donkey, with its head thrust forward to graze in exactly the attitude of the animal in the oil-sketch and *The Cornfield*, is to be seen in the *Dedham Vale, Morning*, of 1811; and a faint pencil drawing in the 1813 18
sketchbook shows a similar donkey, although without a foal. It has been argued on stylistic grounds that the oil-sketch was made at about the time that Constable was painting *The Cornfield*; but the indications as to dating seem to me to be too slight to allow of much certainty, and a much earlier date cannot be ruled out. It has also been argued that this sketch cannot have been used for the *Dedham Vale, Morning*, since the donkey in that picture is without a foal; but the foal would in any case have been obscured by the bank, with its undergrowth, on the left side of the picture.

As Graham Reynolds has proposed, the idea of the flock of sheep represented partly in full light and partly in shadow may well have been suggested by Gaspard Poussin's *Landscape near Albano*, now in the National Gallery, a 68
picture that Constable saw when it was exhibited at the British Institution in 1822. In the Mediterranean (as is shown in Gaspard Poussin's picture) shepherds lead their flocks; in Northern Europe they drive them; and while the sheep-dog waits for him, Constable's shepherd-boy has left his flock for a moment in order to slake his thirst. This is a lovely piece of drawing, and even the rustic awkwardness of the boy is charming and expressive. The 64
forms are handled broadly and sculpturally, with an emphasis upon simplified planes. It is altogether an unforgettable image—first stated with a few strokes of the brush in the early sketch, which would have been painted on the spot, and then, many years later, given complete realization in the great composition now in the National Gallery.

In view of the probable dependence of the central passage, containing the sheep, upon the picture by Gaspard Poussin, it may be apposite to note at this point Constable's observations to Fisher upon the exhibition at the British Institution in 1822, when the picture by Gaspard was on view to the public. In a letter to Fisher written on 31 October of that year, Constable expressed

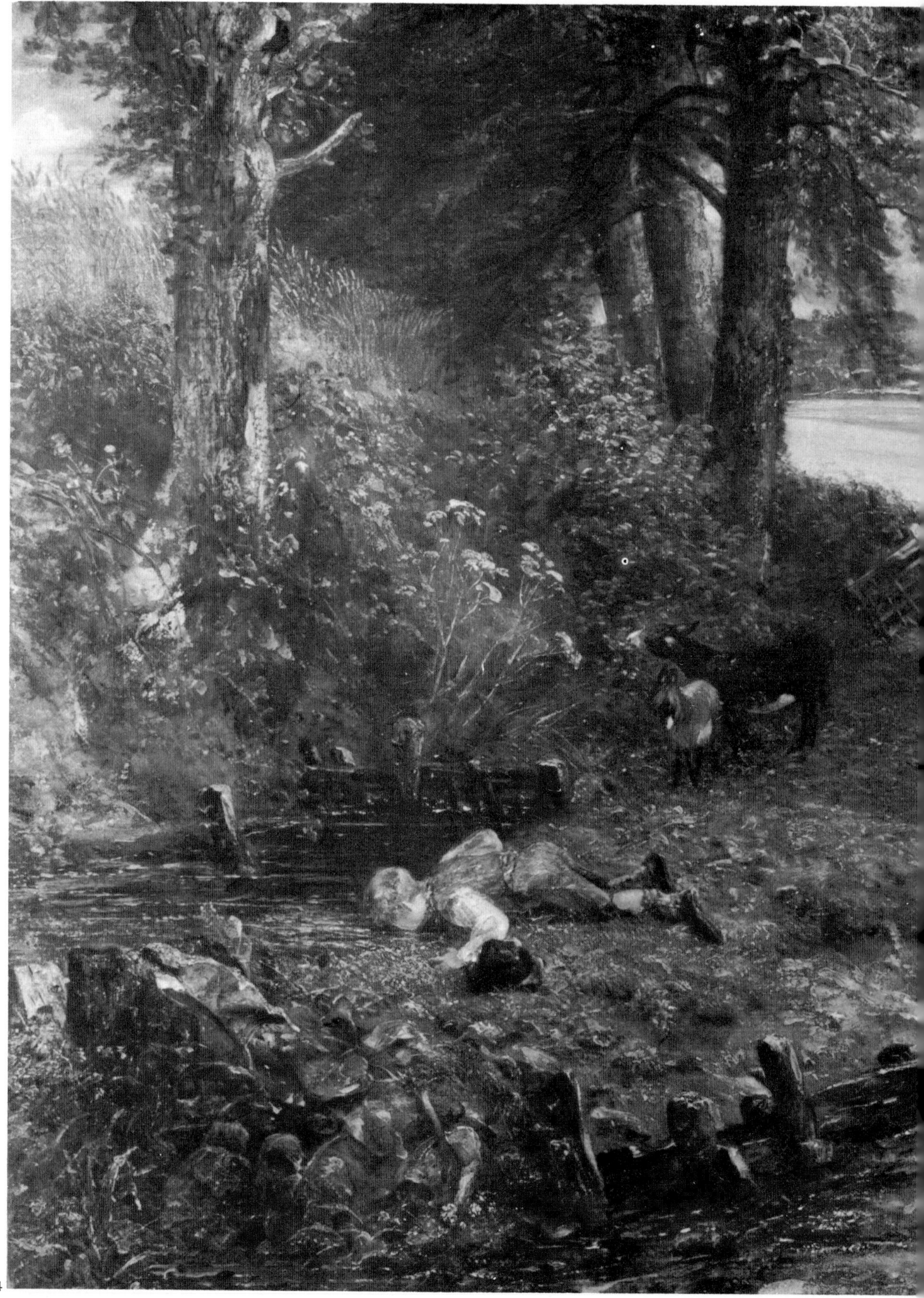

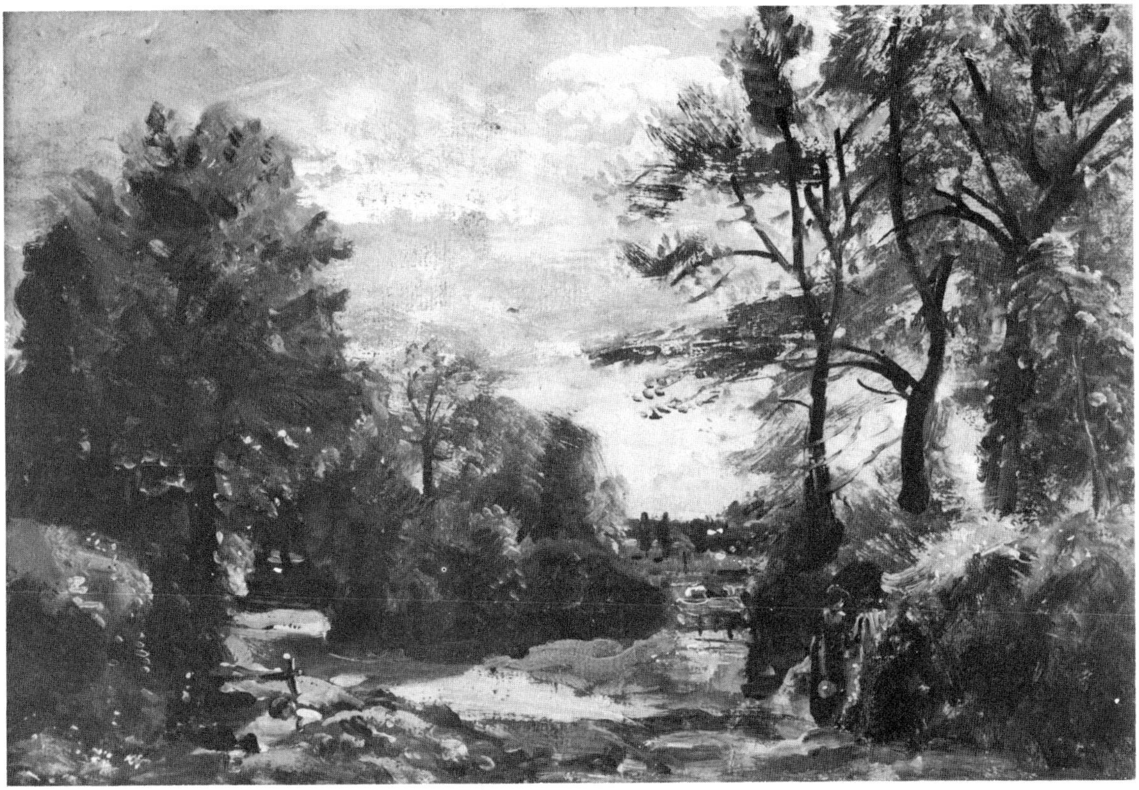

65

67

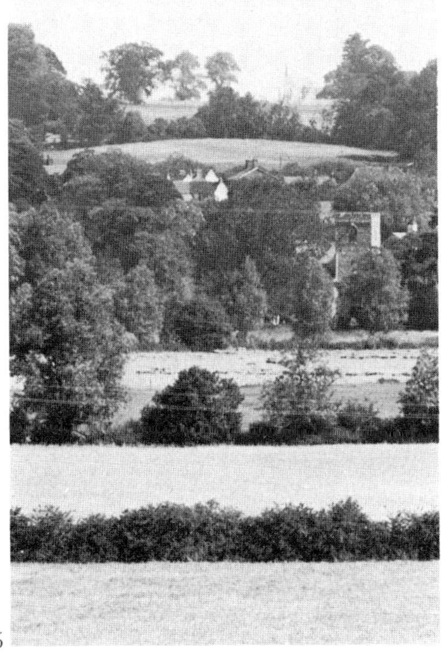

66

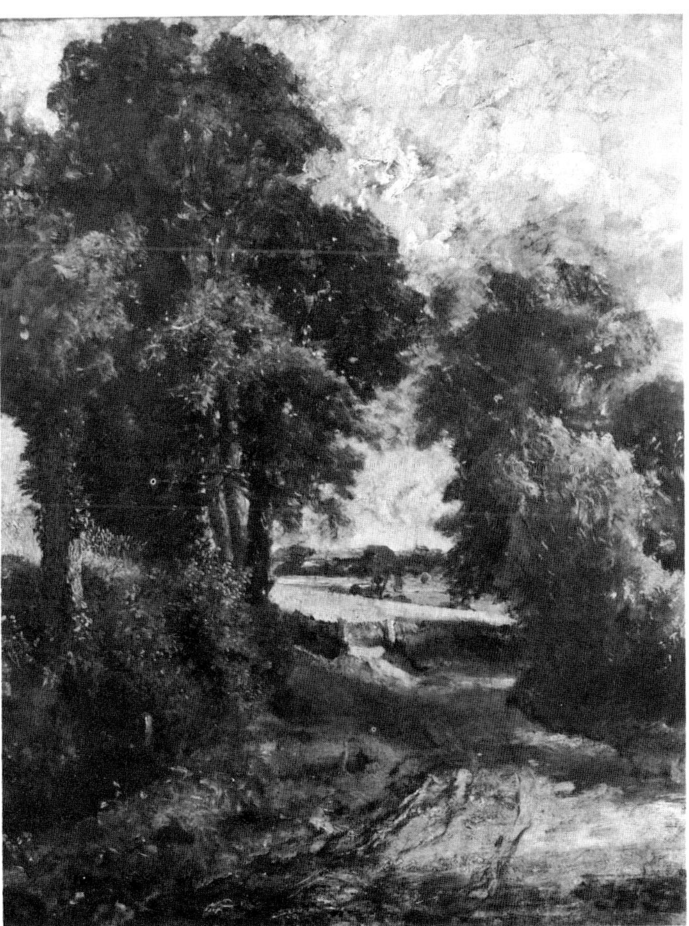

The Cornfield
Captain Charles Constable, the painter's son, commenting on this painting in 1869, started the myth that Constable was not an accurate painter by saying that "the little church in the distance never existed". The lane concerned turns off to the right

about 200 yards down the road from East Bergholt Church to Flatford, then bends to the left, and this is the point where it enters the picture. Just beyond, it bends right again with a gap looking over the valley, where there is indeed no sign of a church nestling among trees as in the painting. Yet it seems eminently possible that Constable obtained his inspiration for the church in the final work from Higham Church (66), seen from the high ground across the valley from Langham about two miles away, a view he knew well. The church was therefore transposed from one point of Constable's country to another.

The idea of painting a flock of sheep passing through shadows to sunshine may have come to Constable after seeing Gaspard Poussin's *Landscape near Albano* (68) in 1822. Yet his study of 1825 shows no sheep at all (67): and he went back to an early study of a country lane to recapture the motif of a boy drinking (65), to a sketch for the plough (69), and to his painting of Helmingham Park over twenty years earlier (23) for the brightly lit tree on the left. It is hard to believe, when we look at the accurately painted details of flowers, grass and wheat, that this was not painted in Suffolk but was done in London through the sheer power of Constable's creative imagination, which combined disparate elements and brought them together in a perfect composition.

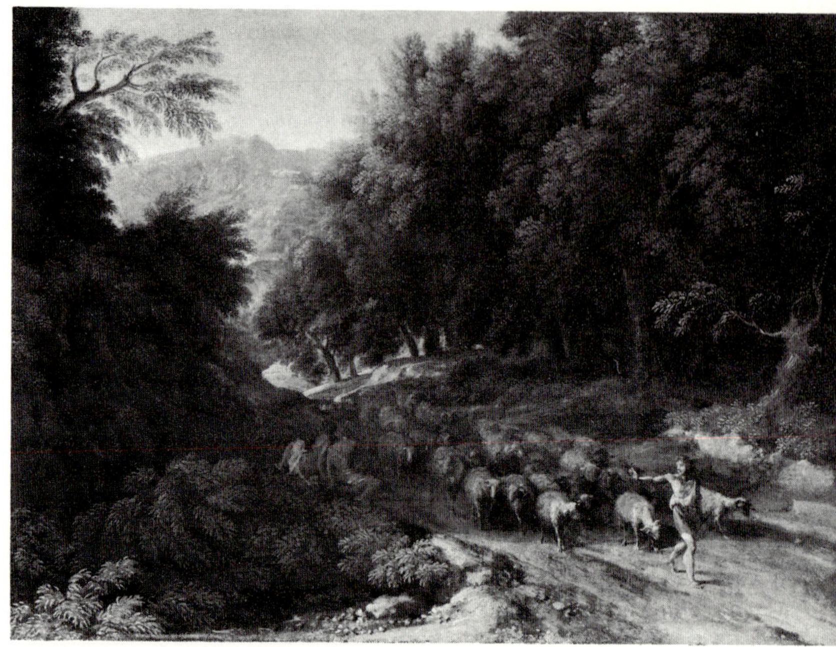

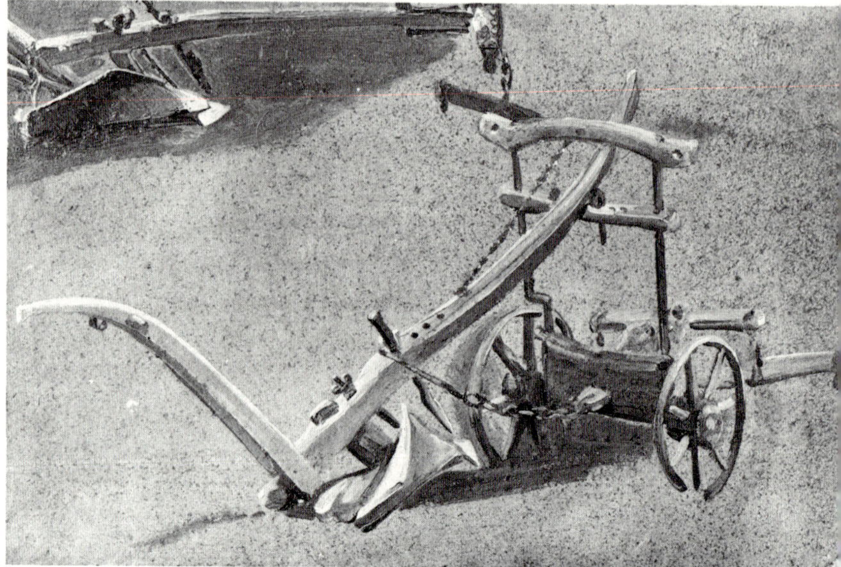

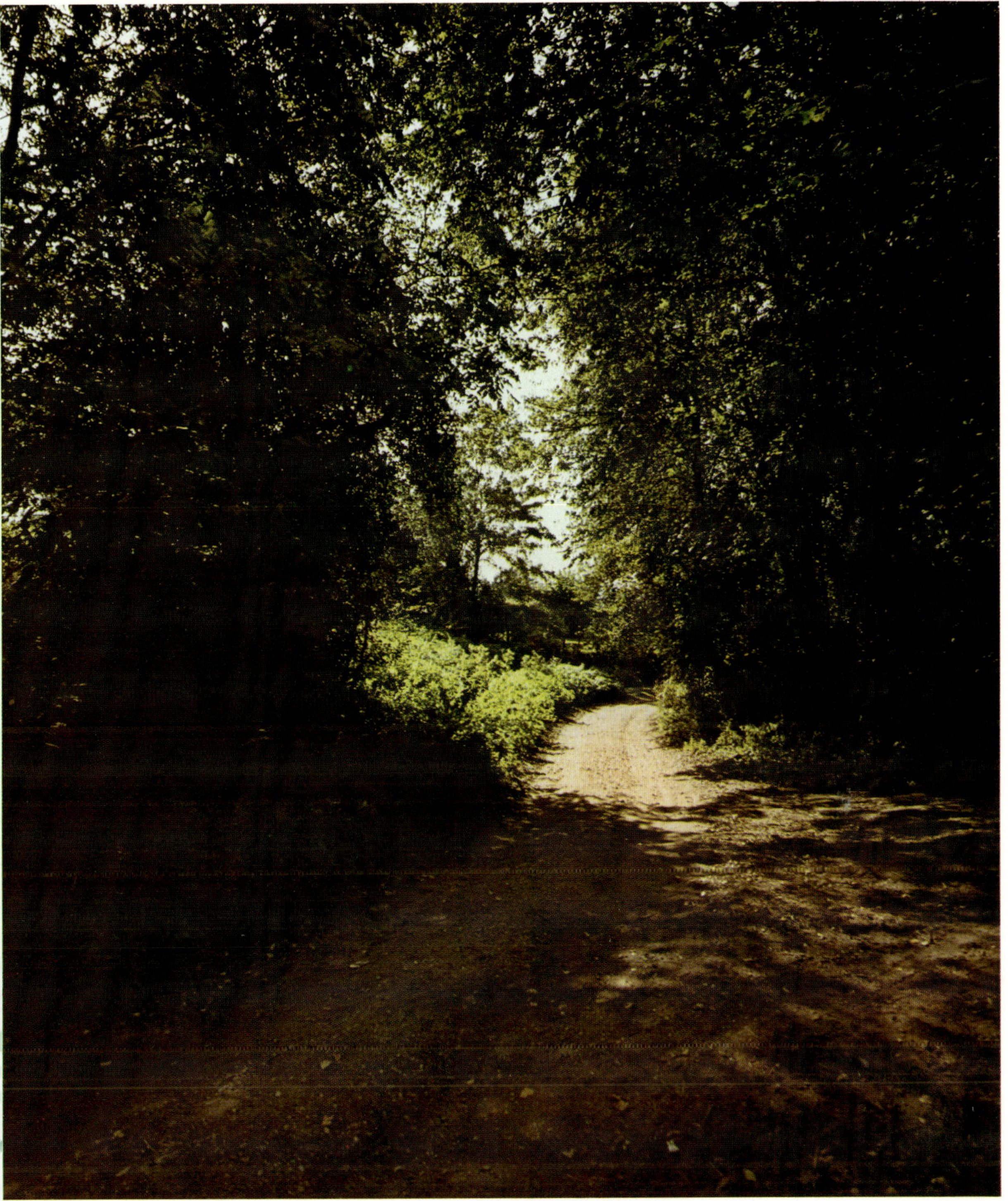

III-IV *The Cornfield* (*see over*) The lane leading from East Bergholt to Fen Bridge is still recognisable as the site of *The Cornfield*: the ditch running along at a higher level on the left is the remains of the stream where the shepherd boy lies to slake his thirst, and the gap in the hedge looks over the valley which Constable painted.

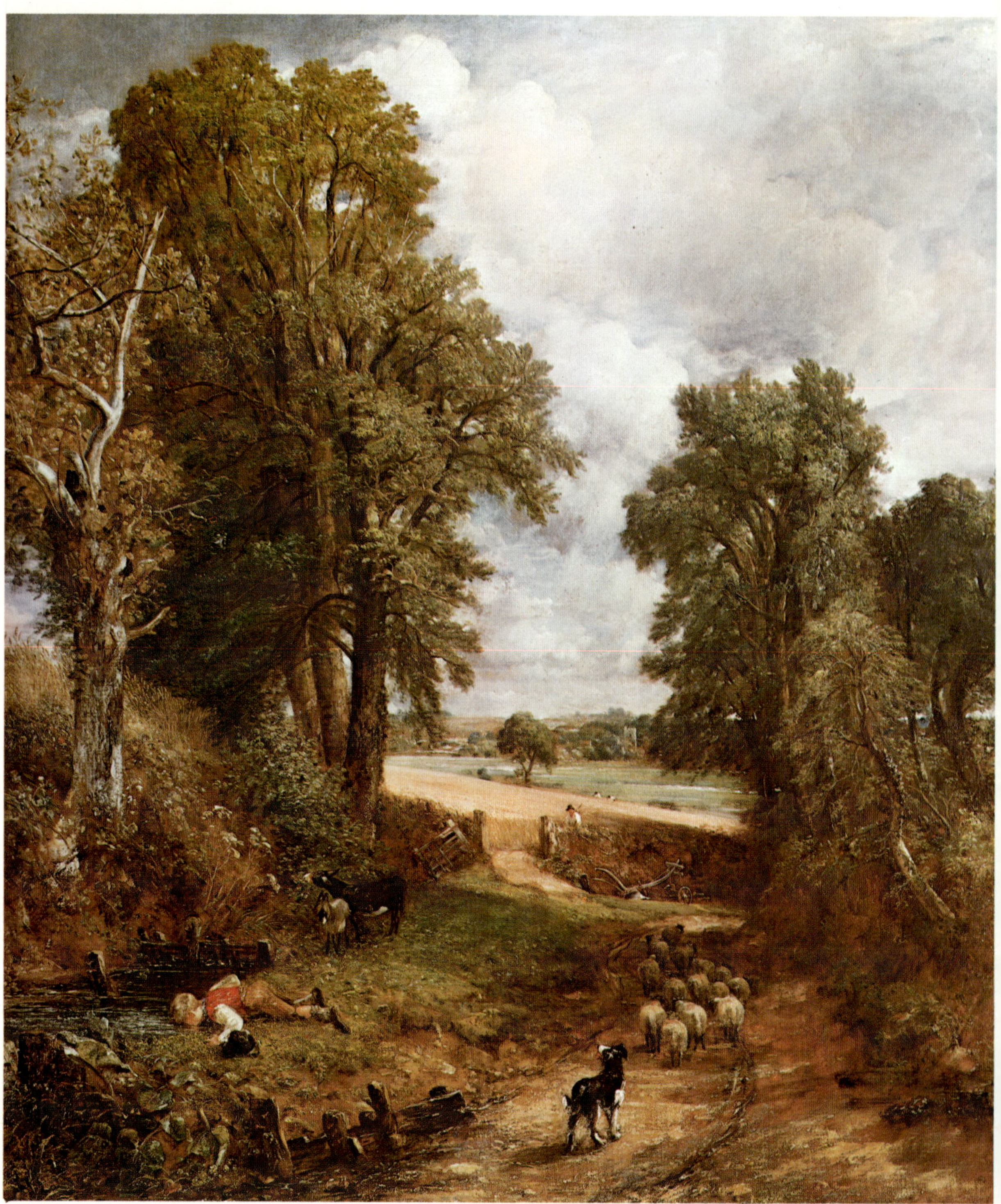

his dismay that English artists were busy at the British Institution making inferior copies, for sale, of works by such masters as Van de Velde, Gaspard Poussin and Titian. One of the artists, Thomas Christopher Hofland, had, he said, sold "his shadow of Gaspar Poussin" for eighty guineas: "It is nothing more like Gaspar than the shadow of the man [is] like himself on a muddy road." Constable was anxious, besides, lest the practice of slavish copying from the Old Masters would have a deleterious effect upon students; and it was for this reason that he was to become sceptical of the ultimate value to the arts of a National Gallery. But such opinions on his part should not be misunderstood as implying any lack of recognition of the importance to be attached to a true study of the art of the past: indeed in the early winter of 1823—the year after the British Institution exhibition—he was himself copying pictures by Claude at the Leicestershire seat of Sir George Beaumont, Coleorton Hall near Ashby-de-la-Zouch. And the design of Claude's
Hagar and the Angel, of which Sir George had permitted him to make a 28
copy in 1800, appears to have influenced the composition of *The Cornfield*, IV
just as it lies behind the *Dedham Vale* compositions of 1802 and 1828; for the trees beside Constable's lane, massed against the sky, are reinterpretations, in a modern style, of the Claudian convention whereby a distant vista is glimpsed between larger and smaller masses of silhouetted trees in the foreground or middle distance; and the church beyond the cornfield is the pictorial equivalent of the tower which acts as the focal point in Claude's picture.

Constable evidently felt the need for greater variety on the left-hand side of his composition than was provided by the small compositional study. Here too he may have learnt from the example of Claude's *Hagar*, where the arching trunk of a brightly lit tree in the right foreground presents an effective contrast to the dark areas of foliage behind it. There were precedents also in the landscapes of Ruisdael and Hobbema. Constable's source was a representation of a similar tree in a picture of Helmingham Park, Suffolk, which 23
he had painted over twenty years earlier: as in *The Cornfield*, the tree forms a prominent feature at the left-hand side of the composition. This addition produced not merely a contrast in lighting but variety of another sort: the tree is almost dead, like the ash-tree which Constable was to introduce in a similar manner into *The Valley Farm*, and both in its nakedness of form and in its uncertain life it becomes a foil, suggestive of the habitual rhythms of Nature, to the healthy magnificence of the great elms beyond it.

An equally important development from the stage represented by the compositional sketch can be deduced from the significantly different format of the finished composition in the National Gallery, which is proportionately wider. Constable was thereby enabled to broaden the lane and, indeed, the whole scene, letting in a much larger expanse of sky between the two principal masses of trees—a sky almost filled with those rolling cumulus clouds which were for him the chief 'organ of sentiment' in a landscape. Never had he made studies of clouds like these at East Bergholt: here again the Suffolk landscape lies under a Hampstead sky, splendid and spacious, swelling up from the horizon, in concert with the noonday mood of this most memorable, and most moving, of all evocations of the country lanes of England, and of their shifting lights and shades.

The Cornfield is all this: it is also the most masterly—certainly up to this date—of Constable's explorations of spatial composition: once again, a dog in the foreground helps to establish the spatial rhythms of the design, which wind back through passages of alternate light and dark towards the imaginary church—or, if not entirely imaginary, transposed, as Attfield Brooks has suggested, from its actual site in Dedham Vale; for, as he points out, this 66
seems to be Higham Church, which stands in a quite different part of the valley. Perhaps the sheepdog, which is so essential to the composition, and which leads us into the scene while at the same time directing our attention, by the turn of its head, to the drinking boy, was in part inspired by the little dog in the foreground of Gainsborough's *Market Cart*, now in the Tate Gallery: but if this was so, the influence of Gainsborough's masterpiece, which is all the more plausible in view of the resemblance of the birch-tree in the right foreground of *The Cornfield* to the tree in the corresponding area of the Gainsborough, would no doubt have made itself felt much earlier, since not dissimilar dogs appear in such pictures as *The Hay Wain* and the *Boat passing a Lock*. However that may be, *The Cornfield* is to the art of Constable what *The Market Cart* is to that of Gainsborough: never, since the time of Gainsborough, had that most endearing of English scenes, a simple and quite ordinary country lane, been made the subject of so affecting a landscape.

Once again, as in the case of *The Hay Wain*, it is strange to realize that this Suffolk picture, redolent of summer, was painted during a London winter. It is strange also to reflect that the picture seems to have owed something to the advice of Constable's friend Henry Phillips, the botanist and landscape designer. Phillips lived at Brighton, where the artist had met him in 1824, and it was to his household that Constable sent his ailing son John, so that he could benefit both from the sea air and from the kindliness and instruction which the Phillipses, who had opened an academy for young ladies at their house, were able to give him. Phillips became a warm admirer of Constable's art, and the painter in turn expressed his enthusiasm for Phillips's botanical writings, notably his *Sylvia Florifera, or the Shrubbery*, which had appeared in 1823. On his visits to London, Phillips would call in at the house in Charlotte Street to see Constable's latest paintings, and it was on one of these visits, early in the year 1826, that he saw *The Cornfield*, still unfinished on Constable's easel. On 1 March he wrote to him:

I think it is July in your green lane. At this season all the tall grasses are in flower, bogrush, bullrush, teasel. The white bindweed now hangs its flowers over the branches of the hedge; the wild carrot and hemlock flower in banks of hedges, cow parsley, water plantain, &c; the heath hills are purple at this season; the rose-coloured persicaria in wet ditches is now very pretty; the catchfly graces the hedge-row, as also the ragged robin; bramble is now in flower, poppy, thistle, hop, &c.

Some of the plants and flowers to which Phillips drew Constable's attention
can be recognized in the National Gallery picture. The pointed leaves of the 64
large plants in the left foreground suggest that what is represented is water plantain, although other rounded leaves nearby may belong to butterbur; the very large leaves might indicate the common burdock, but this plant is not usually found on wet ground—and, as the two wooden dams show, the bank between the lane and the stream from which the boy is drinking is very wet indeed. Further back, we see brambles and cow-parsley; and the corn is full, as in July. The donkey on the left is feeding from the suckers produced by the tall English elms farther back. English elms—as distinct from the smooth-leafed elm (which does not produce suckers)—are comparatively rare in some parts of East Anglia; but that they were to be seen in the neighbourhood of East Bergholt in Constable's time is certain. As they were common in Hampstead, Constable would have had ample opportunity to make fresh studies.

The Cornfield—the richest in tone and colour of all Constable's major Suffolk landscapes—was exhibited at the Academy in 1826. On 8 April the painter wrote to Archdeacon Fisher:

I have dispatched a large landscape to the Academy—upright, the size of my Lock—but a subject of a very different nature—inland—cornfields—a close lane, kind of thing—but it is not neglected in any part. The trees are more than usually studied and the extremities well defined—as well as their species—they are shaken by a pleasant and healthful breeze—"*at noon*"—"while now a fresher gale, *sweeping with shadowy gust the fields of corn*" &c, &c. I am not without my anxieties—but they are not such as I have too often really deserved—I have not neglected my work or been sparing of my pains—they are not sins of omission. . . . My picture occupied me wholly—I could think of and speak to no one. I was like a friend of mine in the battle of Waterloo—he said he dared not turn his head to the right or left—but always kept it straight forward—thinking of himself alone—I am much worn, having worked very hard—and have now the consolation of knowing I must work a great deal harder, or go to the workhouse. I have, however, work to do—and I hope to sell this present picture—as it has certainly got a little more eye-salve than I usually condescend to give to them. . . .

Constable sent to the Academy, along with *The Cornfield* (which appeared in the catalogue simply as 'Landscape'), *A Mill at Gillingham in Dorsetshire*. The critic of *The Times* praised both pictures as the best landscapes in the exhibition, and described *The Cornfield* as "singularly beautiful, and not inferior to some of Hobbema's most admired works". Despite Constable's expectations, however, the picture remained unsold; and he exhibited it again at the British Institution in the following year (as 'Landscape: Noon'), subsequently showing it at the Paris Salon (in 1827) and at Worcester (in 1835). In the catalogue of the British Institution exhibition the lines from James Thomson's *Summer* which Constable had quoted in his letter to Fisher, evidently from memory, were printed in their correct form:

A fresher gale
Begins to wave the woods and stir the streams,
Sweeping with shadowy gusts the fields of corn.

It was fashionable for painters of the time—Turner among them—to accompany their pictures with apt quotations from the poets, of whom Thomson was one of the most popular; and Constable chose a passage which evokes the moving lights and darks of Nature, when clouds send shadows scurrying across the open fields.

The Cornfield has much 'eye-salve', as Constable called it—much detail and finish—but a great deal of it is suggested, instead of being "retailed out" (to quote the expression he had used in speaking of his intentions in *The Mill Stream*): Constable's technical mastery was never more in evidence than in

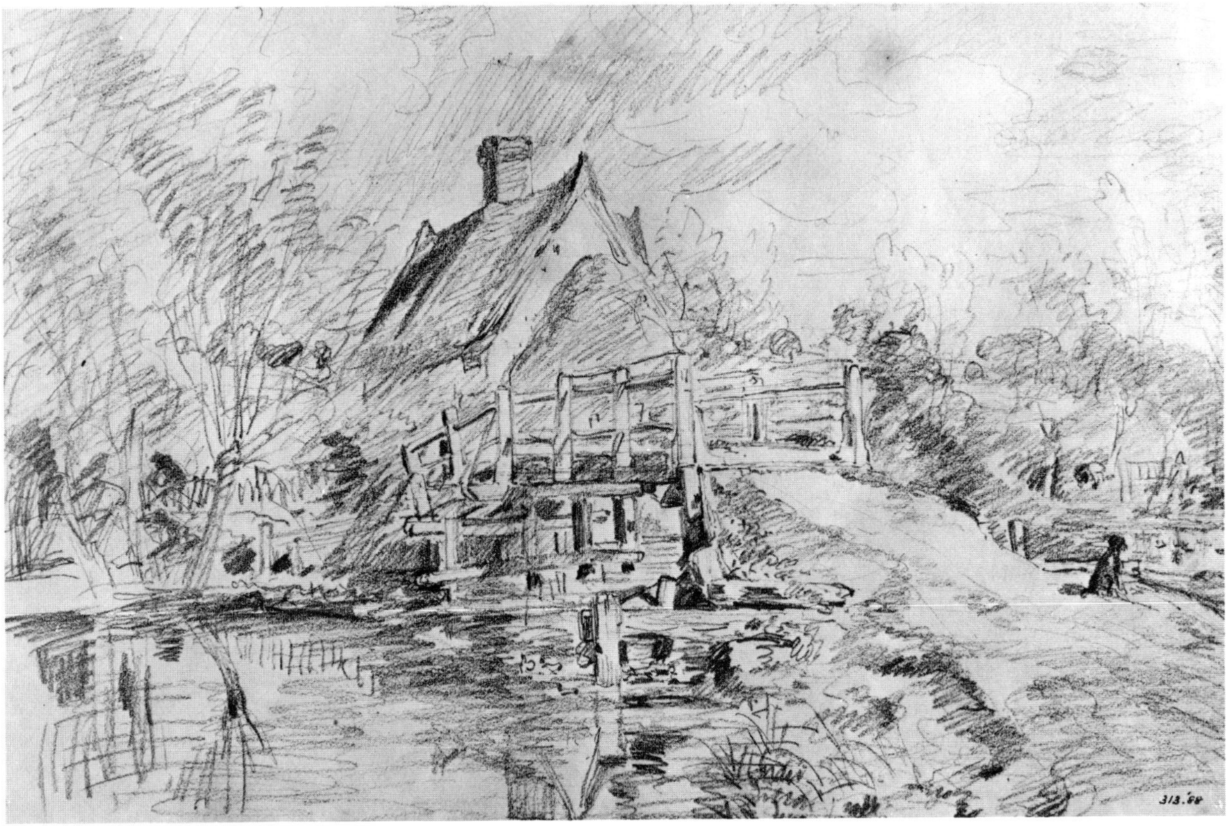

70

71

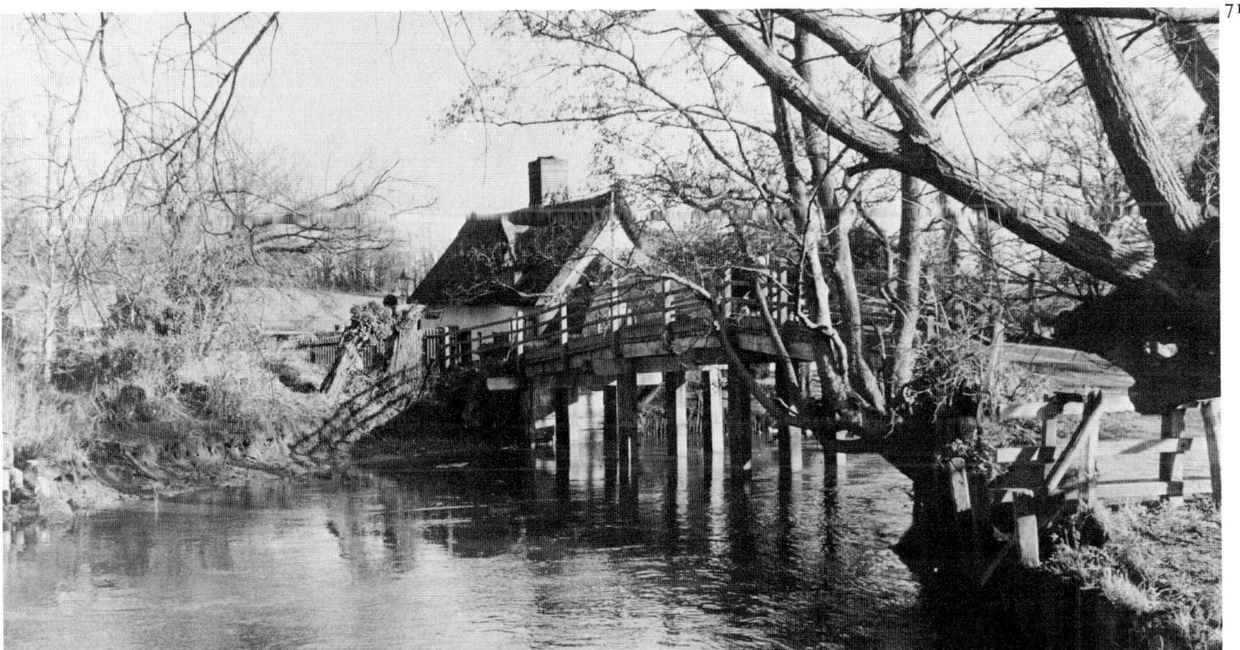

Flatford Old Bridge and Bridge Cottage
This drawing formed part of the sketchbook of 1827 (cf. 2, 57, 59). It shows the bridge from an angle different from that in any of the other works discussed. Although the cottage has been preserved, it must be noted that the bridge in the photograph was constructed in the 1930s by East Suffolk County Council to replace one that had become unsafe and which may or may not have been the one in existence in 1827.

his ability to combine an impression of the variety of Nature with an expression of her ceaseless life and motion. Moreover, every suggested detail of leaf or flower or golden corn takes its place within a coherent whole, a conception at once comprehensive and sublime. It was fitting that this work, which when it was first seen elicited comparisons with Hobbema himself, should have been the first painting by Constable to enter the National Gallery.

Constable told Fisher, "The voice in my favour is universal—' 'tis my best picture'." Yet it could still be treated with a certain amount of disrespect by the humorous Francis Chantrey, the sculptor and founder of the Chantrey Bequest, who was emboldened to try to touch up Constable's pictures in the Academy. Before the exhibition opened, according to a story recounted by David Lucas, Constable's engraver, Chantrey went up to Constable and, observing the dark shadows under the tails of the sheep in *The Cornfield*, remarked, "Why, Constable, all your sheep have got the rot: give me the palette—I must cure them." He then made an attempt to 'improve' the picture in this passage, but failed to do so; whereupon he threw the palette at Constable and departed. Constable himself told Fisher a similar story: "Chantrey," he wrote, "loves painting (better perhaps than stone). . . , and he works now and then on my pictures. . . ; and yesterday he joined our group and after exhausting his jokes on my landscape, he took up a large dirty palette rag and threw it in my face and was off."

Constable's exhibits at the Academy in the following year did not include a Suffolk scene; but he showed *The Glebe Farm* at the British Institution: as Shirley pointed out, this is a highly imaginative composition in which two distinct viewpoints are combined. The picture was inspired by the church and farmhouse at Langham, and was freely composed from much earlier studies. In the light of Constable's transformation of the subject it is no wonder that, when Leslie visited Langham with a friend three years after the artist's death, he found everything "so much changed excepting the church, that we could scarcely recognize it as the scene of the 'Glebe Farm' ". Constable's principal exhibit at the Academy in 1827 was *Marine Parade and Chain Pier, Brighton*, not the happiest of his compositions and one that gives the impression of laboured effort. Constable never took to Brighton, which was probably too much associated in his mind with his wife's declining health. That year he became more and more anxious about her, and settled her in what was intended to be a permanent residence at Well Walk in Hampstead. He was anxious also about his financial situation, especially after the birth of another boy towards the end of the previous year; a seventh child was to be born in January 1828. Constable's worries over money, which had compelled him to seek a loan from John Fisher, were to be ended on the death in 1828 of Maria's father, who left her a considerable fortune: but the sadness of the occasion was compounded by the clear signs that Maria's own life was hanging by a thread: in March of the same year she was too weak to make the journey to Brighton, where, it was still hoped, the sea air might benefit her. In February she had seen her husband's professional hopes again dashed, when Etty was preferred to him in the election for a vacancy in the list of Royal Academicians. When, in the following year, he was at last elected, the honour had come too late: his wife had died in the previous November, and he could no longer impart it.

Dedham Vale

It was in the midst of these troubles that in April 1828 Constable sent to the
Academy the great *Dedham Vale* now in the National Gallery of Scotland, 75
together with the *Hampstead Heath: Branch Hill Pond* in the Victoria and Albert Museum, which was based on an oil-sketch painted in 1819 (also in the Victoria and Albert Museum). The two paintings, although widely different in composition, have in common a gravity of tone and a meditative poetry akin, to some extent, to the mood of many landscapes by Ruisdael, one of whose pictures had lately impressed Constable so deeply that he had been unable to get it out of his mind; and in each we find the same mastery of lighting, under skies which darken ominously overhead.

In October 1827 Constable had taken his children to Flatford, to show them the haunts of his boyhood and to relax in the company of his brother Abram (who in some anxiety had done everything to put him off, pleading lack of adequate accommodation and even voicing the fear that the children might fall into the pond between the Mill and Willy Lott's House). Constable appears to have enjoyed this respite; he made some drawings by the Stour; and we known that on 6 October he and his brother visited a friend at Ded ham. It is clear, however, that when he began work on the Edinburgh *Dedham Vale* on his return to London, Constable based the composition upon the small picture showing the same view, which he had painted in
Suffolk in 1802. 27

He made numerous changes, modifying his original conception in important respects, adding certain details and removing others. He had at his dis-

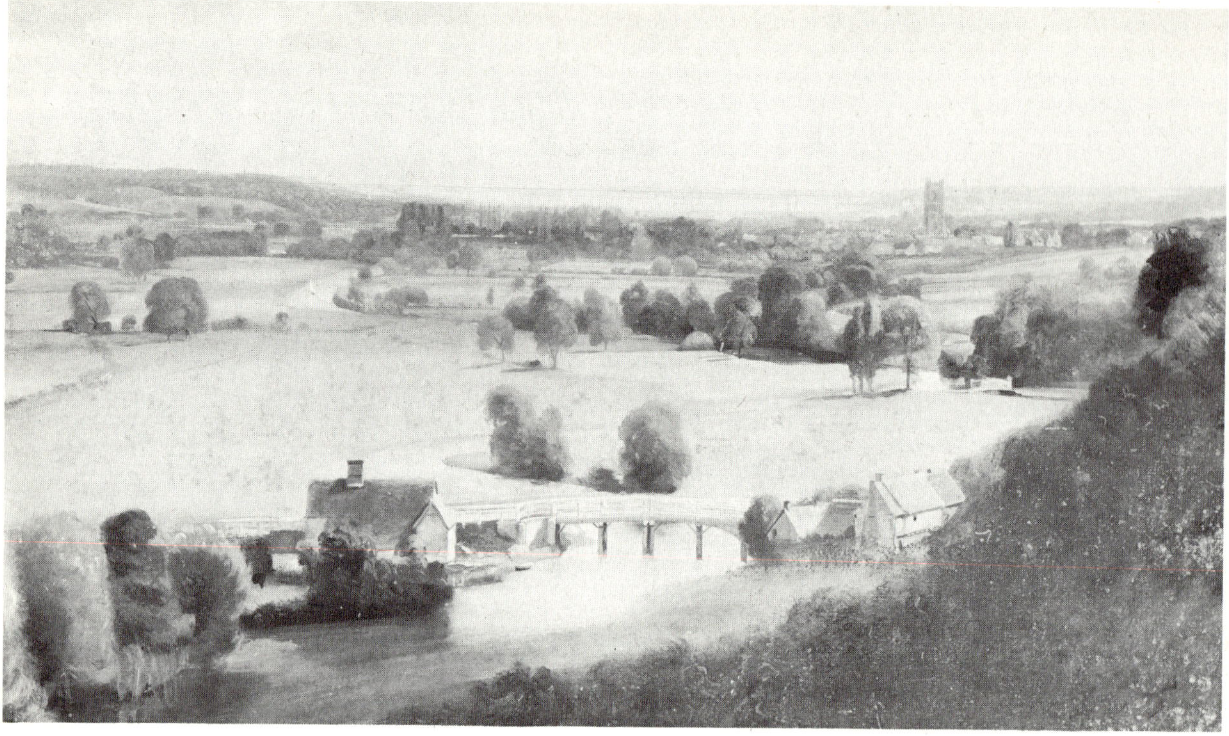

72

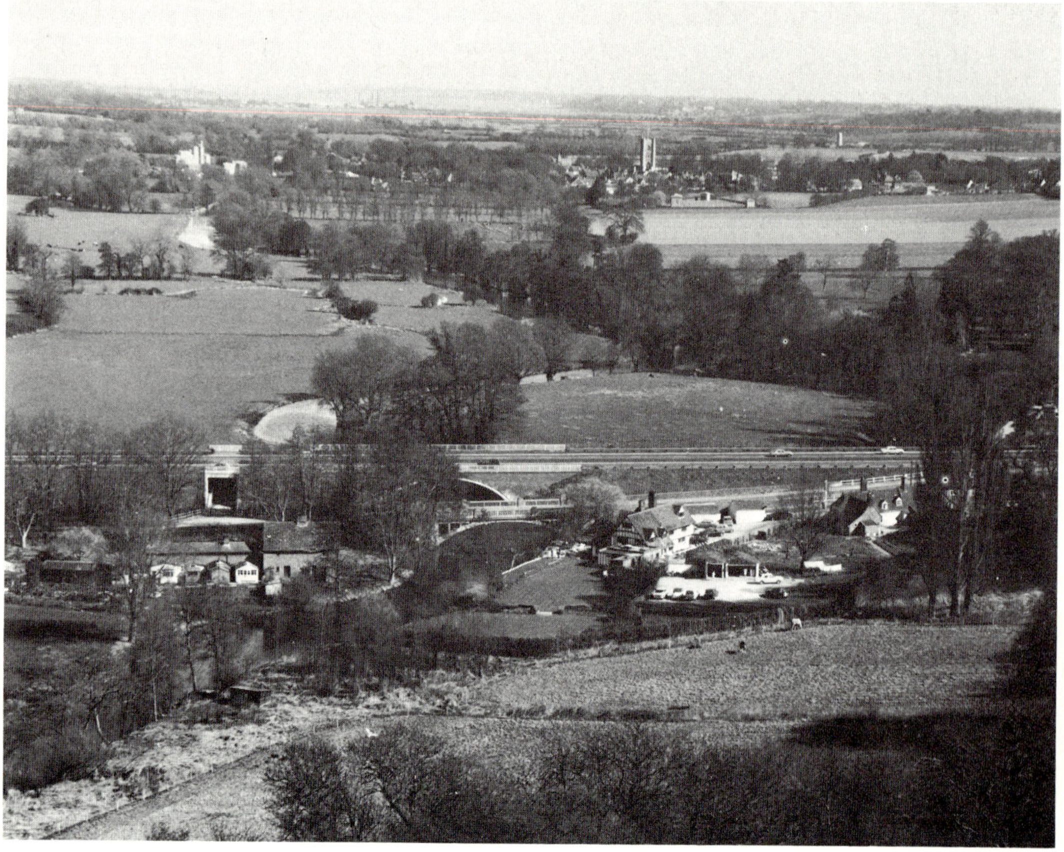

73

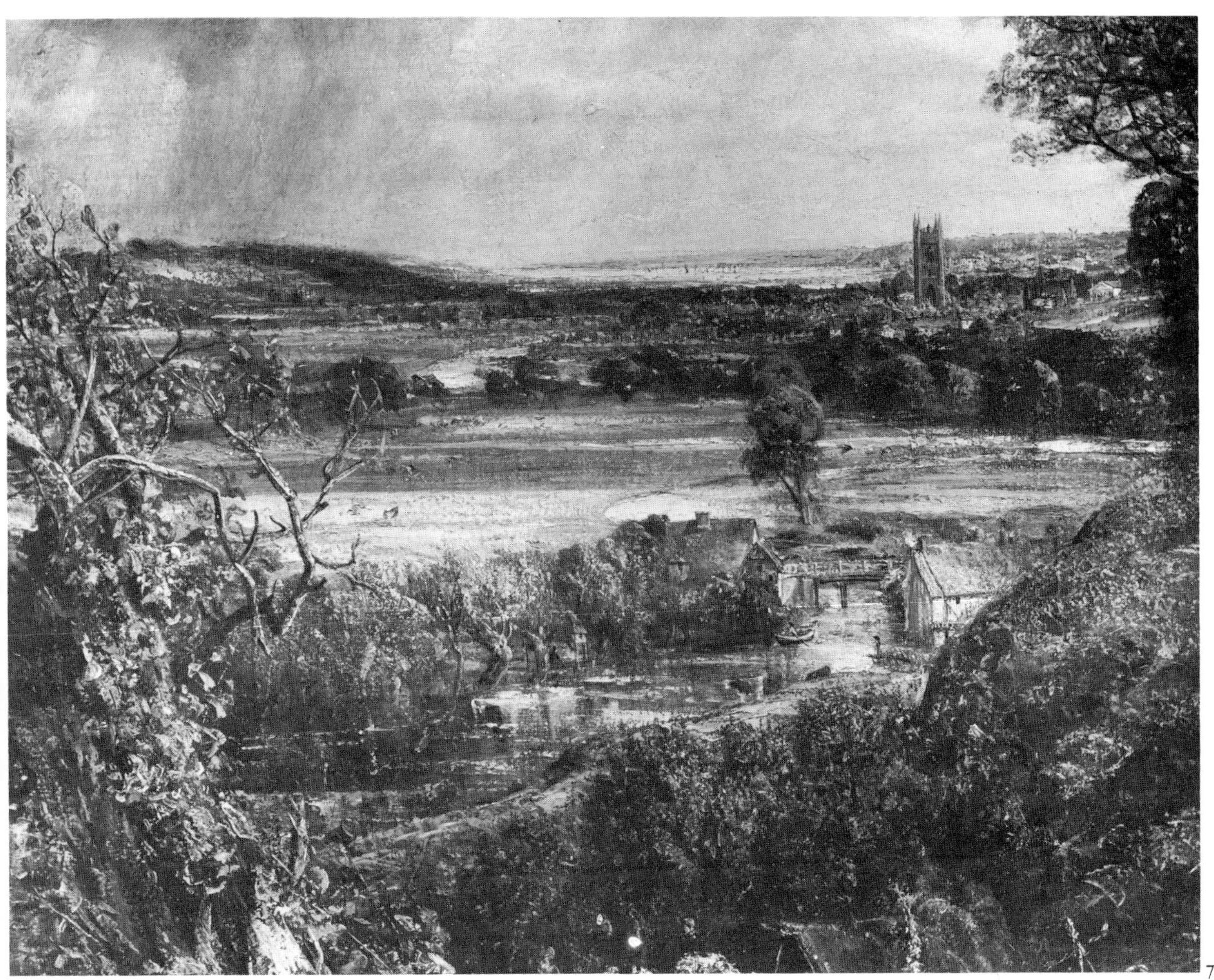

74

Dedham Vale 1828 (see over) This great painting, which Constable described as "perhaps my best", is quite obviously based upon the small one he painted in East Bergholt in 1802 (27). But the artist has also drawn upon other works executed from the same basic location on Langham Coombs, as the now wooded hills are called, such as the very detailed *Valley of the Stour with Dedham in the distance* (72), assigned to about 1804. The view has long been obscured by trees: so it is seldom realised how accurate the landscape details are, not only in the early works but in the exhibited painting as well. The helicopter photograph (if we allow for the changes due to the extra height from which the scene is viewed) illustrates this very clearly, for not only the two houses on either side of the river bridge but also the river itself, the hedges and fields, Dedham Village, and further off the shores of the estuary at Mistley and right down to Wrabness Point are all most accurately shown. Full details appear in the note in the Appendix. That Constable could include such detail and accuracy in such a splendid and beautiful composition executed in London shows how triumphantly he had become the "natural painter" he had set out to be.

75

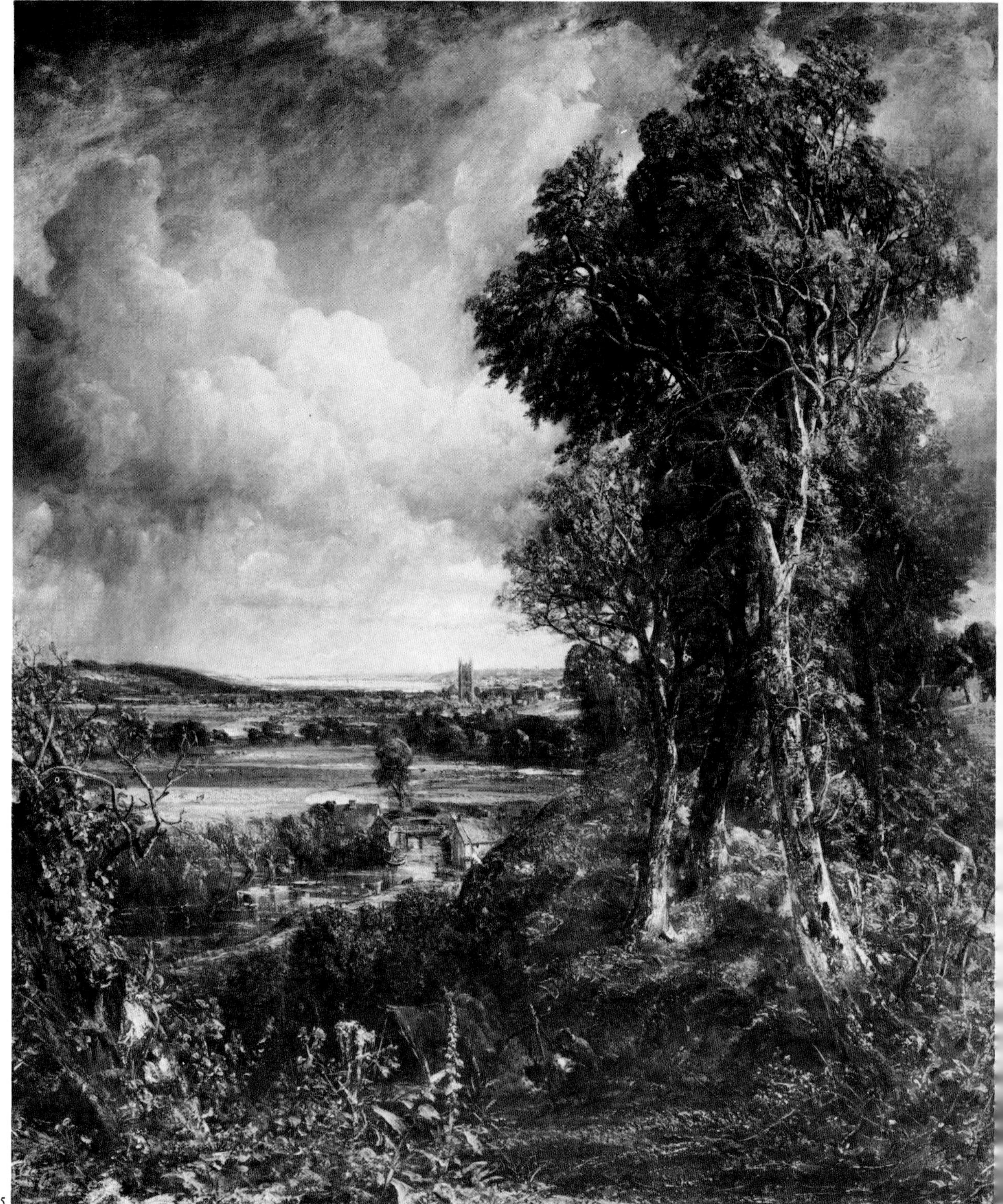

posal other oil-sketches giving a similar view from the hill behind Dedham, of which one, also in the Victoria and Albert Museum, is datable in the period 72
1800–5. This sketch, which is rather odd in style for Constable, includes the bridge spanning the Stour between two cottages—these features being omitted from the picture of 1802. Constable added them to his composition, making them into an effective point of interest in his middle distance, and creating in the red roofs of the cottages an effective foil to the vivid greens 75
of the nearby willows and of other verdure in the same general area of the picture—those dark, cool greens so characteristic of the valley of the Stour. The solitary tree beyond, already recorded in the picture of 1802, was retained, together with the general aspect of Dedham and its church: but the sense of distance is increased, and the church tower rises up more dominantly against the estuary, as the focal point of the design.

As in the case of *The Cornfield*, Constable chose a canvas proportionately wider than that of the picture which was his principal source; and he now opened out the landscape to the left (much in the manner in which he had revealed the meadowlands in *The Hay Wain*) by reducing the prominent tree in the foreground to one of smaller size, and half-withered. At the same time Constable redesigned the large group of trees on the right, giving them greater substance, and again introducing a dying ash-tree, which seems almost to lean for support against the great elm behind it. The majesty now assumed by this principal group of trees is enhanced by the addition of a little vista to their right, leading to a cottage on the hill, and of the figure of the woman nursing her child by a fire in the foreground, which at once enlarges their scale.

The billowing cumulus clouds so beloved of Constable now replace the far less dominant sky of the earlier *Dedham Vale*. We may recall again Constable's words to Fisher: "I have often been advised to consider my Sky as a 'White sheet *drawn behind the Objects*'." But the sky in a landscape, he went on, must be its "key note", "the standard of 'Scale'", and the chief "Organ of Sentiment": "You may conceive then what a '*white sheet*' would do for me, impressed as I am with these notions." The 'white sheet' was a convention inherited from Claude or at least from his imitators: but Constable's aims respecting the new conquests attainable by a "natural painture" had long since made such academic considerations irrelevant. The rather static and timid conception of the early *Dedham* now gives way to a magisterial evocation of windblown skies and quivering trees, whose leaves sparkle in the changing light; and when Constable opened out his landscape to the left, he related it more closely to this majestic sky. The whole composition has, besides, a new firmness of structure and an almost sculptural sense of the relationships of planes and forms within an ample space. The paradox is that the picture executed in London presents the scene with a greater force and immediacy of impact than the picture painted in Constable's studio at East Bergholt within walking distance of the *motif*. The picture was well received at the Academy, and Constable referred to it as "perhaps my best". He was gratified, furthermore, that his other exhibit, the *Hampstead Heath: Branch Hill Pond*, was purchased by Chantrey.

Later paintings

After his wife's death in November 1828 Constable never ceased to wear mourning. A few days before her death Leslie had visited the Constables at Hampstead, and he recollected the occasion in his *Life* of the painter: "She [Maria Constable] was then on a sofa in their cheerful parlour, and although Constable appeared in his usual spirits in her presence, yet before I left the house, he took me into another room, wrung my hand, and burst into tears, without speaking." The dark mood of Constable's late style has long been associated by students of his art with the desolation of spirit which he now felt. The pictures he had painted of the sea and beach at Brighton from 1824 onwards had begun on a happy note, and their freshness and spontaneity anticipate Boudin; but by 1827, when he painted the *Marine Parade and Chain Pier*, another quality was apparent to a discerning friend such as John Fisher. In the following year he advised Constable to put it back on his easel: "Mellow its ferocious beauties," he wrote, "calm your own mind and your sea at the same time, and let in sunshine and serenity." But these "ferocious beauties" were to remain a characteristic feature of Constable's style after his wife's death. "Every gleam of sunshine is withdrawn from me," he wrote in despair. ". . . Can it be wondered at . . . that I paint continual storms?"

In 1829, in this mood, Constable painted the expressive *Hadleigh Castle*, using as a guide a small pencil drawing made fifteen years earlier. Perhaps he remembered, when choosing this wild and unprecedented subject, the words he had written to his future wife after he had visited the spot: "I was always delighted with the melancholy grandeur of a sea shore." It is to this period also that belong those dark sepia-wash sketches of Dedham and the Stour—
among the final evocations, infused with a brooding melancholy, of the 81
scenes of his boyhood—and others in oils, fantastic and almost incredible

in their expressive freedom and daring. There often comes to great masters, in their last years, a capacity for immediate expression; a gift that is bestowed, it would seem, on a few rare spirits, like an accession of wisdom, and which no longer requires the rules and props that must guide youthful endeavour. We find it in late Michelangelo, in late Titian, in late Rembrandt, in late Goya, in late Turner, and not least in late Constable. I would shrink from the attempt to define this phenomenon any further, except to suggest that it never appears to occur without a passage through suffering.

In the years immediately following his wife's death, Constable was much occupied by the preparation of his *English Landscape Scenery*, a collection of mezzotints after his own works which were executed by David Lucas. This publication, which appeared in five parts between 1830 and 1832, had a precedent in Turner's *Liber Studiorum*; the scheme was encouraged by John Fisher (despite his doubts about the appropriateness of black-and-white mezzotint as a means of reproducing the pictures of an artist who depended 44
so much upon colour); and hopes were raised that the publication would do much to establish Constable's reputation. Constable took great trouble with the letter-press and closely supervised Lucas's work, constantly revising and retouching the plates, and in the process impressing upon them the stamp of his anxieties and melancholy states of mind. *English Landscape Scenery* disappointed Constable's expectations, and it scarcely did justice to the full range of his art. Nevertheless he gained some reward in 1832, soon after the publication of the fifth part, when there occurred the famous incident that gave us the expression 'Constable's Country'. Constable described the circumstances in a letter to Lucas:

> In the coach yesterday, coming from Suffolk, were two gentlemen and myself, all strangers to each other. In passing the vale of Dedham, one of them remarked, on my saying it was beautiful, "Yes, sir, this is Constable's country."

In 1829 Archdeacon Fisher and his wife had invited Constable to visit them at Salisbury. He stayed with them there in July and—for the last time—in November, making numerous sketches. The great, brooding, rainbow landscape, *Salisbury Cathedral from the Meadows* (Lord Ashton of Hyde), which Constable exhibited in 1831, was one impressive product of this renewal of close contact with his old friends. But in August of the following year Fisher died suddenly, after a short and painful illness; and it was thereafter to Charles Leslie, his future biographer, that Constable turned for friendship and solace. Yet one senses that the links which had been broken were pressing upon his sensitive nature all the more bitterly. In 1836, Constable exhibited at the Royal Academy for the last time.[6] The works that he showed included a large watercolour of *Stonehenge*, made in 1835, and a major oil-painting, *The Cenotaph*, painted in 1836, a few months before his death.

The sheer power of the *Stonehenge* is extraordinary for a watercolour, and its expression of the pathos of human aspiration on the one hand, and, on the other, of the vastness that lies about us belongs wholly to the Romantic sensibility. From the mysterious monuments of Stonehenge it is a far cry to the genteel monument to Sir Joshua Reynolds, the first President of the Royal Academy, which is the subject of *The Cenotaph*. The monument had been set up by Constable's old friend Sir George Beaumont at Coleorton Hall, and it bears some lines of tribute by Wordsworth. The busts at the sides of the picture are of Michelangelo and Raphael. The exhibition of 1836 was to be the last held at Somerset House before the removal of the Royal Academy to rooms in the National Gallery and eventually to Burlington House. Hence this picture, painted from a small pencil drawing which Constable had made some twenty years earlier. As Constable explained, " I preferred to see Sir Joshua's name and Sir George Beaumont's once more in the catalogue for the last time at the old house." We may see the picture virtually as the epitaph of an age that was passing away; and Constable himself died in the year in which Queen Victoria came to the throne.

Yet still more significance attaches to the one painting that he showed at the Academy exhibition in the previous year and at the British Institution
in 1836—*The Valley Farm*, in the Tate Gallery, which reflects the deepest 76
preoccupations of his working life. For here Constable returned in spirit to Flatford Mill, creating out of his memories, and from the materials supplied by earlier sketches, an epitome of the subject-matter which had been the constant source of his inspiration over the years. The subject is Willy Lott's House, magnified and glorified. The viewpoint is from the river bank to the right of the pond seen in *The Hay Wain*, so that we see the other side of the house. But Constable greatly increased the scale of the house, and introduced windows into the front, while making the cottage-windows at the side more imposing.

A number of earlier studies relate to this composition, exhibited at the Academy in 1835. These include a pencil study in the 1813 sketchbook, two oil-sketches of the general view (both in the Victoria and Albert Museum),
a drawing of about 1802 at the Courtauld Institute of Art, a beautiful oil- 77

sketch of about the same date, in the collection of the Earl of Haddington, a detailed pencil drawing (in the Victoria and Albert Museum) of the ash tree 78
which appears on the right in the Tate Gallery picture, and a pencil and watercolour study of a little girl (inscribed on the mount 'Suffolk Child'; also 79
in the Victoria and Albert Museum), which was used, in reverse, for the figure in the boat.

A further, very late and quite large drawing of an ash tree in the Victoria and Albert Museum seems to have been based upon the earlier drawing, as Graham Reynolds has surmised. Reynolds has also drawn attention to a letter written by Constable on 14 February 1835 to his old friend John Dunthorne, referring to some studies by the younger Dunthorne, who had died three years earlier, in which he made the following request: "If you can lend me two or three of poor John's studies of the ashes in the town meadow, and a study of plants that grew in the lane below Mr Coleman's, near the sprouts which ran into the pond, I will take great care of them and send them safe back to you soon. I am about an ash or two now." These studies—like the drawing of a hay-cart which Constable had requested from Dunthorne when he was painting *The Hay Wain*—were evidently required either as aids to the finishing of the composition or for use in lectures: but otherwise the matter is somewhat obscure. A second large drawing of an ash tree, also in the Victoria and Albert Museum, is a companion-piece to the first, and includes a notice fixed to the trunk, the last word of which is *LAW*. We are reminded of Leslie's account of Constable's last lecture at Hampstead, given on 25 July 1836, in which he says:

> Constable then gave some practical rules for drawing from nature, and showed some beautiful studies of trees. One, a tall and elegant ash, of which he said "many of my Hampstead friends may remember this *young lady* at the entrance to the village. Her fate was distressing, for it is scarcely too much to say that she died of a broken heart. I made this drawing when she was in full health and beauty; on passing some time afterwards, I saw, to my grief, that a wretched board had been nailed to her side, on which was written in large letters: '*All vagrants and beggars will be dealt with according to law.*' The tree seemed to have felt the disgrace, for even then some of the top branches had withered. Two long spike nails had been driven far into her side. In another year one half became paralysed, and not long after the other shared the same fate, and this beautiful creature was cut down to a stump, just high enough to hold the board."

Basil Taylor may be right in supposing that the two drawings of an ash tree

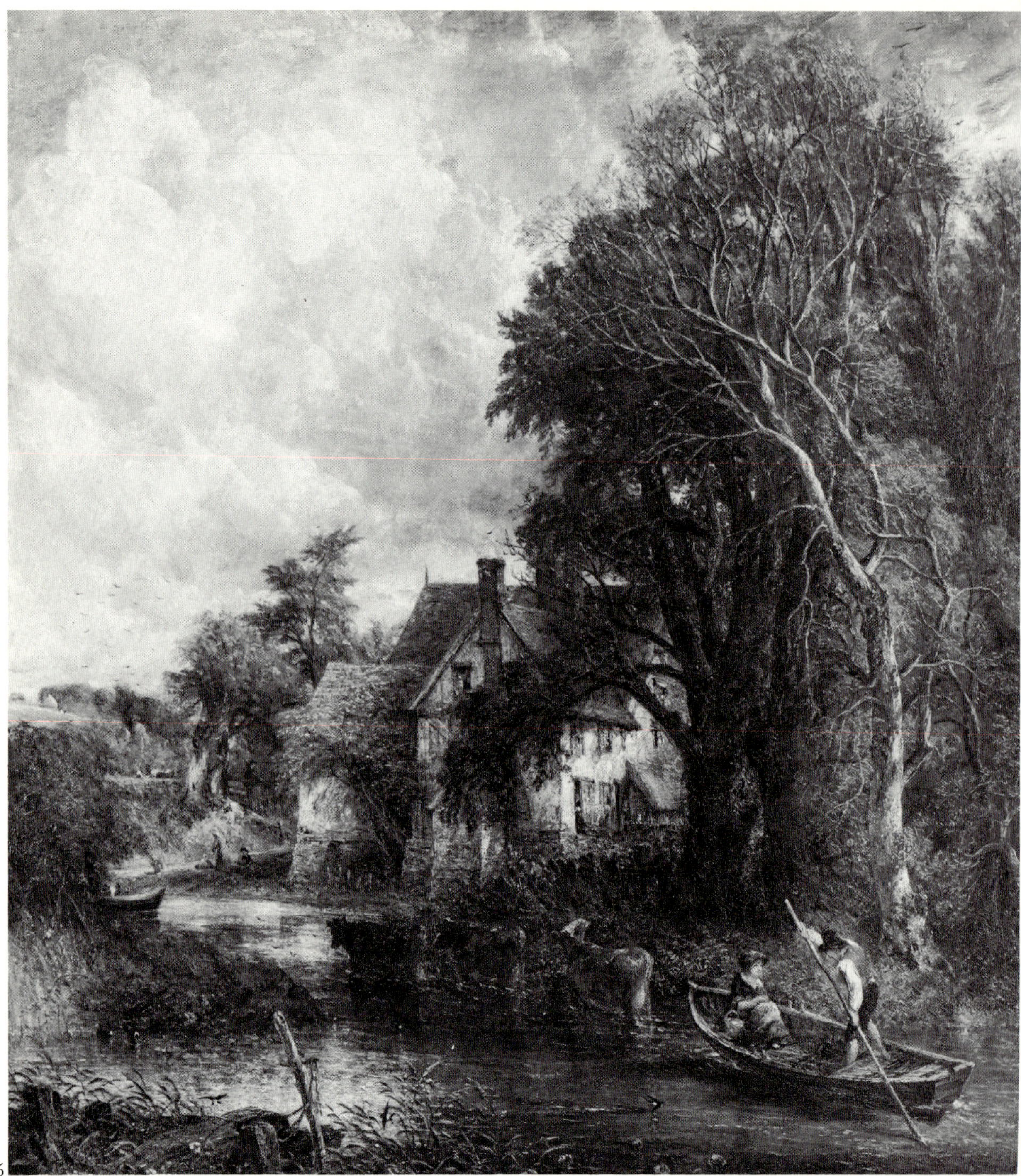

76

The Valley Farm
This is a representation of a magnified and glorified Willy Lott's Cottage seen from downstream (from the river bank to the right of the mill-pond in *The Hay Wain*). There are several preparatory pencil and oil sketches for it, dating from many years earlier, which show how Constable enlarged the house and increased the number of windows. He also did a pencil and watercolour sketch for the girl in the boat (79), a pencil drawing of the ash tree on the right (78), and an expressive oil study of a solitary man poling the boat along (80). A combination of imagination and accuracy characterises this late work, which was perhaps carried out in a period of particular nostalgia for Suffolk in the years before the painter's death. Visitors to the area should be warned that the 'Valley Farm' which appears on Ordnance Survey maps is an entirely different though adjacent building, and was named in this way long after Constable's death.

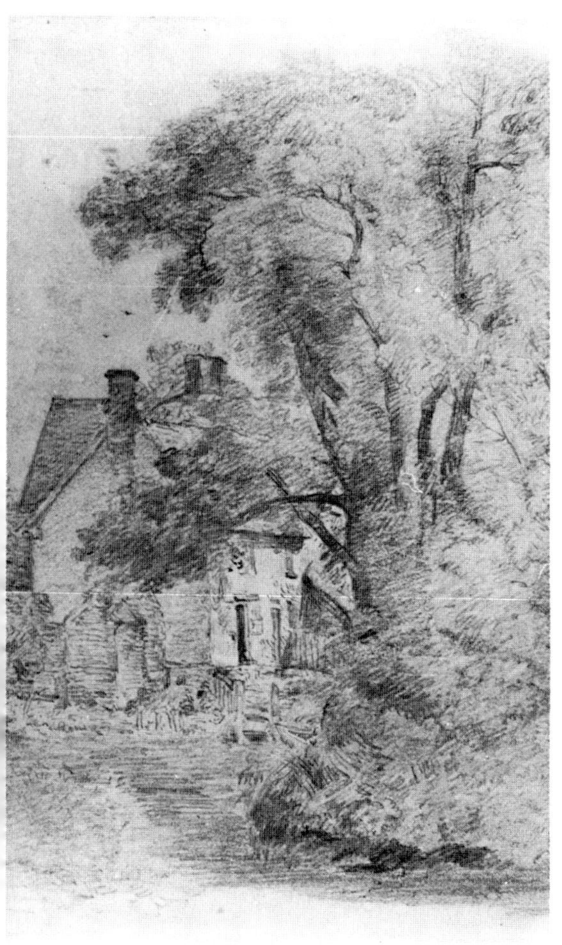

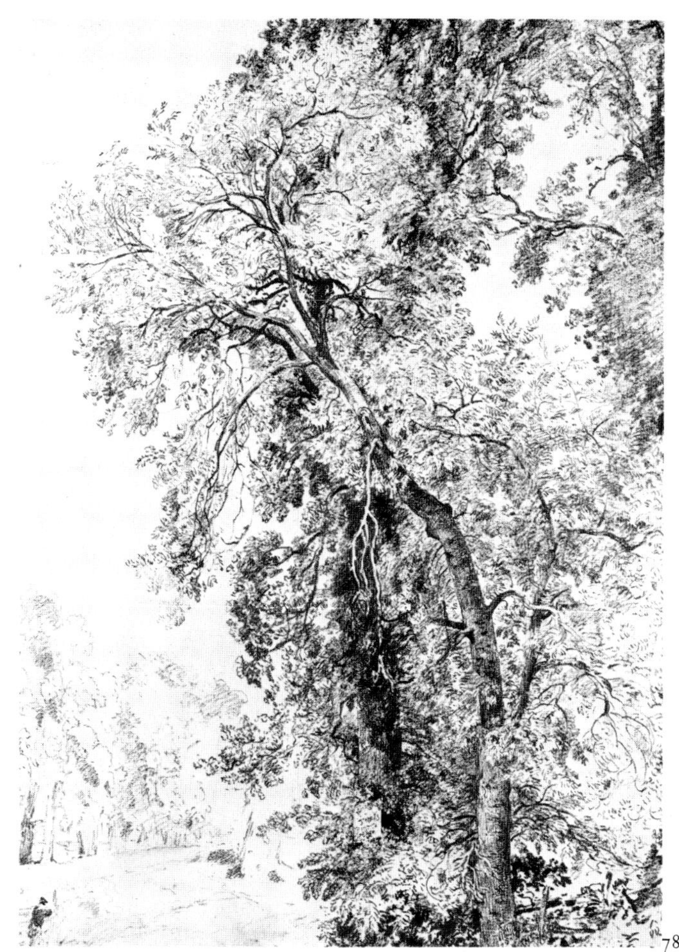

78

80

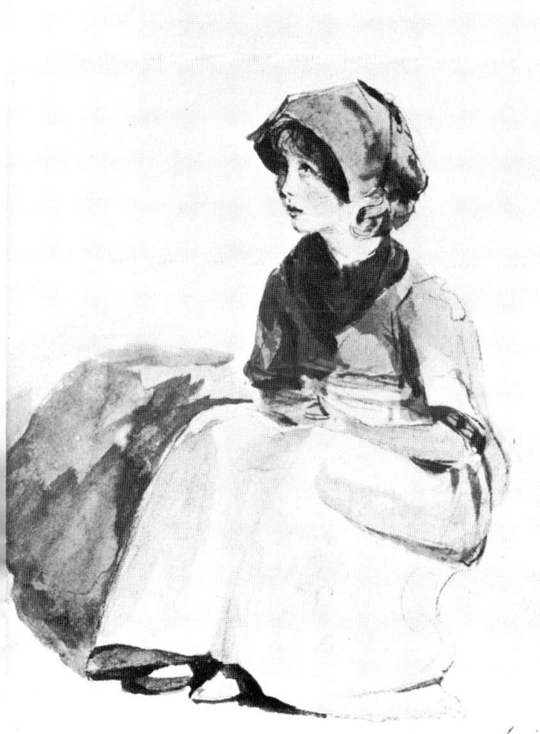

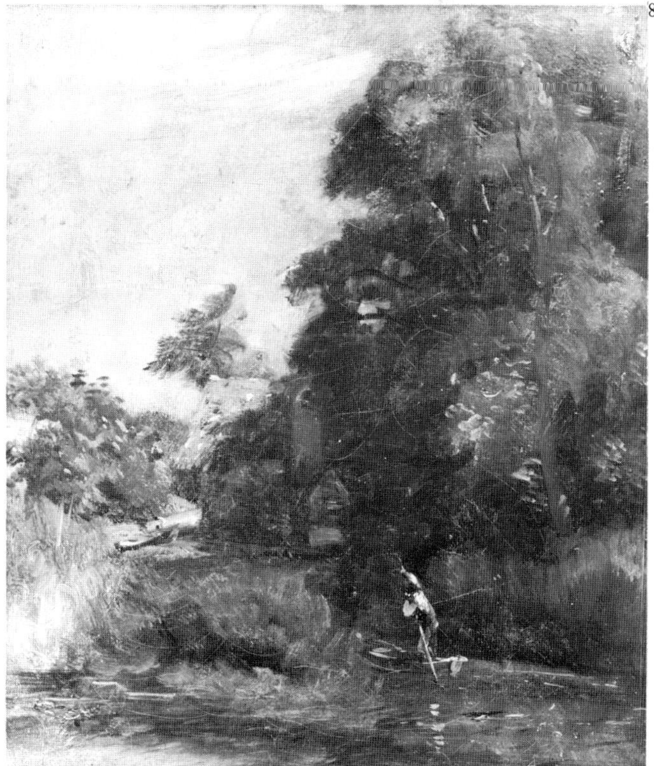

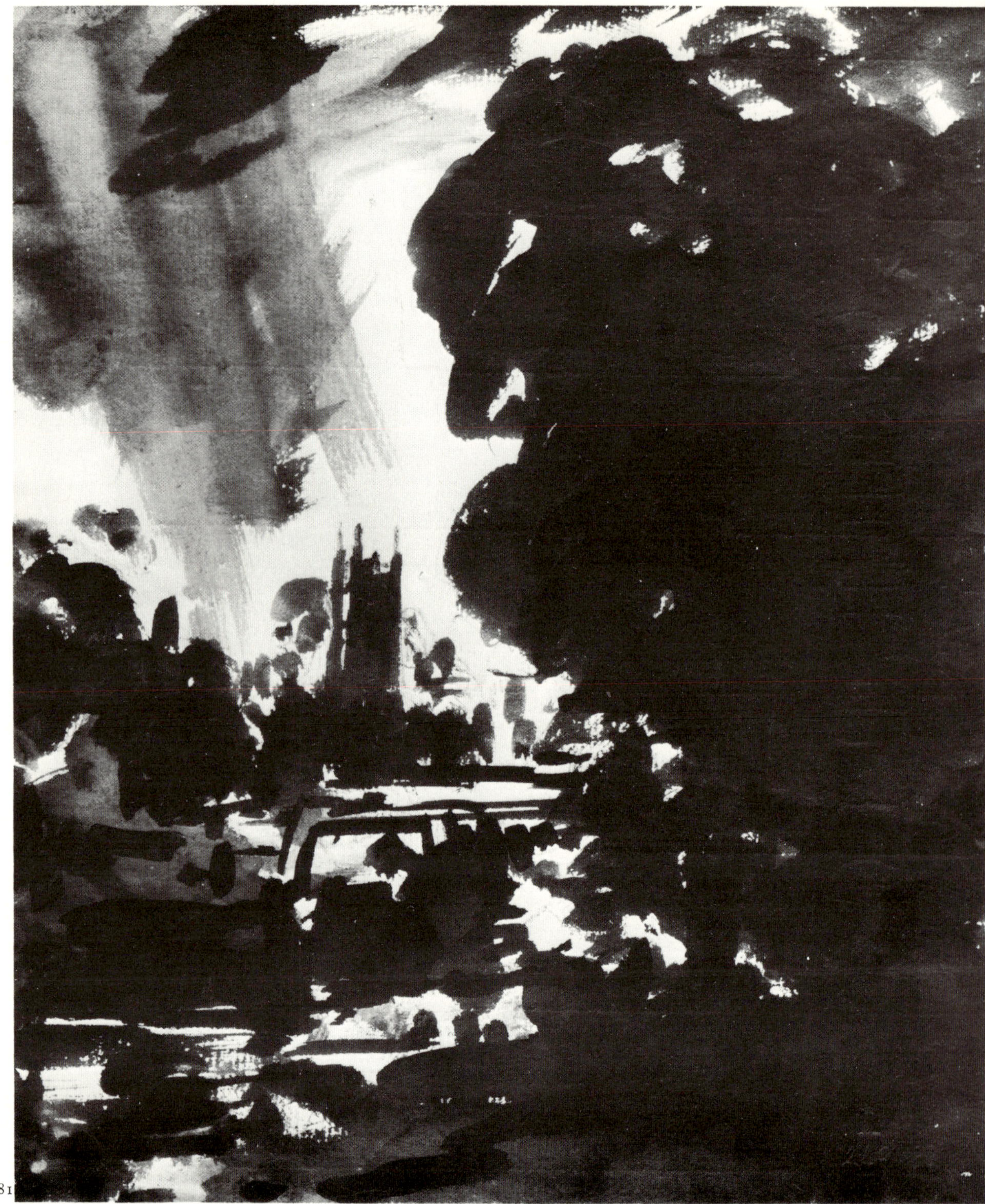

81 *A View on the Stour, Dedham Church* Comparison with *Dedham Lock and Mill* (23) indicates that this expressive study is probably a reworking of that painting. The church tower is seen above the lintel of the lock gate and the right-hand tree is very similar. It is the last work in which he is known to show Dedham Church—the focal point in so many of his great paintings. Graham Reynolds wrote: "These late sepia drawings prove that he did not necessarily require the actual presence of the original subject to inspire some of his most effective and moving renderings of the scenery with which he was most familiar." (*Apollo*, 1972).

that relate to *The Valley Farm* were made at Hampstead; in which case the phrase I have used in describing the great Stour pictures—"Suffolk scenes under Hampstead skies"—requires amplification in this case, in order to embrace so essential a feature of the landscape setting as the dying ash tree. Of course, we know from Frith's *Autobiography* that Constable was accustomed to bring branches, leaves and so forth into his studio when he was at work on a painting, so that much of the detail in the Suffolk compositions would have been studied out from such natural forms, gathered presumably in London or Hampstead. Graham Reynolds has interestingly adduced Frith's evidence in commenting upon a late oil-sketch of foliage in the Victoria and Albert Museum, which he relates in a general way to the foregrounds of such pictures as *The Lock* and *The Leaping Horse*. Frith thus describes his visit, as a youth, to Constable's London studio:

> There was a piece of the trunk of a tree in the room, some weeds, and some dock-leaves. "And what line of the art do you intend to follow?" said Constable to me. "I don't know, Sir," I replied. . . . "Well, whatever it may be," said the great landscape painter, "never do anything without nature before you, if it be possible to have it. See those weeds and the dock-leaves? They are to come into the foreground of this picture. I know dock-leaves pretty well, but I should not attempt to introduce them into a picture without having them before me."

Constable may well have had *The Valley Farm* on his easel when the young Frith called upon him.

The *motif* of the young man punting a girl in a boat occurs already in
The Mill Stream, where the figures are seen from a different angle. With the
help of the watercolour drawing of the young girl and no doubt a further 31
study of the male figure, Constable revised the image; and earlier stages in the
development of his idea can be seen in the oil-sketches of the general view, in
which first a solitary seated man and, then, a standing figure appear in a boat 80
towards the centre of the composition, rather than well to one side as in the finished picture. The scene in the Tate picture is autumnal, and the lighting somewhat bleak. A dark mood reigns over the composition as a whole, as in so many of the works of the final period. Constable now seems to be looking back upon the scenes of his boyhood and youth with an ineffable sadness, through the years of loneliness and bereavement. Although it found a purchaser before it left his studio, the picture was not too well received at the Academy, and Constable returned to work on it after the exhibition had ended, before showing it again at the British Institution.

The Valley Farm, although differing from the earlier Suffolk pictures both in style and in mood, shares with them that striving after a synthesis between his aims as a "natural painter" on the one hand, and his concern with expressive composition on the other, which lies behind all Constable's major works. In the great Suffolk pictures the ordinary and the familiar are elevated towards the sublime; and in them there is reflected, more clearly than in any of Constable's paintings of other subjects, the very processes of his mind, as the scenes of which he formed pictures as a boy, and which he recorded on the spot in his early sketchbooks and studies, are developed in his painting-room into perfected compositions. In the process we become aware that some of these scenes, which *in situ* strike us by their intimacy, have become enlarged by the operation of the painter's imagination. When, in the summer of 1840, Constable's biographer C. R. Leslie visited East Bergholt and Dedham with a mutual friend, William Purton, who was one of the painter's least prejudiced admirers and himself an amateur artist, they were both struck by the verisimilitude of some of the pictures they knew so well and by the artistic licence apparent in others:

We were received at Flatford with the greatest hospitality by Mr Abram Constable and his sisters, and were accommodated with facilities for exploring what to us was classic ground, in which we had the advantage of being accompanied by Constable's eldest son, and his nephew, the Rev. Daniel Whalley. . . . We found that the scenery of eight or ten of our late friend's most important subjects might be enclosed by a circle of a few hundred yards at Flatford, very near Bergholt. . . . So startling was the resemblance of some of these scenes to the pictures of them, which we knew so well, that we could hardly believe we were for the first time standing on the ground from which they were painted. Of others, we found that Constable had rather combined and varied the materials, than given exact views. In the larger compositions, such as "The White Horse" and "The Hay Wain", both from this neighbourhood, he has increased the width of the river to great advantage; and wherever there was an opportunity, he was fond of introducing the tower of Dedham Church, which is seen from many points near Flatford. . . . Travelling is now the order of the day, and it may sometimes prove beneficial—but to Constable's art there can be little doubt that the confinement of his studies within the narrowest bounds in which, perhaps, the studies of an artist ever were confined, was in the highest degree favourable. . . . His ambition, it will be borne in mind, was not to paint many things imperfectly, but to paint a few things well . . . Chiaroscuro . . . was an all-important thing in his estimation. Many artists see it nowhere, but Constable saw it everywhere, and in all its beauty. Why then should he go in quest of subjects, when the spots endeared to him from his infancy, or from the associations of friendship, had not only in general great attractions of their own, but where they had least of beauty could be elevated by this power to sublimity?

Chiaroscuro—it may be added—was only one of the elements of a pictorial language moulded both by the study of Nature and by the lessons of such masters as Claude, Gaspard Poussin, Rubens and Ruisdael, beside whom Constable takes his place within the great European tradition. By the same token, the ideal of Landscape created by Claude and Gaspard from visions of the Roman Campagna, or by Rubens and Ruisdael from their response to the scenery of the Netherlands, has its counterpart in all that Constable drew from a small corner of Suffolk, which even in the artist's lifetime was becoming known as 'Constable's Country'.

Notes

1 Since this passage was written, and at the time that the present book was going through the press, much the same comparison between *The Hay Wain* and the *Château de Steen* has been drawn by Mr Richard Tyler, but in a more extended form: cf. Richard E. G. Tyler, 'Rubens and "The Hay-Wain"', *Connoisseur,* clxxix, 762 (August 1975), 271 ff.

2 The famous sentence at the end of this quotation, together with other parts of the letter, requires some comment. Leslie, in his *Life of Constable*, gave the sentence in the well-known form: "*There is room enough for a natural painter.*" But in the manuscript of the letter—formerly in Lord Plymouth's collection, but now lost—the sentence read: "There is room enough for a natural painture." The spelling "painter" appears, then, to have been due to Leslie—as was the italicization of the whole sentence, as a means of emphasizing this important affirmation of the artist's aims as a painter. The spelling "painture" is given both by Shirley, in his edition of Leslie's *Life*, and by Beckett, in his edition of Constable's correspondence (although Shirley, as Leslie's editor, deliberately preserved the latter's italics).

It is quite usual now to interpret "painture" as meaning a 'style of painting'. Shirley, however, records the same spelling—"painture"—in two other passages in the letter: (1) "... Sir Joshua Reynolds's observation that 'there is no easy way of becoming a good painture'"; and (2) "... the french [*sic*] painture mentioned by Sir J. Reynolds, who told him that he had long ceased to look at nature ..." It is obvious, as Graham Reynolds points out, that in both these instances Constable must have meant 'painter'. On the other hand it should be noted that in each of these two passages Beckett transcribes the word as "painter", giving the spelling "painture" only in the sentence, "There is room enough for a natural painture".

It may be added that elsewhere in the letter such misspellings as "shurest" and "beleive" (the latter being less remarkable than the former) are recorded both by Shirley and by Beckett. I believe that, in the absence of the original manuscript, it is wisest to keep an open mind upon the central question—as to whether Constable meant 'style of painting' or (as Leslie assumed) 'painter'. It would be interesting to know whether the manuscript formerly in the Plymouth collection is in Constable's own hand, since a copyist might perhaps have transcribed "painter" as "painture".

There are two further points relating to this letter that seem to be worth making. First, did Constable mean to say that Nature was "the source from which all *originally* [my italics] must spring" (a passage omitted by Leslie but given both by Shirley and by Beckett)? The word *originality* might appear to make better sense in the context. Possibly there was a slip of the pen here: but without further evidence one can do no more than to raise the question, rather than to advance a definite hypothesis.

Secondly, where according to Beckett (whose version of the letter I again follow here) Constable writes, "I . . . have neither endeavoured to make my performances look as if really executed by other men," Leslie—followed by Shirley and Mayne—gives the following: "I . . . have *rather* [my italics] endeavoured to make my performances . . ." (etc). Beckett's rendering reverses the meaning as Leslie understood it; it is also awkward stylistically: but, in view of Beckett's general reliability, the only strong reason for questioning this reading would be some definite proof that the manuscript itself was in some way faulty.

3 I am deeply obliged to Mr Leslie Parris, Deputy Keeper of the Tate Gallery, for his helpfulness in considering the questions that I put to him about the drawing of 1817 and the problems that seemed to me to be posed by it. *Inter alia*, I raised the question whether any existing X-ray photograph of *Flatford Mill, on the River Stour* had thrown fresh light upon the matter. None then existed, but Mr Parris subsequently arranged for such a photograph to be made at the Courtauld Institute. Unfortunately it does not help with the problem of the 1817 drawing, although it does reveal a painted-out horse. I am grateful to Mr Stephen Rees-Jones, of the Courtauld Institute of Art, and to Mr Parris, for making the photograph available to me for inspection. I defer to Mr Parris's judgment that the drawing cannot be a preparatory study made in advance of the painting, in view of the absence of any suitable 'candidate' for the Academy exhibition of 1817, other than the picture in the Tate Gallery. If, of course, an alternative candidate were to be found, my hypothesis that Constable revised the Tate picture after the 1817 exhibition would not be necessary.

4 It is now generally accepted that Constable would have been acquainted with contemporary scientific inquiries into cloud formations and their classification, and he may well have read Thomas Forster's *Researches about Atmospheric Phenomena* (1812) and Luke Howard's *Climate of London* (1818–20), which opens with an 'Essay on Clouds': on this whole question see Kurt Badt, *John Constable's Clouds* (London, 1950).

5 For Reinagle see Alastair Smart, 'Ramsay Richard Reinagle', *The Antique Collector,* xlvi, 2 (February 1975) and 3 (March 1975). This curious figure among Constable's contemporaries deserves further investigation.

6 The not quite finished *Arundel Mill and Castle* (Toledo Museum of Art), on which Constable was still at work on the day before his death, was hung in the Academy exhibition of 1837 as a memorial to him.

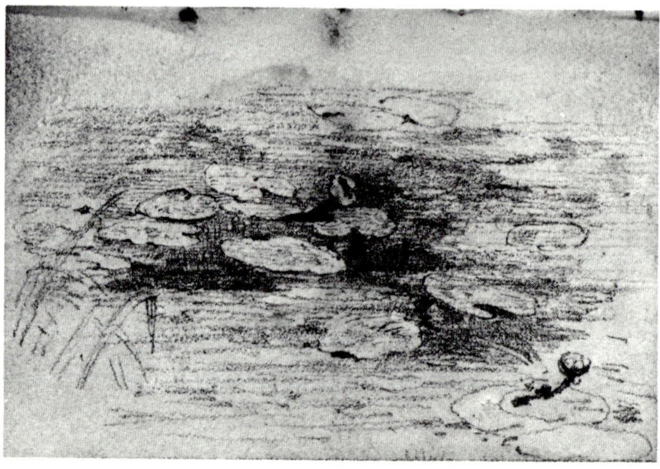

Study of water-lilies from 1813 sketchbook, used later in *The White Horse* and *Stratford Mill.*

Appendix:

further topographical notes

Attfield Brooks

The Hay Wain

There are seven known works and sketches which were available to John Constable for the full-size study and the finished painting of *The Hay Wain*. The topographical feature common to all is Willy Lott's Cottage which can be seen today unchanged in its basic form. The sketches can be broadly classified according to the angle at which the small (northern) gable and the large (western) gable (bisected by the brick chimney) are seen. In this way distraction which might be caused by Constable's variation in the length of the roof line can be avoided. References throughout are to Graham Reynolds's catalogue: see Bibliography.

Three of these:

1 *The Mill Stream*, *c.* 1813–14, Tate Gallery (32)
2 *The Mill Stream*, exh. 1814, Christchurch Mansion, Ipswich (31)
3 *Willy Lott's House*, *c.* 1810–15, V.A.M. GR110a (*verso*) (46)

show the small gable comparatively narrow and the large one comparatively broad, indicating viewpoints on the forecourt of Flatford Mill.

The other four:

4 *Willy Lott's House*, *c.* 1810–15, V.A.M. GR110 (*recto*) (45)
5 *Willy Lott's Cottage*, dated 29 July 1816, Christchurch Mansion, Ipswich (49)
6 Landscape sketch *The Hay Wain*, *c.* 1821, Collection Mr and Mrs Paul Mellon
7 *Willy Lott's House*, *c.* 1830, V.A.M. 329a (*verso*) (47)

all show the small gable broadly and the large gable narrowly, indicating viewpoints through the farmgate and along the track leading to Willy Lott's Cottage and the farm.

Before we embark upon a detailed examination of the topography of each of these seven works there are two general points to be made. First is the relationship of the various channels of water seen in *The Hay Wain*. The main stream entering the picture at the lower right, and flowing across to disappear to the left behind the cottage, is the tail water of the mill, which after passing over the mill-wheel and down the tailrace escaped from the archway under the centre of the Mill courtyard. It broadens out into the pool in which the waggon is standing before running to join the main river down the channel seen clearly in *The Mill Stream* (No 2). The channel (with light on the water above the waggon) was quite shallow and led to the main river which is on this side of the meadows and hidden behind the low bushes. From the point where it joined the river there was a ford across to the meadows. The trees and bushes to the left of the light patch of water were on an island called 'The Spong'. It is recorded in *The Suffolk Stour* by Ambrose Waller (Norman Adland & Co, 1957) that three or four years after the artist's death Abram Constable agreed with the Navigation Authority to the closing of the ford and this channel, on the Authority undertaking to pay fifty shillings per annum forever. This is the reason that many visitors now look in vain to find it. The layout is clearly shown in the reproduction of the East Bergholt Enclosure Award dated 1817 (page 19).

Second is the question of whether the waggon and horses would have been in the water, or is this a piece of artistic licence? Certainly they could have been there for at least two good reasons. The first is that they were about to cross the ford. Haymaking on the far meadows supports this explanation. The alternative is that, in accordance with common local practice, the horses in warm weather were allowed to cool their feet and fetlocks. This was considered to keep the joints in condition and prevent the trouble known as 'grease'. In very dry weather, too, farmers often took waggons and carts into water to keep the wood of the rims from shrinking and allowing the 'fellies' or segments to work loose on each other and from the spokes.

It is convenient to consider Nos 1 and 2 together before proceeding to the others. No 1 is obviously the sketch for No 2 and was probably done on the spot. The view down the stream of the tail water to open meadows on the far side of the river, together with the disturbed water in the centre foreground as compared with quiet water on either side, pinpoints the viewpoint on the Mill forecourt as exactly over the arch where the water escaped from the tailrace of the mill-wheel. In both the water level is neither excessively high nor excessively low so it can be judged to be about a normal level. The glimpse of the far meadows indicates that were it not for the undergrowth and foliage on the right-hand side there would be the opportunity to see much more of them. The same would apply today except for the large flood-protection wall erected about twenty years ago on the far bank of the river. The figure of the girl doing her washing in the river by the fence just to the right of the cottage is not shown in sketch No 1 but is introduced into the finished picture. She also appears in all the other sketches except Nos 3 and 7 where the high water level renders her presence inappropriate.

As No 5 bears a date two years after 1814 when No 2 was probably exhibited, it is likely that it is three years after the painting of No 1. This is the only *dated* work showing Willy Lott's Cottage at almost the same angle as in the finished painting. The tail water, due to the change of viewpoint, now disappears to the left behind the cottage but the meadows are clearly shown because the undergrowth which appeared on the right of Nos 1 and 2 has disappeared. It can be argued that this was a compositional device by the artist, but I prefer the hypothesis that during the three years the undergrowth had been cut. Today such undergrowth is looked upon as a nuisance and is only cleared when it has to be, but 160 years ago it was cared for because when cut, the produce (faggots) was a valuable commodity as fuel for cooking on the old open hearths in cottages and houses, and especially for burning inside the old brick ovens for baking bread, etc. It is worth quoting from the *General View of the Agriculture of the County of Essex*, an official report to the then Board of Agriculture published in 1807, where it records (Vol I, p. 183) hedges "torn up, destroyed and burnt, stake, withers, bushes and all by the destitute poor, who, from deficiency of wages, are utterly unable to purchase fuel and compelled to steal it, or perish with cold". Elsewhere it records woods near Hadleigh Castle where part of the underwood was cut regularly each year at fourteen years' growth, made into faggots and sent to London to produce on an average five guineas an acre—no mean income in those days. The fact that this is a dated sketch probably means that it was executed on the spot, thus strongly supporting this suggestion. The level of water is lower than in any of the other works in this series which may have some bearing on why the sketch was made in the first place.

Turning to No 7 I must record that my first impression on seeing this reproduced in Graham Reynolds's catalogue was "My word, what a flood!" and my immediate thought before consulting the text was "Constable surely worked quickly to make a record of that scene before the water went down". Since then, the facts recorded by Graham Reynolds have been and still are a puzzle, as they seem so at variance with that strong impression. But even he records that here was possibly a return to nature rather than a reworking of No 4. Constable seems to have taken immense care over the painting of the lower half of the sketch especially the water, but the trees seem to have been sketched in far less detail, possibly even rather hurriedly.

Graham Reynolds considers this work to have been used by David Lucas for the engraving *Willy Lott's House* whilst Andrew Shirley takes the sketch No 4 to have been used. However, the engraving does not follow either of them with sufficient exactitude for anyone to be certain. In No 7 the treatment of the trees seems to have some similarity to that of the trees on the left of *Spring, East Bergholt Common* (V.A.M. GR 122) and those in *Stoke by Nayland* (V.A.M. GR 330). Both these were engraved by David Lucas and the treatment of the trees in the three engravings is very different in each case. The two latter were engraved and published during John Constable's life but *Willy Lott's House*, though well advanced, was probably not in its final state before he died. The treatment of the trees by Lucas on this plate seems closer to both No 3 and No 4 than to No 7 and does not, as might be expected, resemble that in *Stoke by Nayland, Suffolk*, although the painting of this resembles No 7 and its engraving seems to follow the painting. The elderberry bush by the cottage differs from the bush shown in all the sketches whilst the water level most resembles that in No 3. The figure to the right of the house is also quite different in the engraving. Neither in this sketch nor in the engraving is there any sign of the far meadows which are quite hidden by the undergrowth.

The next sketch, No 4, is from almost if not quite the identical viewpoint as No 7, but here the similarity ends. It is a very peaceful scene of a quiet summer day with the river at a very low level, though not quite as low as in No 5, which again is from the same viewpoint. The foliage is low, showing the meadows. The 'path' described by Graham Reynolds along which the dog is trotting appears more likely to be the gravelly shelving bank of the river exposed because of the low water level. The outline of the trees in the engraving seems to have been taken from this sketch rather than any of the others.

Before leaving this viewpoint which is virtually the same as that used for *The Hay Wain* itself, it is preferable to consider No 6. This is clearly a first essay for the whole composition. In the centre the foliage seems perhaps low enough to show the far meadows, but on the right they are completely obscured. The water level seems to be about the same as in No 5, that is to say about normal. The figure of the woman to the right of the cottage is shown and the waggon appears for the first time. The sketch, which appears to be a studio work does not seem to have any other topographical features worth noting. There is in the Paul Mellon collection another sketch, oil on panel size 7½in × 12in (19cm × 30.5cm), which foreshadows the final composition very closely.

Finally No 3 returns to a viewpoint close to that of Nos 1 and 2 but slightly to the left. The swirl of the water escaping from the tailrace at the right lower corner indicates a viewpoint still on the mill forecourt rather than on to the farm track. The foliage is low, allowing slight glimpses of meadows at the far end of the tail water and under the right-hand tree. The water is high, though not as high as in No 7. This sketch is on the verso of No 4 and Graham Reynolds considers both were painted about the same time as or just before Nos 1 and 2.

The next question is the relationship of these seven works to each other and to *The Hay Wain* itself. The first point is that Nos 1 and 2 seem to form a pair without any direct relationsip to *The Hay Wain*, which they antecede by seven years. No 7 may also date from approximately this period as all three show the considerable growth of bushes and undergrowth that is absent from the others. Thus far the conclusions are fairly obvious, though in the case of No 7 it is possible that it could have been done some nine or more years after the bushes began to grow again, i.e. well after the completion of *The Hay Wain*. The dated sketch No 5 may well be the first real germ of *The Hay Wain*. Its very close relationship with the left-hand side of the finished painting has already been pointed out. No 4 does not somehow seem to have the immediacy of a sketch done on the spot. No 5 must, it seems, be contemporary or very nearly so with No 4, though having greater immediacy, but it cannot compare in this respect with No 7. Can it therefore be that Nos 3–4 were done in the studio to assist Constable in making up his mind whether his great picture should be a composition based on a rather livelier version of *The Mill Stream* (No 2) or a rather quieter version of No 5? Stylistically this solution may not be completely satisfactory but topographically it has its attraction. Be that as it may, No 6 and the larger sketch, both in the Paul Mellon Collection, are clearly adjuncts to the composition Constable adopted.

So far consideration has really been confined to the left-hand half of *The Hay Wain*. The right-hand side poses two questions in today's conditions: were the meadows really visible from the viewpoint; and had the artist any material available to him when he was painting? So far as the possibility of seeing the meadows is concerned I certainly seem to remember standing near Willy Lott's Cottage some forty or so years ago and seeing at least glimpses of them where now all is hidden by undergrowth, and I have never had the least doubt that this was possible at least sometimes. Memory is fickle, but Sir Martin Davies writing in the second edition (1959) of the National Gallery catalogue of the British School describes the viewpoint of *The Hay Wain*, "whence still there is something of a view across the flat valley". Of course, as mentioned earlier, there is now an additional obstacle to a view of the meadows in the form of a flood-protection wall erected after the very severe East Coast Tidal Flood of 31 January 1953. In addition to causing 119 deaths and making 21,000 people homeless in Essex alone, the salt water flooded land at Flatford and killed off many splendid trees. So this new flood wall is very substantial and almost the same height as the top of Flatford Lock; quite enough to prevent a glimpse of Constable's view in the future even if the bushes are cut down.

No drawings or sketches of the meadows to the right of *The Hay Wain* viewpoint are now known, though as there is no outstanding special feature there may be one or more awaiting recognition. However, it must be remembered that *Boat-building near Flatford Mill* was taken from less than 200 yards away and the angle of view is such that the meadows on the left of that painting are the same as those on the right of *The Hay Wain*. *Boat-building* was exhibited at the R.A. in 1815, but Constable still had it later on as it was included in the sale by the Executors on 16 May 1838. There was also the sketch on p.37 of his 1814 sketchbook, as well as p. 25 and p. 61 of very similar areas.

So, to sum up, *The Hay Wain* is a marvellous artistic composition of topographical realities so blended as to be one of the most satisfying of works of any age to the lover of typical English countryside.

View on the Stour near Dedham

The title of this great painting, obviously originally given because of the recognisable tower of Dedham Church as a focal point, is rather misleading as to its location which is at Flatford just below the little dock where the barges were built. Graham Reynolds pointed out that the sketch on p. 52 (54) of Constable's 1814 sketchbook (V.A.M. GR 132) which like the painting and its full-size study shows Dedham Church, Flatford Bridge and Bridge Cottage, but does not cover the left side of the painting, was used by Constable seven years later for this work. The foreground of the sketch is however rather indistinct, but when compared with pp. 27 (53) and 59 (55) its significance becomes very much clearer. That on p. 59 shows the bow of a barge previously thought to be in the river: but close examination reveals that it is in fact a barge being built, as shown on p. 57 but seen almost at right-angles. The figures on the right of p. 59 are on Flatford Bridge and the dark shadow in the centre foreground of this page and pp. 27 and 52 becomes clearly recognisable as the barrier which is keeping the water out of the little dock. So pp. 27 and 52 are both seen to be sketches very closely connected with the composition of the final painting, though in this the artist has substituted different trees on the far bank of the river. The 'bank with cows' in p. 27 which Graham Reynolds describes is now seen to be Flatford Bridge and this appears probably to be a very good example of Constable following the advice given to him some twenty years before by J. T. Smith: "Do no sit about inventing figures for a landscape taken from Nature: for you cannot remain an hour in any spot, however solitary, without the appearance of some living thing that will in all probability accord better with the scene and time of day than any invention of your own." The cow, albeit facing the opposite direction, appears again in the full-size study and in Lucas's engraving of the work, while the exhibited painting has a man instead. The view of Dedham Church and the meadows is now completely obscured by willow trees and ivy-covered stumps and beyond the bridge overgrown pollard willows shut out the bends in the river. However, careful study of the map and a walk along the towpath reveal how accurately Constable has shown the course of the river and the shape of the distant hills. The right foreground shows an 'eel-pritch' resting on the barrier of the little dry dock which he has thickened up to form a pathway.

However, this was not the end of the matter, for in October 1827, five and a half years after *View on the Stour near Dedham* was exhibited, John Constable spent a holiday at Flatford and whilst there made a series of sketches in a sketchbook which has since been dismembered. There are fifteen pages from this book recorded by Graham Reynolds in his catalogue, eleven of them being in the Victoria and Albert Museum, two in the British Museum, one in the National Gallery of Ireland, Dublin, and one in a private collection. At least three of these have been shown by modern photographs to be exceedingly accurate (including *Flatford Old Bridge and Bridge Cottage on the Stour*) (70). Others are very recognisable including the one in Dublin which has the misleading title of *Flatford Lock with Flatford Old Bridge and Bridge Cottage* (57). The viewpoint of this is almost identical to that used for this great painting but just a few feet further from the river so that the structure in the foreground, mistakenly described as Flatford Lock, can easily be recognized as the barrier of the barge-building dock. All the other basic topographical features of the painting, the course of the river, Dedham Church tower, Flatford Bridge and Bridge Cottage are clearly visible in their correct relationship to each other. However, there is considerably greater growth of trees and bushes on both sides of the river as compared with the pages of the 1814 sketchbook of thirteen years before, from which it is likely that the painting was developed. The artist inscribed this drawing "Flatford Octr. 5 1827" and there is every reason for assuming that it accurately represents the scene on that day.

The Lock

In the original vertical version (private collection) of *The Lock* (1824) there is a barge in the lock itself which is full of water and a man is operating the shutter in the gate to release it. Dedham Church is seen across the meadows in the correct location. There are large trees on the right in which the wind is blowing and the sky is full of billowing cloud. Constable then made several versions of this painting and changed the format to horizontal. One which he painted for a dealer in 1826 he was able to get back in 1829 for presentation to the R.A. as his diploma work. He made several changes without losing the basic topography of the scene. The barge is now moored on the left to a post below the lock, waiting while the water escapes ready for it to enter and proceed upstream. The man operating the lock is in a different stance, the trees have been changed to ashes or willows and are much smaller, there is a stormier sky with a shower to the left, whilst the horizontal format allows the scene to be extended to include the upstream gate of the lock above which Flatford Bridge and Bridge Cottage appear.

Apart from the full-size study for the exhibited painting, few if any preliminary sketches are known at the present time. The oil-sketch *Barges on the Stour* (V.A.M. GR 104) *c.* 1811 is from a very similar viewpoint looking slightly further to the left. Another in sepia, reproduced in *John Constable R.A.* by Hon. Andrew Shirley (Medici 1944), is horizontal in format and appears related to such versions. There is also a pencil drawing in the British Museum (59), but this was done during his visit to Flatford in October 1827 when the various versions had all been completed. To judge from the accuracy of detail in other drawings from the sketchbook he used on that occasion, this one shows that the basic details in the diploma work represent the scene in a very realistic manner.

Flatford Lock appears in many of Constable's sketches, drawings and paintings from many different angles. What is curious is that the lintels over the lock gates appear and disappear in them with no apparent consistency over any given period. In this study it is seen in *Flatford Mill from a Lock on the Stour,* 1811 (I), *Boat-building near Flatford,* 1814 (33), *Flatford Mill on the Stour,* 1817 (35) and the two sketches of trees (37–38), *The Lock* 1826 (58) and the drawings of 1827 (2, 59). Plate I and 58 show no lintels whereas all the others show them very clearly. There are at least ten or twelve others which are almost equally divided between the two types, and the sepia sketch for *The Lock*, referred to above, is unique in that it shows a lintel to the posts below the lower gate but not above the gates themselves. Sketches presumably made on the spot both in oil and in the sketchbooks used in 1813, 1814, and 1827 are all more or less evenly divided. In some of them, like *The Lock* (58) for example, it is easy to see that lintels would seriously interfere with the composition, as is confirmed by comparison with *Barges on the Stour* which does have them. They do not interfere in this oil-sketch because of the slightly different viewpoint and angle of view. In others, however, such as the drawing *Lock on the Stour* (V.A.M. GR 293), which omit them, it is difficult to see that they would have interfered very seriously. This was contemporary with *Men loading a barge*, which shows the lintels (2).

The most likely solution appears to be that in Constable's early days the lock was not in very good repair and there were no lintels. The oil-sketch *Flatford Mill from a Lock on the Stour* assigned to 1811 seems to date from this period. The lock may have been repaired about this time, and *Barges on the Stour* which is assigned to the same year may have been the first to show it in the fresh state. Thereafter it seems, from the 1813 and 1814 sketchbooks as well as the other works, he showed the lock in whichever state suited his subject best. It is doubtful if this conundrum can ever be resolved with certainty.

The Leaping Horse

Unlike *The Cornfield*, this painting has never been associated by the artist's son or anyone else with a specific site. Dedham Church tower, on the right-hand side of the exhibited painting, is an obvious addition for balancing the composition, as it does not appear in the full-scale sketch in the Victoria and Albert Museum. The other main clue is the sluice—or weir—where water is escaping from the main course of the river to a lower channel. There are not many such weirs left today, so it seemed likely to me that this one may be the sluice at the spot where the old river channel, forming the county boundary between Suffolk and Essex, leaves the navigable river between the site of New Fen Bridge and Dedham. Naturally the barges were required to go to the mill to load flour—hence this sluice.

The full-size study (51) for the painting in the Victoria and Albert Museum gives possible help in establishing the facts. Amongst the trees near the right-hand edge there are some brush marks of red which can be possibly taken as indicating a low building such as Flatford Mill seen through the trees. Flatford Mill cannot be seen if one stands near the existing sluice, but its general direction is obvious and can be confirmed from the map. Furthermore the course of the river conforms to that shown by the artist in both the study and the exhibited painting. However, there is no sign in either of New Fen Bridge, which he knew so well. It seems to be masked by the horse or its rider. When we examine one of the two chalk and ink wash sketches in the British Museum it will be found that in one of them (63), whose viewpoint is perhaps a yard or two further left and nearer the river, the bridge appears quite clearly behind the horse. In the photograph taken on 23 February 1975 (61) the site where the bridge stood is just over the posts at the right-hand edge of the sluice. Water still flows through the new sluice into the old river channel which was rather narrowed with spoil when the river was dredged in about 1940. The horse-chestnut tree growing on its banks is probably around seventy years old. The left-hand side of the painting and the sketches do not form part of this scene. The river does not widen out and there are no grounds for thinking that large trees existed at this spot. But the evidence for the site set out above appears conclusive as regards that area of the painting to which it refers.

Dedham Vale 1828

This great painting is one of the most interesting of all Constable's works from a topographical point of view. The view from the hills bordering the Stour Valley, between Langham Church and Gun Hill, Dedham, is one that interested John Constable from his earliest days. The series of four watercolours which he presented as a wedding present to Lucy Hurlock in 1800 were done at the eastern end of these hills and included one overlooking Dedham Church and the estuary (14). The other three watercolours are now in the Victoria and Albert Museum. Two years later in 1802 he executed the small oil painting *Dedham Vale 1802*, also in the Victoria and Albert Museum (27), which obviously laid the foundation for the great picture of 1828, now at Edinburgh; he also drew from almost the same spot pencil sketches now in Cambridge and Florence, and painted at least three horizontal versions in oil of the scene. These are undated but are variously assigned to the period between 1800 and 1810.

One of them *The Valley of the Stour with Dedham in the distance*, now in the Victoria and Albert Museum (73), is particularly detailed in its portrayal of the topography. The two buildings on either side of the river bridge are still in existence, that on the right-hand side being Le Talbooth Restaurant. This building lines up with Dedham Church tower in the distance and the other building lines up with the stretch of river and Dedham Mill beyond it; and these two converging lines give an indication as to the viewpoint on the ground. By plotting these lines on a large-scale map it is possible to find the location of this viewpoint, but unfortunately it is in the middle of a wood which has grown up since Constable's time and is now carefully preserved for pheasants. From the map it is obvious that Constable has portrayed quite accurately all the bends in the river as well as many other features of the landscape. A visit to the spot with the permission of the owner at a time when the leaves were not on the trees enabled glimpses to be obtained which confirmed the line-up of the buildings previously indicated, but no possibility existed of a proper view of the scene. In 1971, however, Major Alan Bower of Colchester kindly took a photograph from a helicopter hovering above the area. The extraordinary accuracy of Constable's painting is clearly shown by this photograph. Although the trees have naturally changed considerably since Constable's time, the hedgerows, the river, the fields and the outline of the estuary in the distance are all the same. The old wooden bridge was, of course, replaced long ago and a reinforced concrete bridge built about fifty years ago, designed to cope with the heavy traffic between London, Ipswich and Yarmouth, stands in its place. Close behind, the new dual-carriageway, constructed in 1965, really affects the scene surprisingly little.

It is worth enumerating some of the identifiable features of this painting. Above the left-hand cottage, Dedham Mill is clearly seen in the middle distance. Further away still, a windmill is visible which has been identified as a mill which stood in the parish of Brantham, close to the edge of the estuary. Across on the opposite shore of the estuary Wrabness Point, almost nine miles away, can be clearly spotted, and then further to the right, near Dedham Church tower, can be seen the wooded hill of Mistley, below which in Constable's day wooden ships were built. The white structure of Mistley Church, designed by Robert Adam, of which the two towers still remain, is very clearly identifiable. Dedham Church tower, standing up amongst the roofs of the houses of the village is, as in so many works of Constable, a prominent feature and accurately portrayed. In the far distance to the right of the church tower, Manningtree Township can be identified. The white building to the right of Dedham village is Dedham Assembly Rooms which are now the Hewitt Memorial Hall at the village. These are just a few of the readily identifiable features of the landscape.

Although the 1802 painting does not give as detailed a representation of the landscape, the essential features such as the river bends, the church tower and Mistley Church, and the estuary in the distance, are all there quite accurately. To return to the 1828 picture there is not so much detail of hedges in the nearer meadows bordering the river, but greater and accurate detail in the village and the church tower. The Dedham Assembly Rooms stand out particularly clearly. Mistley Church, too, with Manningtree Township, is very detailed; and there is an additional feature which appears in none of the other paintings, the windmill on the far skyline, almost above Dedham Assembly Rooms. This mill is of particular interest to the author as it was bought by his family in the 1880s and used for grinding animal food. Although the machinery and sails were dismantled the structure still stood until after the First World War. Constable has placed it in the correct geographical position. So this great painting, which Constable himself described to his friend Archdeacon Fisher as "perhaps my best", in addition to being by any standards a great work of art does retain nevertheless the highest degree of topographical accuracy.

Selected bibliography

C. R. Leslie, *Memoirs of the Life of John Constable, R.A.* (London, 1843; 2nd edition, 1845)

C. R. Leslie, *Memoirs of the Life of John Constable, R.A.*, edited and enlarged by the Hon. Andrew Shirley (London, 1937)

C. R. Leslie, *Memoirs of the Life of John Constable, R.A.*, edited by J. H. Mayne (London, 1951)

The Letters of John Constable, R.A., to C. R. Leslie, R.A., edited by Peter Leslie, with an introduction by Sir Charles Holmes (London, 1931)

John Constable's Correspondence, edited by R. B. Beckett (six volumes, Suffolk Records Society, the first volume jointly with H.M.S.O., 1962–8) (Suffolk Records Society, vols. IV, VI, VIII, X, XI, XII)

John Constable's Discourses, compiled and annotated by R. B. Beckett (Suffolk Records Society, vol. XIV, 1970)

Hon. Andrew Shirley, *The Published Mezzotints by David Lucas after Constable* (Oxford, 1930)

C. J. Holmes, *Constable and his Influence on Landscape Painting* (London, 1902)

Sir Kenneth Clark [Lord Clark], *John Constable: 'The Hay Wain' in the National Gallery, London* (The Gallery Books, no. 5, London, 1944)

Martin Davies, *The National Gallery Catalogues: British School* (London, 1946) (including entries on works since transferred to the Tate Gallery); 2nd edition (revised) (London, 1959)

Charles Johnson, *The Growth of Twelve Masterpieces* (London, 1947)

S. J. Key, *John Constable: his Life and Work* (London, 1948)

Kurt Badt, *John Constable's Clouds* (translated by Stanley Godman) (London, 1950)

Mary Chamot, 'The Constable Room at the Tate Gallery', *Connoisseur*, cxxxvii (May 1956), 258 ff.

Michael Kitson, 'John Constable, 1810–1816: a chronological study', *Journal of the Warburg and Courtauld Institutes*, xx (1957), 338 ff.

Lawrence Gowing, *Constable* (New York, 1960)

Graham Reynolds, *Victoria and Albert Museum: Catalogue of the Constable Collection* (London, 1960; 2nd edition, 1973)

Phoebe Pool, *John Constable* (London, 1964)

Basil Taylor, *Painting in England, 1700–1850: Collection of Mr and Mrs Paul Mellon* (Museum of Fine Arts, Richmond, Virginia, 1963)

Carlos Peacock, *John Constable, the Man and his Work* (London, 1965)

Graham Reynolds, *John Constable, the Natural Painter* (London, 1965)

John Hayes, 'The Drawings of George Frost (1745–1821)', *Master Drawings*, iv (1966), 163 ff.

John Baskett, *Constable Oil Sketches* (London, 1966)

Charles Rhyne, 'Fresh Light on John Constable', *Apollo*, lxxxvii, 73 (March 1968), 227 ff.

John Sunderland, *Constable* (London, 1971; 2nd edition, 1972)

Leslie Parris and Conal Shields, *Constable: The Art of Nature* (exhibition catalogue, Tate Gallery, London, 1971)

Ian Fleming-Williams, 'A Runover Dungle and a Possible Date for "Spring" ', *Burlington Magazine*, cxiv, 831 (June 1972), 386 ff.

Conal Shields and Leslie Parris, *John Constable 1776–1837* (Tate Gallery, London, 1973)

Basil Taylor, *Constable: Paintings, Drawings and Watercolours* (London, 1973)

Richard E. G. Tyler, 'Rubens and "The Hay Wain" ', *Connoisseur*, clxxix, 762 (August 1975), 271 ff.

Luke Herrmann and Felicity Owen, *Sir George Beaumont of Coleorton, Leicestershire* (Leicester Museum and Art Gallery, n.d.)

E. H. Gombrich, *Art and Illusion: A Study in the Psychology of Pictorial Representation* (London, 1960; 3rd edition, 1968)

Ambrose J. R. Waller, *The Suffolk Stour* (Ipswich, 1957)

A. F. J. Brown, *Essex People, 1750–1900, from their diaries, memoirs and letters* (Essex Record Office Publications no. 49) (Essex County Council, Chelmsford, 1972)

Index

Plates are indicated by italic type

Adam, Robert, 140, *5*
Algarotti, Count, 39, 51
Allen, Thomas, 39
Angerstein, John Julius, 66
Arrowsmith, John, 60

Barbizon School, 35, 61 f.
Beaumont, Sir George, 43 f., 47, 49, 53 f., 80, 83, 109, 126
Bicknell, Charles, 57 f., 60, 118
Bicknell, Maria (wife of Constable), 14, 52 f., 55, 57 ff., 60, 81, 118 f., 124, *29*
Boucher, François, 45
Boudin, Eugène, 124
Brantham, 21, 74
Brighton, 36, 54, 104, 107, 114, 118 f., 124

Cattawade, 21
Chantrey, Sir Francis, 118, 124
Claude Gellée (*or* Lorrain), 37, 44, 46, 49 f., 53 f., 66, 90, 100, 113, 123, 133; *28*
Coleorton Hall, 44, 113, 126
Constable family: Abram (J.C.'s brother), 38, 56, 77, 91, 119, 132; Anne (J.C.'s mother), 43, 49, 57, 91; Capt. Charles (J.C.'s son), 108, 111; Golding, snr. (J.C.'s father), 13 f., 17, 20, 31 f., 37 ff., 43, 56, 59, 73, 83, 91, *3*; Golding, jnr. (J.C.'s brother), 38; Maria (J.C.'s wife), *see under* Maria Bicknell
Constable, John, Works by: *Arundel Mill and Castle,* 135; *Autumnal Sunset, 1,* 27, *16; Boat-building near Flatford Mill,* 12, 66 ff., 72. 101 f., 137, *33*; studies for, 68, *34*; *Branch Hill Pond, Hampstead,* 77, 79 f., 119, 124, *44*; *The Cenotaph,* 125 f.; *Christ blessing Little Children/Bread and Wine,* 54; cloud studies, 79, 80 f., 134, *43*; *The Cornfield,* 21, 33, 36, 38, 44, 46, 50, 52, 65, 88, 98, 107 ff., 123, *64, IV*; paintings and studies related to, 107 ff., *23, 65, 67, 69*; *A Cottage,* 100; *A Country Lane,* 107 ff., *65*; *Dedham Church and Vale,* 26, *14*; *Dedham Lock and Mill,* 32, 83, *22*; *Dedham Vale* (1802), 44, 49, 54, 107, 113, 119, 121, 123, *27*; *Dedham Vale* (1828), 21, 33 f., 52, 54, 88, 94, 113, 119 ff., 139, *74, 75*; *Dedham Vale, Morning* (1811), 16, 28, 43, 55, 109, *18*; *Dedham Vale with a Ploughman,* 68; *East Bergholt Church,* 24, *12*; *East Bergholt Street,* 23, *10*; drawings of Flatford (1827), 101, 138, *2, 57, 59, 70*; *Flatford Mill from a Lock on the Stour* (V & A), 12, 63, 139, *I*; (R.A.), 63; *Flatford Mill, on the River Stour* (1817), 12, 34, 55, 68 ff., 91, 93 ff., 96 f., 101 f., 134, *35*; studies related to, 69, 70 f., 134, *37, 38*; *Flatford Old Bridge and Bridge Cottage,* 117, 138, *70*; *The Glebe Farm,* 118; views of Golding Constable's garden, 14, 68, *4*; *Hadleigh Castle,* 124; paintings of Hampstead Heath (see also *Branch Hill Pond*), 47, 89, 119; *The Hay Wain,* 21, 31 ff., 36, 42, 46 f., 52, 55 f., 61, 63 ff., 73, 76, 80 ff., 94 ff., 102, 107, 114, 123, 126 ff., 132 ff., 135 ff., *30, 48, II*; studies related to, 81 ff., 135 ff., *45, 46, 47, 49, 51*; X-ray photograph of, 84, *48*; *Helmingham Park,* 41, 112, 113, *23*; *The Leaping Horse,* 12, 21, 52, 81, 102 ff., 131, 139, *60*; studies for, 102. ff., 105, *62, 63*; *A Lock on the Stour with Dedham Church in the distance* (1827 drawing), 99, 101 f., 138 f., *59*; *The Lock* (1824 and 1826 compositions), 52, 94, 97, 98 ff., 101, 102, 131, 138 ff., *58*; *Malvern Hall,* 55; *Men loading a barge* (1827 drawing), 12, 102, *2*; *Marine Parade and Chain Pier, Brighton,* 118, 124; *A Mill at Gillingham,* 116; *The Mill Stream,* 56 f., 64 ff., 81, 84, 87 f.; 116, 131, 135 ff., *31*; study for, 64 f., 135 ff., *32*; Mistley river scenes (drawings), 14, 16, *5, 6*; *A Road near Dedham,* 107; *Salisbury Cathedral from the Bishop's Grounds,* 48, 98, *25*; *Salisbury Cathedral from the Meadows,* 125; self-portrait drawing, 22, *9*; sketchbooks of 1813 and 1814, 55 f., 68 ff., 73, 76 f., 91 ff., 109, 126, 137 f., *1, 34, 37, 53, 54, 55, 82*; *Spring, East Bergholt Common,* 136; *Stoke-by-Nayland,* 125 f., 136; *Stonehenge,* 126; *The Stour Valley and Dedham Church,* 68; *Stratford Mill,* 52, 55, 60, 75, 76 ff., 81, *41*; studies related to, 76 f., *82*; *Study of Trees,* 100; *Trees at East Bergholt* (1817 drawing), 69, 71 f., 133, *38*; *The Valley Farm,* 55, 64, 81, 91, 113, 126 ff., *76*; studies related to, 126 ff., *77, 78, 79*; *80*; *Valley of the Stour with Dedham* 121, 139 f.; *View of Dedham from lane,* 29, 34, *20*; *View at Epsom,* 55; *View on the Stour near Dedham,* 12, 21, 33, 52, 55, 81, 83, 91 ff., 98, 102, 106, 137 f., *56*; studies related to, 92, 94 ff., 137 f., *52, 53, 54, 55*; *View on the Stour, Dedham Church,* 124, *81*; *Village Fair at East Bergholt,* 14, *7*; *Waterloo Bridge,* 107; *The White Horse,* 46, 52, 60, 73 ff., 77, 91, 132, *39*; studies related to, 73, *82*; *Willy Lott's House,* oil sketches of, 55, 63, 82 ff., 135 ff., *45, 46, 47, 49*; *Wivenhoe Park,* 33 f.; *English Landscape Scenery,* 125, *44*
Cozens, J. R., 44, 50
Cranch, John, 43

Dedham, 13, 16, 20 f., 26, 28 f., 32, 37 f., 44, 49, 54 f., 74, 83, 94, 105, 107 f., 114, 119 ff., 132, 139 f.; Assembly Rooms, 140; Grammar School, 38, 105, 107; Lock and Mill, 32, 83
Dedham Church Tower, 26, 32, 34, 38, 54, 94 ff., 98 ff., 108, 132, 137 ff.
Delacroix, Eugène, 35, 42, 61 ff., 103
Dunthorne, John, snr., 33, 37 f., 53, 65, 126 f.
Dunthorne, John, jnr., 38, 83, 126 f.
Dysart, Earl and Countess of, 54 f.

East Bergholt, 13 f., 20, 23 f., 27, 29, 31, 36 ff., 44, 54 f., 59, 66, 73, 77, 80, 91, 107, 112 f., 115, 121, 124, 132; Church, 24, *13*; House 14, 73; Street, 23, *11*
Etty, William, 118

Farington, Joseph, 66, 69, 77, 81, 98, 100
Fisher, John, Archdeacon of Salisbury, 36, 50, 57, 59 f., 62 f., 75 f., 80 f., 89 f., 95 ff., 100, 106, 109, 115, 118, 124 f., 140
Fisher, Dr John, Bishop of Salisbury, 36, 59, 98, 107
Flatford, 13, 16, 21, 29, 32, 37, 74, 92, 98, 99, 101, 111, 119, 132, 137 f.; Bridge Cottage, 67, 92, 94, 117, 138, *71*; Lock, 67, 98 ff., 102; Mill, 20, 31, 52, 64 ff., 68 ff., 72, 77, 81 f., 91, 93, 96 f., 102, 119, 126, 139; Old Bridge, 68 ff., 74, 92, 97, 99, 101 f., 117, 137 f., *71*
Forster, Thomas, 134
Frith, William Powell, 127
Frost, George, 38 f.
Fuseli, Henry, 100

Gainsborough, Thomas, 38 f., 43, 45, 50, 100, 114, *24*
Géricault, Théodore, 34 f., 60
Girtin, Thomas, 44, 50
Glover, John, 90
Goya, Francisco de, 124
Gray, Thomas, 36
Gun Hill, Dedham, 49, 139

Hampstead, 30, 36, 45, 47, 50, 77, 79 ff., 89 f., 101, 127; Lit. and Sci. Soc. 43 ff., 50, 55, 127
Higham Church, 20, 112, 114, *66*
Hobbema, Meindert, 100, 113, 116
Hofland, Christopher, 113
Hoppner, John, 54
Howard, Luke, 134
Hum, James, 17
Hurlock, Lucy, 139

Lake District, 36, 54, 56
Langham, 20, 59, 78 f., 94, 118
Lawrence, Sir Thomas, 62
Leonardo de Vinci, 39
Leslie, C. R., 10, 37, 42, 44 ff., 51, 66, 76, 124 f., 127, 132, 133
Lewis, Henry Greswold, 55, 81
London: British Institution, 69, 72 f., 75 f., 109 f., 116, 118, 126; Burlington House, 126; National Gallery (in Constable's times), 46 f., 110, 118, 126; Royal Academy of Arts, 36 f., 54, 60, 62, 66, 68 ff., 73, 91, 95, 98, 101 ff., 116, 118 f., 124 ff., 134, 137; Royal Academy Schools, 38, 42 f., Royal Institution, 43 ff., 47; St Martin in the Fields, 60; Somerset House, 126
Lucas, David, 47, 77, 79, 118, 125, 136, *44*

Malvern Hall, 55, 81
Manningtree, 140
Matthews, Henry, 89
Michelangelo, 124, 125, 126
Mistley, 13 f., 16, 21, 49, 121, 140

Nayland, 20, 54
Nollekens, Joseph, 39

Osmington, Dorset, 60

Paley, William, 55
Paris: Musée du Louvre, 62; Salon, 35 f., 62, 102 f., 116
Peak District, Derbyshire, 36
Phillips, Henry, 52, 114 f.
Poussin, Gaspard (Dughet), 50, 89, 109 f., 113, 132, *68*
Purton, William, 132

Raphael, 44, 126
Reinagle, Ramsay Richard, 45, 98, 134
Rembrandt, 35, 37, 50, 53, 77, 80, 101, 125
Reynolds, Sir Joshua, 51 ff., 90, 126, 133
Rhudde, Rev. Durand, 59 f., 77
Rosa, Salvator, 90
Rubens, Sir Peter Paul, 47, 50, 53, 83 f., 88, 133, *50*
Ruisdael, Jacob van, 35, 42, 45 ff., 50, 53, 100, 113, 119, 133

Salisbury, 36, 48, 51, 59, 73, 81, 125
Smith, John Thomas, 39, 42 f., 51, 91, 138
Stoke-by-Nayland, 20, 29
Stour, River and Valley, topography of, 20 f., 26-29, 32, 49, 67, 70, 74, 78 f., 84, 94 f., 99, 105, 111 f., 117, 121, 128, 130, 135 ff.
Stratford Mill, 20, 76 ff., *42*
Stratford St Mary, 20, 27 ff., 74

Thomson, Henry, 66
Thomson, James, 116
Tinney, John Perne, 76, 81
Titian, 48, 50 ff., 90, 109 ,125, *26*
Turner, J. M. W., 35 ff., 75, 100, 116, 125

Velde, Willem van de, 100, 109

West, Benjamin, 75
Wilkie, Sir David, 100
Willy Lott's House (*or* Cottage), 10, 31, 47, 55, 63 ff., 81 ff., 87 f., 94, 96, 119, 126, 128, 135 ff., *II*
Wilson, Richard, 50, 100
Wordsworth, William, 126
Wrabness Point, 121, 140